Just Being There

Just Being There *(Based on a True Story)*

Copyright © 2013 by Jan Amos.

Library of Congress Control Number: 2013947435
ISBN: Softcover   978-1-61856-298-2
               Pdf   978-1-61856-299-9
               Epub   978-1-61856-304-0
               Kindle   978-1-61856-305-7

Cover Design: Jenna Hooper

Jenna Hooper
Web & Graphic Designer
www.jennahooper.com

Editor: Laura Monroe

Rev. date: 08/20/2013

BookWhirl.com Publishing
PO Box 9031, Green Bay
WI 54308-9031, USA
www.BookWhirl.com

Just Being There

(Based on a True Story)

by

Jan Amos

Dedication

*I dedicate this book to all the mothers, fathers,
grandparents, aunts, uncles and all the people
who are raising our children. As it is
we that have the power to change the
world with just being there for our kids.*

Introduction

As I sit and start to write the introduction to this book, an essence of peace, joy, and love fills my soul. Yes, as I bring the four children who are in my life into my awareness and combine the pages of this book my essence fills with happiness and the light shines throughout. Next I reflect on all of the children who have touched my life, as there have been many, and I am grateful for each and every one of them. The main message threaded throughout this book and through my personal experience is the power of parental love, especially maternal parental love. When I think of Mother Teresa, I have confirmation of this power, as she remains an example of this type of love to each and every one of us.

As I reflect on my life and my experiences, I wonder how I knew the power of parental love because it is not something we are taught. But somehow I just knew; I just knew the power behind it and how to give it to my kids. I ponder right now about the natural ability for motherly instinct, and I realize at this moment that I was very blessed to have this amazing attribute or gift within (yes, I believe I was born with a very strong motherly instinct). As we look at the people of the world, we can see that we are all one and the same in many ways, and we are all teachers for the children.

This book will take you on a journey that follows an amazing story based on true events. It will invite you to open to the realization of the powerful connection between a parent and a child, and what can happen to both child and parent due to this amazing association. Moreover, it is my greatest hope that it will explain the mantra behind good parenting and open up the doors to healthy relationship for all.

The Beginning

It was September 2011, Labour Day weekend: a time of moving into a new season of change and a time for hope and a time of new beginnings. I could smell fall in the air, and the leaves were just starting to change colour. The water that surrounded us was now taking on a darker look: a look of the winter to come. Young kids were starting school, young adults were leaving the nest bound for post-secondary education, and summertime romances were coming to an end.

I was at this time a single woman just trying to survive the failure of my twenty-year marriage—a failure that occurred due to circumstances beyond my control. I now finally had my own house with all my belongings returned to me and I had begun to move on. My path through this transition had been quite interesting as five years ago, I put all my efforts and finances into developing a youth program. It was a youth program that helped a lot of kids but didn't end up making it. Also during this time, I discovered my passion for writing inspirational books that had the ability to heal the people. My first book, A Woman's Passage to Freedom, had helped and healed a lot of women, which I was very thankful for.

Right now, I found myself working part-time at a restaurant called Mama's Restaurant located in Middletown, Ontario. I at times wondered why I was still working in the restaurant business, as I knew that my path and purpose in life (which had been shown to me quite a few times over the past few years) was to help the women and kids of the world. I had been through quite a lot and during this journey of healing I had discovered my passion as an inspirational writer, yet I still found myself for the past six months working in the restaurant business. I was thankful for this job, as I unfortunately had to learn the hard way over the past few years that even though you have found your passion or purpose in life you still have to make money and pay the bills—and for me right now, the restaurant business was providing this. However, I must say that every time I got into my car and drove to work, I did ask the question why, and the answer that always came to me was the same, yes always the same: to trust the universe and live in faith.

My life had been blessed with two beautiful children. My eldest daughter Kate was in her fourth year at Arizona State University, and our journey together over the past twenty years was hard to comprehend and amazing to look back to (both through the rewarding and trying times). Kate was a fantastic athlete and also strong-willed, with the gift of an amazing math brain. I could see her fulfilling her dreams of waterskiing, becoming an engineer, and living the life she deserved.

My youngest daughter Emily was starting her second year at Queens University in Kingston, Ontario. Emily was an amazing young woman, a young woman filled with strength, love, and determination. I could see her walking the beautiful campus of Queen's University shining her light, and I saw the people following her in her path. Emily was living with four other students in a university house, experiencing all the fun that comes with that.

I was at this time home but not alone, as I had Christine. Christine was a very special young woman who had entered into my life five years ago and had become a complete gift to me. At this time in her life, she had just experienced a tragic loss, the loss of her wonderful father. At our first meeting, Christine and I had an instant connection of friendship and camaraderie. I then started to notice that Christine was one of the kids who was always around the house, and so she came to be a part of my life. Now, five years later, she had given us all a special gift, a gift of a child: the gift of baby Paul, who is very special to me.

I also have my eighty-five-year-old mother in my life, which is a gift and also a very large responsibility. We had just moved her into a retirement home, which for some reason did not feel very good. Mimi was still quite healthy, although she was unable to grocery shop, cook for herself and take care of the day to day activities. But she was still driving and able to get herself, around which I was definitely not sure of.

Part of my life consisted of entering Mama's Restaurant for my scheduled shift four times a week. The owners, Frank and Sandra, were European, which meant that the restaurant came first before anyone or anything else. They had a lovely home on the water that sat empty most of the time, as they basically lived at the restaurant. Frank was great with the customers and understood the importance of being good to them; Sandra was a little quieter and lived her life from this place.

Most of the staff had been at Mama's Restaurant for years, and so I was, as they say, the new kid on the block (although I was thankful I wasn't the oldest kid on the block). There was Diane who was like a manager and the go-between for most of the staff. There was Margaret, who had been there longer than Frank; James, who had to put up with all us women; and Helen, who was really in charge. There was also Chrissy who I was very fond of, who was younger and reminded me of a firecracker. Right now, Chrissy was learning the difference between a healthy relationship and one that was not so healthy. She had written down in her cashbox what she was looking for in a man to create a healthy relationship. I also worked with a woman named Joanne, who kept us laughing and who was taking control of her life, which was a very good thing. We also had Meghan, Emily, and Angie: the hostess staff. Meghan was very special to me, as I drove her home after most of her shifts (she lived one street over) and we had become close. The kitchen staff consisted of Nick, who was the kindest spirit I had ever come across and who reminded me of a teddy bear; Wayne, who was ready to retire any minute, Tyler, who was a genius; and Simone, who had endured enough for any woman in a lifetime. When I thought of the staff at Mama's Restaurant, I thought of family a bit dysfunctional and yet still a functional family.

This September, Mama's Restaurant was in a time of transition, as some of the staff were moving forward to pursue different schooling opportunities (although the kitchen staff was always in transition, because it was the nature of the business). At this time, I had been paying attention to the new kitchen staff, as I was indirectly responsible for closing duties, so I had made a point of getting to know them.

It was a Saturday night just like any other Saturday night. I had arrived at work early and was preparing for my shift and checking the buffet (on Saturdays we offered a roast beef buffet). At this time, Frank, the owner, introduced me to a new closing dishwasher. About fifteen minutes later, I found this young man beside me putting away some coffee cups. I turned to him and said, "Sorry, what is your name again?" He then stood tall beside me—dark haired, thin, with his whites on and a black tailored cap—and a smile appeared on his face and he gave me the name Dylan. I stopped for a split-second and looked right into his eyes; he smiled at me and I smiled back at him, and I said thank you and moved to the next counter. He then returned to the kitchen, and I stopped and thought to myself, that was a little strange. The night then continued normally, without anything unusual, and Dylan did a fantastic job as the closing dishwasher.

The following Sunday, I found myself once again driving to Mama's Restaurant wondering why and still living in faith. As I entered the restaurant, I settled into the Sunday night atmosphere, which was traditionally a little more relaxed, and I noticed that Dylan was working once again. I said hello to him, and we exchanged a smile. At this moment, I saw something in him, a strength of energy, and I noticed his unique and special essence, and thought to myself, nice, how very nice.

About a week later, I really noticed the clear energy coming from Dylan, an energy that was so welcoming that it brought us into a conversation. During this conversation it came forth that Dylan knew my daughter Emily from their high school days. With this connection established, we found that we also enjoyed a connection of spirit and similar energy. Most of all, I knew there was something special about Dylan; I could see it as he entered into a room. But I did not understand at this time what this connection really meant and I could never have imagined where we were headed.

Dylan started to become a part of the family at Mama's Restaurant, forging a brother-type bond with Nick and an older sister bond with Chrissy. I also started to notice the crush Meghan the hostess had on Dylan; she would blush every time he walked into the room. I noticed that Frank was a little hard on Dylan, as he was with most of the new dish staff. I also felt a little jealousy over the attention that was starting to form around Dylan.

As the days passed, Dylan and I found ourselves quite often in conversation during our shifts at work, and we began to find out about each other's personal lives. I started to open up about my writing of inspirational books and all the kids in my life. I talked about Kate, Emily, Christine, and baby Paul, and shared that one of my passions in life was to help youth. I talked about the youth course I had developed and facilitated with my good friend Marilyn, and I also talked about Marilyn—who I had met during a Face Program training (a diversion opportunity from the court systems for our youth)—and how we had become family. I emphasized to Dylan that I believed it was all about the kids.

Dylan then started to tell me about his life: that his mom had left him at age two, that his dad raised him, and that he had been living on his own since he was seventeen. I at this moment, totally stopped in my tracks and looked right into Dylan's eyes; I could feel his pain, as it was spilling all over the place. I then told to Dylan how sorry I was. There was silence for a while, and all I could think was, who could leave their child at the age of two and how could this young man have gone through most of his life without a mother? I could even picture him as a young boy missing the love of a mother or just the presence of a mother in his life, I then felt how wonderful it was that he was still a person full of love. I then looked around to see if anyone else had heard our conversation, but it seemed that Dylan and I were the only ones in the room. I also felt that somehow I was taking away some of the pain that had been in Dylan's heart for a very long time.

Days passed, and Dylan started opening up about his love for music. He first started to talk about his love for the piano and that he had been playing piano for the past ten years. He said that when he turned fifteen he opened his mouth and realized he had a voice as well. I can remember asking him lots of questions about his music and abilities, and seeing the joy in him as he was expressing his love for music. I also knew to just listen to him, and it was fantastic just being there for Dylan and listening to him talk (I feel that it's so important to listen to our kids of today, as they have so much to share and so much passion in them if we as adults would just take the time to acknowledge it). And so I listened and learned as well, because Dylan was a fountain of knowledge and information. I did notice that Dylan would steer the conversation back to me more often than not, as he had the natural ability to be humble.

We then began to notice the similarities between our paths. Even though we were thirty years apart in age, we were still both artists with a passion: me as a writer and Dylan as a musician. I would find myself talking about the progress of my book Having Faith and Dylan would be talking about the progression of his album—this being a dream come true for Dylan, as recording his songs was something he had dreamed of for quite a few years. I also realized at this time that I was teaching Dylan conscious behaviour, the things I had taught my girls, and he was loving all of it. Yes, I must say that he was one of my best pupils, as he understood and got everything I was saying right away. I could actually see him getting it. Then his questions became more frequent, and I knew he was applying this knowledge to his music and the passage of his musical career. I could at times see the relief come across his body and the change in his energy, as he was receiving the answers he needed to hear.

A Life-Altering Moment

Two months had now passed, and it was October 31, Halloween, when Dylan had a life-altering moment. When I arrived for my shift at Mama's Restaurant, Dylan was not there. I then heard that he had been hit by a truck and that he was okay but in the hospital, and I immediately felt this enormous hole in my heart.

Two weeks later, Dylan was finally back at work, in his whites with that cute black cap, with a cut above his eye and scrapes all over him. I didn't even know he was working that night, and there he was beside me. I gave him a big hug, sending all my healing energy into his body that felt like only skin and bone.

I then asked Dylan what happened, and he said he had his head down and was in a hurry, and all of a sudden there was a truck and then he was under it. I was standing there listening to him, and he said, "Yes, it went right over me, and I can still hear the tires racing by." I reminded him that we are always in the right spot at the right time and that there's no need to hurry anywhere. The next day, Emily loaded the hospital pictures from Dylan's Facebook page, and a sick feeling entered my heart and my gut when I saw them.

Dylan's Music

It was November when a man named Neil who had been helping Dylan with recording his songs came in for dinner at Mama's Restaurant. Dylan and Neil were recording songs that Dylan had written, and Neil had a CD and player in hand and he also needed a good meal. Neil sat at the table and told me how fantastic and talented Dylan was; he actually said Dylan was the most talented kid he had ever encountered and that he had worked with a lot of kids. I thought to myself how impressive this was and wondered if Dylan had heard this; I then walked back to kitchen to tell him. Now the look on Dylan's face was full of surprise, and so I repeated it again, looking him right in the eyes so he would know it was true.

The next thing I knew, Neil was at the front counter of the restaurant with the CD player, asking me if I would like to hear some of Dylan's music. Of course I said yes, I would love to. As I leaned over to put on the earphones, a feeling of excitement came across my entire essence. As Neil hit the play button, I found myself hearing this amazingly sweet, strong voice accompanied by wonderful piano and rhythm. All I could think was, wow, this was good, really good. I then let the music take me away as I lost all thought of being at work and Mama's Restaurant.

When I returned to the kitchen, Dylan must have for a split-second wondered what had happened to me because I was excited and going on about listening to his music and how fantastic it was. He then said to me, "Really, Jenny, you think so?" and I said yes. I then noticed a slight bit of disappointment on Dylan's face but I just kept going on about my musical background, and the excitement just kept pouring out of me. Dylan just smiled at me and didn't say much, and then I was needed back in the restaurant.

Five minutes later, I found myself back in the kitchen standing beside Dylan asking him if everything was okay. He said yes, although I knew the answer was no. I then asked him again, and this is what he told me. He said he was very grateful for Neil's help, but he would go to Neil's studio and ghost voice and ghost piano, when he would return the next day Neil would have added other instruments. Thus, to Dylan, the songs were not what he heard in his head and definitely not how he wanted his music to sound.

I thought for a minute and then shared that I had an editor and that she did make some changes to my writing. They were made in a different colour, and I had to okay every change, as it was always me who was in control of my writing and my books. Dylan just looked at me, hugged me, and said thank you. As I walked away, I knew at that very moment that it needed to all be about Dylan and his music.

On my way home in the car, I started to wonder why Dylan had come into my life and why he was becoming such a large part of it. Many kids and even adults had passed through my life in the past— some for a short time, some for a long time, and some had actually become a permanent part of my life, like Christine and Paul. I also believed that everyone comes into your life for a reason. Kids had been entering into my life for thirty years, and at this stage I already knew I had a gift with the kids. However, in this case I totally knew that this was all about Dylan's gift and that this was something I needed to remember.

Something had changed in me. It was as if I knew something different was happening and that it was going to be big, very big. It was a feeling that was good and scary at the same time. I also knew it was to be about music, all about music. Just then I remembered I had just bought the Justin Bieber DVD (Justin Bieber: Never Say Never), and I just knew that Dylan needed to watch this movie.

The next day, I brought the DVD to the restaurant for him to borrow. I can remember saying, "Now, this movie is very important to me," and Dylan immediately saying, "I will take good care of it!" Dylan must have thought that it was kind of strange that a mom-like person had Justin Bieber's DVD and that it was important to her. Two weeks later,

Dylan handed the DVD back to me with a sparkle in his eye, saying he had watched it twice and that he didn't want to be like Justin Bieber, as he was a unique musician. But he had learned a lot and now knew that he had to get on YouTube with his music.

Early Winter

The seasons were changing again as fall slid into winter. One fine morning, our community woke up to a light blanket of snow on the ground. I looked out the window of my beautiful house, marvelling over how there was something very special about the first snowfall. It was the peaceful, joyful feeling that filled my entire body as I looked out into the street. I thought about my kids and my mom, and I was comforted knowing Kate would be home for Christmas soon and Emily as well. The world was just beginning to enter into the hustle and bustle of getting ready for the Christmas season. I had always loved the Christmas season, as it had always been about family, love and, of course, the stockings.

However, it was my eighty-six-year-old mom who was now the main focus of my energy, as she had been in a retirement home for the past four months and was not enjoying any of it. I must say they were wonderful at the retirement home; it just wasn't for her. I think maybe it was because she was too healthy for her age and that she didn't want to be in there. So she and I had arranged for her to move in with me on December 28, and the plans had been set into motion.

The restaurant was also busy with Christmas parties and people just generally being out and about and choosing to enjoy a dinner out. Moreover, due to the change in the weather, I started driving Dylan home on Sundays, which was only a five-minute drive out of my way. During this time, we would talk, and one Sunday Dylan made the comment, "Where have you been for the past twenty years of my life?" Then he answered his own question, "Well, you are here now," and a smile appeared on his face.

The next Sunday trip home to Dylan's house, something very special happened to me, as this Sunday he had the first copy of the first CD of the songs that he had written. Dylan really said nothing to me during our shift and just asked at the end if I was able to drive him home, and I said yes, of course. As he was getting his coat on, he pulled out his CD and mentioned that he had something for us to listen to on the way home. I could see that he was just bursting at the seams and was so very proud at this moment—this was the first copy and I was the first person who was going to listen to it!

We then closed up the restaurant and got in my car, and he put the CD into the player and turned up the volume (as he already knew I liked to listen to music loud). Then he smiled like I had never seen him smile. The music started, and it was so good, so great—it was amazing. Dylan was beating his foot against the car floor and sang along, and his voice was strong and beautiful. Dylan then moved quickly through each song, showing me his favourite parts and even some parts he would like to change. The joy that was pouring out of this kid was simply amazing.

When we arrived at Dylan's house, he informed me that the CD was a gift for me to keep. I was extremely surprised and happy and very grateful, and I thanked him for the CD. I then gave him a hug for the gift of being able to listen to this talented young man who had become such a part of my life! I listened to the CD on my way home and then later in my house; I must say that I played that CD at least ten times within twenty-four hours and enjoyed it every time—and there was no guilt that my Justin Bieber CD was lying on the backseat of my car.

Two days later, I had to loan the CD to one of the other employees for their enjoyment. I didn't want to part with it, but the more people who heard it, the better. I then started sharing it with more of the other staff members, always keeping track of it and always knowing when it was time to it to be returned to me. I can remember Frank, the owner, commenting, "Isn't that copy for the restaurant?" and me just quietly saying, "No, this is my copy." The strangest thing was that I hadn't seen Dylan in a least a week and wasn't able to tell him how wonderful his music really was.

Christmastime

As Christmastime fell upon us, Kate and Emily returned home for the holidays. This was a very special Christmas for me and my girls, as I now had my own home with bedrooms for my girls to call their own. Christine and baby Paul also came, as Christine had been living with her mom over the past few months since her relationship with Paul's dad had become unhealthy. I knew that this was painful for Christine, as family was so very important for her. I gave Christine my first book A Woman's Passage to Freedom, as I believed the teachings in this book were eye opening and life changing, and could help her.

Brandon and Emily were together this year: Brandon being Emily's first love and Christine's brother. How this all unfolded was a miracle in itself. It started five years ago when my ex-husband and I were on a waterskiing trip with Kate and the neighbours, who had a daughter named Maggie (who was also someone who spent a lot of time at my house was looking after Emily). Emily and Maggie were on the dock enjoying the sun when two nice guys pulled up in a fishing boat. A spark was set off between Emily and Brandon, and a party was lined up for the evening. Emily and Maggie attended the party, and this was the start of Brandon and Emily. Emily and Brandon dated for three years, and then it was over and Emily found herself in another relationship with a great guy. I was at this time happy for Emily, although I wasn't sure if she hadn't already given her heart away. Moreover, I guess you would have to say that if Emily and Brandon hadn't dated, Christine and I would have never met. However, these two years later, Emily and Brandon were just finding their way back together and were still a little unsure of the path of their relationship.

Christmas Eve came, and it was the most special Christmas Eve, as I was with my girls and, of course, Mimi, my mom. We headed out to attend the wonderful Christmas Eve ceremony at the United Church located in Middletown. The service was full of love, song, and hope of the passage of Christ, and it only took a few minutes before I was brought to tears of joy (as I always wore my heart on my sleeve).

We returned home and were joined by Brandon, Christine, Stephanie, and Bryan. (Stephanie was Brandon and Christine's mom, and also one of my closest friends, and Bryan was her new husband). The evening was a time of family, great food, and some cards. The kids got into a euchre tournament, and the house was filled with joy—although we were missing Matt, Kate's boyfriend, who she met at Arizona State University and had been dating for the past few years. Matt was actually scheduled to visit in a few days for a family wedding on my ex-husband's side of the family. We were all very excited to have Matt come to visit us in our new home. I had experienced a wonderful visit with Matt and his family that past summer in the California area, although at this time I was not sure if Matt and Kate had the makings for a long-term relationship.

Our Christmas morning was wonderful, with great stockings to open, and we continued to enjoy the holiday season with the best CD ever playing in the background—Dylan's CD! I didn't actually see Dylan at all over the holiday's season, as our shifts had changed, although Dylan was still a part of my heart and still part of my daily music routine.

Moving Day

December 28 was moving day for Mimi! I once again turned to faith and my belief that this was meant to be—that this was the correct path and that I was to look after my mom. When I looked back, I could see that I had basically already been looking after her for the past few years as her caregiver, as well over the past twenty years as her support. During this transition period, I came up with an idea for a new book, "Taking Care of the Golden Years," which I felt would be very beneficial to all age groups as it would cover topics of preparing for your golden years and bringing elders back into the home. In addition, I thought it might give the much needed insight that I felt my mother was missing, as she seemed to believe that I was responsible for her and did not display much gratitude for all the caregiving. Yet I must say, I had seen an enormous amount of gratitude from my good friend Rosie's mom towards Rosie, who also looked after her.

However, by making this move, my mom and I were actually helping each other, because as a single woman it was hard to pay the bills on one income. It was a relief to know I had the rent covered every month, but at the same time, the energy changes in your house as soon as an elderly person moves in (it is like they bring a cloud of doom and gloom with them). I felt frustrated at this time, because I wasn't sure why my books and the passage of an inspirational writing had not come forth for me. Once again, patience, trust, and faith were going to be my only salvation.

After work on New Year's Eve, I went to pick up baby Paul at Stephanie's house and take him home to my place. On my way there, I began to experience great sadness as Kate and Matt, and Emily and Brandon were at the wedding of my ex-husband's niece. I missed my family that I had to leave. I was thankful for the warmth and love I felt as I entered Stephanie's house and checked on baby Paul. We then make a joint decision for me to join the party with great friends in attendance and then cuddle up with baby Paul for the night. As the clock struck midnight, I felt a wonderful sense that this was going to be a special year and all the sadness left my heart. I was happy to receive three texts from Kate, Emily, and Christine wishing me a Happy New Year.

The next day, we enjoyed a family New Year's Day dinner before the girls returned to school: Kate back to Arizona and Emily to Kingston. Christine and Paul were still here, and I was thankful for that. It was truly the start of a new beginning as the new year was upon us.

A New Year

Just after New Year's, we were back working our regular shifts, and to our enjoyment, Dylan and I were working together again on Saturday and Sunday nights. There was a nice change for Dylan, as he was now serving the buffet and a little bit out of the kitchen. This time provided much-needed catch up time for both of us, and it gave us some time to talk about Dylan's CD that I had listened to quite a bit over the holidays. Dylan asked me what my favourite song was, and I had to pause for a minute, as I loved all of them. I finally settled on the second song, "The Saint." Dylan shared that there was a special story behind that song, and I asked him to tell me.

Dylan started to tell me that he had gone for a victory lap at St Teresa School in Middletown and took a music recording class ("victory lap" meaning like a grade thirteen class). He shared that his teacher was very fond of him and thought that he had great talent, and that this teacher had encouraged him to enter into this music competition. Dylan then explained that you had to pick a painting and write a song about it, and so he picked the Leonardo da Vinci painting called "St. Jerome in the Wilderness." He then explained the painting was about this man who was chosen by God to become a Saint and then went to the desert to fulfill his destiny. Dylan then proceeded to tell me I should look it up on the Internet, as it would be something I would enjoy looking at. I smiled and said okay, I would. He then told me that he had won the competition and that with the prize money of one thousand dollars, he was able to buy the keyboard that he now had. I told him how amazed I was, and Dylan just smiled at me and walked away.

As the rest of the night unfolded, I kept hearing Dylan's song "The Saint" in my head. Dylan must have wondered what had happened to me, as I didn't say that much for the rest of the evening. On my way home, I couldn't wait to turn on my computer and look at the painting he had mentioned. And this was exactly what I did: I sat in my kitchen looking at this painting and hearing the song in my head. It became a unique moment of realization of the extraordinary gift and talent that lay within Dylan Lock.

The next day at work, I immediately told Dylan how I had gone home and checked out the painting, and how fantastic it was and how amazing his song was—and there was just this smile on Dylan's face. A few minutes later, Dylan told me that he was to play the background music for Garfield Dunlop our local MPP (who I had already written about in "The Business Side of Things," and once again, I believe there are no coincidences). Dylan then asked me if I would like to attend this upcoming performance on the following Sunday from 1:00 to 4:00 p.m., and I just looked at him and said, of course, I would love to. Dylan smiled at me again and walked away, and I sort of felt a strange feeling inside, as if there was something going on but I wasn't quite sure exactly what it was.

As the day drew closer, I found myself anticipating the excitement of the upcoming performance. It was now Saturday night, and we were working our regular shifts. As I was standing at the pass-through window waiting for my food, Dylan appeared right beside me and started talking about the new cover songs he had learned for tomorrow's performance. He started naming off different artists and songs he had learned and was practicing, and was going to play the next day. When he mentioned the group Styx and the song "Come Sail Away," I completely lit up!

My memory at this moment took me back to age seventeen, my high school auditorium, and the first live band performance I had ever experienced. A smile appeared on my face, as this had been a very happy time of my life. I had a great boyfriend and a full life. As I returned to the moment, Dylan had a wonderful look on his face; it was as if he found the love that music can bring to a person, as he must have seen the look in my eyes as I returned to a wonderful time of my life. I then said, "I love Styx, and 'Come Sail Away' is one of my favourite songs." As we continued to do our duties at the restaurant, I had a peaceful feeling within. My eyes did met Dylan's a few times, and I could see how excited he was for this performance tomorrow and the fact that I was going to hear him. It was as if he knew something I didn't!

As I arrived at the function, I found that I knew a lot of the people due to my involvement with the community, and this was great. I must say, however, that it was the connection of reassurance that Dylan felt the moment he saw me in the crowd that was amazing, and I know he saw me the instant I walked into the room. I felt and understood this connection, as I had felt it many times before with my girls when they knew I had arrived to watch a volleyball, basketball, or soccer game. I got a cup of coffee and found a great seat close to the stage, exchanging a smile with Dylan and settling in for the performance.

It was probably about a minute into Dylan's performance that I could feel the magic, gift, and brilliance of his talent. I don't really know how to explain it, but I just knew his brilliance. As I looked around at the people in the audience, I could see the joy of his music entering into their hearts. The only thing missing was space—meaning that he needed a bigger area to project his powerful voice. Dylan then took a break, and when he came off the stage, he came directly over to me and gave me a hug. I was so very proud of him, and the feeling of joy was everywhere. He then disappeared into the crowd.

Later, Dylan's dad, Gary, sat down at the table right across from me and introduced himself. I looked at Dylan and saw a smile on his face. Gary then started to talk about his life with Dylan. It was a very strange situation for me, as I already knew everything he was saying. Gary also said that this was the first time he had come to watch Dylan play and that Dylan had asked him to come. I said nothing once again but thought, this is exactly the same thing that had happened to me.

It was probably four songs into the next set that he started to play "Come Sail Away." I froze within myself. Dylan was good, and it was as if he was singing directly to me. It was a very magical moment, a moment I will remember always.

During the performance, Dylan played everything from Elvis, to Elton John, to Queen, to Johnny Cash! We were joined by Chrissy and Angie from Mama's Restaurant, which was more family support for Dylan. Those three hours were extremely magical, and the best part was that when Dylan came off the stage for a break, he would come directly over for a brief visit and, of course, a hug from his dad and me. (Gary must have been wondering who the heck was this woman who was now was a part of his son's life.) Dylan would then move off to talk with people, and I knew exactly that this was a connection of family support. I did exchange a few words with Garfield, who I had known for years, as his Middletown office was located in the building I had owned. We both talked about the amazing talent that was within this kid who had entered into both our lives.

I noticed that it was probably time to head home to get ready for work, but I knew there was no way I could leave, absolutely no way at all. Once Dylan finished up, I left, and on my way home all I could say was OMG over and over again, still not realizing what God really had in his plan for Dylan and me.

Within an hour, we were both in the restaurant working our usual shift, although everything had changed! I can remember telling Dylan how fantastic he was and his responses of, "Really, you think so?" I then said to Dylan, "We need to have a time of reflection of the performance we just experienced," and so we found ourselves in Boston Pizza a few hours later talking about the performance. We talked about the songs, the people, Garfield—all of it. It became plain as day that Dylan needed to get on YouTube. This was also a very special moment, as Dylan now had a little extra cash because of this performance and asked to buy one of my books, which I happily sold to him. I dropped him off at home with a sense of happiness within both of us, a plan to start recording for YouTube, and my book Having Faith in Dylan's hand.

He must have started to read my book within a few days, as during our next shift at Mama's Restaurant he was very impressed and said my book was also brilliant. He also said that it was as if I were speaking to him and teaching what he needed to learn at that very moment.

A Time of Disconnection

One week later, I noticed a shift in Dylan's energy. It was a Saturday night, and Dylan arrived to work at his usual time—right at the minute of his start time. I saw him enter the building through the back door, as I just happened to be there, but I could immediately tell that something was wrong and something had changed. Dylan was unable to really look me in the eye, and I thought to myself that this was really strange and I just let it go. But as the next few minutes unfolded, there was defiantly a coldness that appeared within Dylan's energy and I had no other choice but to respect his feelings. After two similar shifts, I was surprised and still wondering what the heck had happened. I kept going back to our last time together and reviewing the conversation, and I could not figure it out. All I could think of was that the relationship that was developing between us was scaring the heck out of him.

It was a Wednesday night. Dylan had placed a takeout order, and I did not even know about it until he walked in to pick it up. I can remember him looking surprised to see me, and by then I knew to keep my distance and so I stayed back as the rest of the staff went to greet him. He looked over with those eyes that cut into you and said, "Hi, Jenny." I responded, "Hi, Dylan." He got his takeout and was off on his way.

By now I was accustomed to this new relationship, and I had actually started to think it was going to be the norm. But four days later, there once again was another shift in energy. Dylan and I were talking a bit more, and it was getting near the end of our shift. That night it turned out that Dylan, Emily the hostess, and I were all leaving the building at the same time. As the three of us stood close outside the front door, I turned to lock the door. All of a sudden there came an arm around my neck and a hug as well. I reached down after locking the door and placed my hand on top of Dylan's and hugged him back. I thought to myself, I love you too, Dylan. No words were spoken, but from that moment on our connection was right back to where it had left off.

YouTube

Through the Justin Bieber movie, we learned the power of the Internet and social networking. This was the main reason I lent Dylan the movie Never Say Never, so he would find the direction to get on YouTube. I believe he already had this knowledge and the movie just confirmed it. Due to the money earned through the New Year's levy the camera was purchased and the setup was in place.

It was January 30 that Dylan called me and told me he had posted a few videos on YouTube. My response was, "Fantastic, Dylan! That is fantastic!" I then said goodbye and turned on my computer to check out his YouTube channel, which was called Dylan Lockstar. I loved it right away, as I knew he was going to be a star—yes, he was going to be Dylan Lock, a star. As I opened my computer, I had so much excitement about me and a feeling of accomplishment for Dylan as well. Within a month of setting his goal of being on YouTube, he was there.

I found his channel right away and settled in for the show. There was "These Eyes" by the Guess Who, which was good and one of my favourites; "Midnight Special" by CCR, which was a favourite of Dylan's; Pearl Jam's "Last Kiss"; and the Beatles' "I've Just Seen a Face." In excitement, I called Dylan back and told him how proud I was of him and how amazing the YouTube videos were.

Dylan was busy working and practicing when an amazing opportunity came forth and he found himself on the way to Toronto with Neil for a meeting at a recording studio. It took some guidance and faith to keep Dylan centered at this very moment, and I swear I was in the car with him on the way to the studio sending my energy, love, and support. He messaged me the next day with the most wonderful tale of his experience, although he confided that there seemed to be more disease and separation within his relationship with Neil than connection. I just told Dylan to let things unfold and take it a day at a time, and that he would know the right path to take with Neil. It was around this time that the knowledge that things were unfolding as they should started to appear within my awareness, but I truly would not understand the power of this statement until the next event with Dylan!

Back to the Family

Kate was working hard at school, this being her last term at university, and starting to ski again. (I saw the benefits of being a musician, as you can continually practice, while with being an athlete you have to rest the body.) Matt was working in California and adjusting to life as a working man. There was still some unsettledness within their relationship, although they were both working on things.

Brandon had now decided that it was time for a commitment in his relationship with Emily, as he realized that the love he had for her was very strong. He approached Emily asking for her commitment, as he felt this was the next step. While Emily loved Brandon very much, she was also still in the university mindset of "there are many fish in the sea." Therefore, she wasn't sure what to do and was unable to make the commitment. I did ask her to follow her heart, but I think she was following her head. She was unable to decide, so the message to Brandon was that she couldn't make the commitment.

There was wonderful news concerning Christine and Paul's father Ron. They had decided to try again with their relationship, so Christine and baby Paul moved back into the home they had left six months ago. They had put their family back together and were once again working on their relationship, and all seemed well.

Things were going okay with my mom living at my house despite the dramatic change in energy. Although my sister Jill had called and unfortunately called me every nasty name in the book because we hadn't told her about our mom moving in with me. She had a point, but she also said that if she had known she would have never let mom move in, and this is exactly why we didn't tell her. Plus, I felt that Jill should have been calling me every day thanking me for opening my home and looking after Mom. I myself was still trying to understand why this was all happening: why I was now a full-time caregiver to my mom and why I was still working at Mama's Restaurant.

A Trip to the Psychic

My first trip to the psychic was over a year ago, one week after my fiftieth birthday, a trip that was meant to be and a trip that would reinforce my intuition of the passage of my life. I also believe that if we end up at a psychic we are meant to be there to get the direction we need. What led me to Kim was her book, which I noticed on Stephanie's kitchen counter, called Wake Up Call: A Psychic's Guide to a Better Life, which I immediately picked up and asked if I could take home and read. (I also had the knowing to place Kim's number into my phone for future reference.) I found that a lot of the teachings were the same as my book, and I right away wanted to have a reading with Kim. I called and things fell into place quite easily. I found myself one Saturday morning in my car on my way to Kim's house for a reading. I was over-the-top excited for many reasons: one for the reading and also to meet Kim.

As I rolled the dice, the first question she asked was, do you have a son, and I at this time said no. She then went on to say that it took me seven years to leave my marriage and that it was a very good thing. She told me that my aura was fully developed and that I had found my inner self and that was why people were comfortable talking to me. She then offered me her business, as she was busy with other things and she felt I had the ability to do readings as well. I said thank you, but I felt my passage in life was to help the people through my books and gift of insight.

Kim then told me that I was going to write a book that was going to make it, and she saw an audience and financial abundance coming my way. Also, she predicted that there was going to be a fantastic man entering my life and that the relationship was to be strong and healthy. I can remember leaving and having to go to Marilyn's for a shot of whiskey right after.

One year later, Meghan the hostess at Mama's Restaurant heard me talking about my trip to the psychic and asked if I would take her, and my first response was, only if you ask your mom and dad. She said okay and came back to me a week later with a green light. I then made a call, and to my surprise Kim was available and two appointments were set in place. I once again thought, well, it's lining up; therefore, it must be meant to be.

I picked Meghan up, as she only lived one street over. This day was filled with excitement over seeing the psychic. I went first, as Meghan felt this was better for her. I once again rolled the dice, and the first question asked was, do you have a son, but Kim, remembering that I didn't and quickly moved on. Then she basically said the exact same thing as before: that I was healed from my marriage. She once again offered me her business and predicted that my man was going to enter my life, that my books were going to make it, that financial abundance was coming, and that ultimate peace, love, and happiness were in my future. I thought, wow, and thanked her.

I was then blessed with some very wonderful direction. Kim got out a piece of paper and wrote her book distribution company name down for me and told me to send a copy of my book to them, predicting that if they liked it, they would take it on. Moreover, she felt that a distribution company was the best way to go for getting my books to the people. I was very thankful to Kim for the reading and the contact for my books. The next day, I typed up a cover letter and set my book to the same distribution company that had handled Kim's book.

Penetang Idol

It was a Wednesday night, and we had a large reservation at the restaurant. To my surprise, Dylan was working; this made me happy, as during our shifts together it was as if we were at home having a family discussion. Meghan, the hostess, was also happy to see Dylan (the teenage crush that she had on him was somewhat obvious). Chrissy, our firecracker, spirited young woman was also working. Nick was in the kitchen helping, so it was definitely a night of family at the restaurant.

As Dylan and I were finishing up, he mentioned to me that there was going to be a Penetang Idol music competition that weekend. My immediate response was, "Let me know, and I will come and watch." The next day, I saw the information in the paper and messaged this to him.

The following Sunday afternoon, I was busy baking for the kids at Mama's Restaurant when the phone rang. I was surprised that it was Dylan. He first asked me what I was doing and how my day was going, and then started talking about the Penetang Idol competition. He asked, "What do you think, Jenny? Should I go to it?" and my response was, "Yes, Dylan, I think you should go!" He then said in his calm, sweet voice, "Okay, I will try to find out some more information and I will call you back."

As I hung up the phone, I just knew I was going somewhere and immediately started to clean up my kitchen, as I was truly baking and had pastry all over the place. I then popped into the shower, and the minute I was out the phone rang again and it was Dylan. He said that he had spoken to someone in charge and he had until 4:00 p.m. to get there to register, as today was the pre-qualification day and the competition was tomorrow. I said, "Okay, let's get going." Dylan said, "Oh, we have lots of time," and then I explained to Dylan that I had to finish getting ready, clean out my daughter's car (which would be a challenge) in order to transport Dylan's keyboard, pick him up, go to another location to get his keyboard, and get him there in less than an hour and a half.

I hung up the phone and started moving very quickly. I was almost ready to leave when the phone rang again and it was Dylan asking if he could borrow the fifteen dollars for the registration, as he was a little short at the moment. I said of course and that this was no problem at all. It was eight minutes to four when we arrived and Dylan started to fill out the registration papers. His name was added to the roster and we were all set, at least for the next few minutes.

As the performances started, I realized that another situation was unfolding—we were now going to be late for work. As I looked at the time on my iPhone and into Dylan's eyes, I knew he was thinking the same thing but no words were exchanged between us. I just quietly got up and called Frank at work and explained we were going to be fifteen minutes late. I must compliment Frank at this time, as he was very understanding and kind about the situation. As I returned to the room, a smile was exchanged between us of understanding and support, plus a reminder to concentrate on the moment at hand. Dylan ended up performing without his keyboard; he did great, but I must say he was a little lost without it. They were to do two songs, but time did not permit this, and a green light was given for Dylan to return for the competition on Monday (it was a holiday in Canada, Family Day).

On our way to work, I said to Dylan, "Well, tomorrow is at the Legion and you can drive home." Dylan just looked at me and shook his head, and I knew he was telling me no driver's licence. I just looked forward and remembered that my mom had been reading a driver's book to renew her licence, which unfortunately for her was denied (and fortunately for all the people on the road). I at that moment knew to bring Dylan the handbook so he could start preparing to take his G1, which was the start of the sequence to obtain a full driver's licence. This was also the moment I knew I needed to play a more motherly role, as we now needed a birth certificate to obtain the driver's license.

We arrived at work and started our usual shift, although something had changed in the attitude of some of our coworkers, as Dylan and I had arrived to work together and we were also both late as well. I could also feel the judgement that was being placed upon us because people were now publicly aware of our relationship. Now Dylan and I thought nothing about it, because for him he had the support of a mother-type figure—something he had been longing for, for years—and I could actually sense the joy and ease he felt within. I could even see him healing from all the times he had missed having a mother by his side.

The next day, I had to wait over a half-hour for Dylan to finish work at Mama's Restaurant before we headed to the finals. When Dylan got in the car, I handed him the driver's handbook with a smile on my face, and he said, "Oh, you remembered." We then headed towards Penetang for the finals, and it all worked out fine, as we arrived just before his age group was to start. He was last, of course, and I reassured him that they were saving the best for last. The room was filled with just over 200 people, mostly family and friends. I had my mom with me, and we settled down with a glass of wine to watch the show. It was turning out to be a nice day, as here we were on Family Day basically as Dylan's family, waiting for him to take the stage. At this moment, I thought about the many events I had been at over the past twenty years with my girls: waterskiing, downhill skiing, soccer, basketball, and dancing. For me, an idol competition was new, but supporting a child was old hat.

My mom and I sat quietly, and there was a chair for Dylan, but he was in and out of it as he really enjoyed visiting with the people. As I watched him from afar, I saw a different young man, one who felt right at home in a room where it was all about music. The contestants were to sing two songs each, and three would be chosen to move on to the finals. Just before it was Dylan's first turn to sing, I found him sitting beside me looking for support and a short pep talk before he went on stage. (Dylan also needed reassurance, as he had just split with his girlfriend and had tried to contact her with no response.) This totally reminded me of Kate needing a mom pep talk just before she skied, and all I really did was listen, as Dylan did most of the talking, and truly this was all he needed at that very moment. Dylan had also brought his video camera and asked if I minded filming, and I said I would be happy to.

It was now Dylan's turn, and as he took the stage with his keyboard, all of a sudden something strange happened. His pedal was not working, and therefore, there was no loud volume coming from his piano. For only a second Dylan showed signs of fear, and then he was able to tap into his amazing ability to go with the flow and was able to reassure the audience. (Later, someone commented that it was better without the pedal, as it was a singing competition and his voice was the main talent being set forth.) He started with Queen's "Somebody to Love," and this was when the magic started. His gift entered into the hearts of the crowd, and a silence fell all around us as everyone's attention was on Dylan. I was at this time videotaping at the back of the room, and let me tell you, as I was watching Dylan, I could also see the reactions from the crowd and it was amazing. Dylan sung two songs, which were fabulous of course, and when leaving the stage he came over and gave me a hug. I wonder if he saw the look of amazement on my face as I processed what was unfolding. It was the official start of Dylan Lockstar Fever, and it was big and it was everywhere.

Dylan quickly became busy talking with the people, shining, and just being Dylan. I also had people share their joy and love of Dylan with me, as people were coming up to the table saying, "Your son is fantastic." I was a little taken aback, but the first words that came out of my mouth were, "I know," and then, "Thank you." I must say, it was special and a little overwhelming. As the next singer took the stage, there was Dylan sitting beside me with so much joy pouring out of him and with a smile from ear to ear. I hugged Dylan and told him how very proud I was of him, and all I could do was smile from ear to ear along with him.

Dylan did not stay long at the table long and rather joined some friends at the back to watch the other contestants. I found myself watching the people and the stage, and then all of a sudden I saw David walk right in front of Dylan with a hot dog and fries in his hand. I made a hand signal to Dylan, saying "book" and "David from my book," and Dylan understood and smiled. When there was a break in the music, I went over to Dylan and said, "I want you to meet my good friends Marlene and David." We headed over to the table and I introduced them to Dylan, and Dylan said, "Anyone who is important to Jenny is important to me." I then said that Dylan could be singing in the finals and that we would know soon.

Dylan, of course, made the top three, and it was once again time for him to prepare for his last few songs. I asked him what he was going to play, and he said Queen's "Bohemian Rhapsody," and my eyes widened as a very large smile appeared. The crowd was silent as Dylan performed his two songs. He started with "Midnight Special," and this performance was amazing. He completely captured the crowd and was shining like I had never seen him shine before. Next, he started to play "Bohemian Rhapsody," and the people were clapping and hooting and I was holding onto the camera, and then the world stopped for me as the word "Mama" came forth. His voice was clear, sweet, and full of love, and it completely shook my heart. My eyes filled with tears, and somehow the strength came to hold it together. As Dylan hit his last cord on his piano, the crowd rose to their feet; the room just became magical, and this was truly a moment that will be with me forever.

As the crowd was still on their feet Dylan just said thank you, and then t started to unplug his keyboard as if nothing had just happened. He came off the stage and gave me a hug, and then the people were everywhere. I then realized I had a problem: my eighty-six-year-old mother who had had a glass of wine three hours ago and was not in very good shape. I knew I had to get her home. There still were two more performances and the judges' time and awards, but I knew I could not wait. I explained this to Dylan, and one look at Mimi and he understood. We then quickly put his keyboard in my car, and I gave him a kiss and a hug goodbye and said, "Call me when you win," and Dylan replied, "If

I win." I gave him the look of a mother, and Dylan returned the smile of a son.

My drive home was a good twenty minutes and still no word from Dylan, although I did hear from David and Marlene, as they were excited to say how great Dylan was and that Anna Thompson (a well-known vocal instructor) was sitting beside Marlene and had said that Dylan was fabulous and that he needed some work with this voice. Marlene then gave me Anna's contact information, and I said thank you and that I would talk to Dylan about it. I then got a little excited, and knowing Dylan did have a phone but it was not working that good, I tried to text him but got no reply.

Then, all of a sudden, my cellphone started ringing. I didn't recognize the number, but it was Dylan. He first asked how I was doing and how everything was; I said, "Great, did you win?" Dylan then said, "Yes, I won!" We spoke briefly on who came in second and third, and he then said he had to go as he had borrowed someone's phone since his phone was not working. I said, "Okay, thanks for calling," and then Dylan said, "I love you," and my reply was, "I love you, too," and then he was gone.

I immediately sat down and thought how amazing my life had become and that it was full of so much family and so much love. I marveled over what a great weekend it had been and how amazing it was. And then it was like a ton of bricks had hit me, and I realized that most of all I now had a son—yes, I had a son.

A Time of Doubt

Two days later, there came of time of doubt in my path with Dylan, as I had a "mother bear" experience come forth that honestly scared the heck out of me. There was a situation that unfolded with crossing the line of the proper age group leading into a relationship. I at this time found myself reacting and stepping up to voice my opinion to Dylan immediately not even considering the proper time and place. Now I knew I could help him get where he needed to be, support him, and love him as a mom would but when I felt this incredible urge to react as a mother bear might, it put me on my ass. (Sorry, no other word for it!) Therefore, I felt the need to back away, and I thought I could let go of a son that I had just acquired. I returned his equipment when he wasn't home, as I still had it in my car. Then Dylan messaged me saying, "Thank you for everything you have done for me, and I have your book and so I will always have a part of you." This was now Thursday night, and I must say that it was quite an emotional night, a night to reflect and a night to have faith.

I woke up Friday with some uneasiness and an invitation for a girls' night at my dear friend Marilyn's house. She said that this regular girls' get-together was going to consist of fourteen women. I was very open to this, as I had learned to embrace the conversation and camaraderie with women, and had started a book a year ago called "Women" (which had many messages, one being a strong and powerful need for more camaraderie among the woman of the world). I arrived at Marilyn's and was quite happy to see her sister-in-law Anne Marie, as I had always been very fond of her. I had met Anne Marie a couple times before and had felt a special friendship between us. Throughout the night, I found myself in conversation with Anne Marie. We started to talk about dance and dancing in Barrie, a larger town a half-hour away, when the words popped out of my mouth, "I love to dance and would love to join you sometime." We exchanged numbers and plugged them into our cellphones. I had an understanding that this was for something much bigger than both of us knew.

The night was great, although I started to develop this sick feeling inside and I knew it was about Dylan. I also at this moment knew I could never let Dylan out of my heart, never, and so a message was sent saying exactly this. There then was a reply, "Hey, I miss you, too." I think this time of doubt was about the fact that I met this kid six months ago and now I felt like he was my kid and I was even acting like a complete mother to him. It was the strangest feeling; it was as if I had been his mother forever. Or I even thought that maybe I had been his mother in a previous lifetime and we had finally found each other again—which, to be honest, was wonderful and scary at the same time. I decided to step a bit back but still be there for Dylan. Most of all, I didn't want it to be about me; I just wanted it to be about the support of a mother, the power of parental love, and how important our role as parents are in our kids' lives. Plus, I wanted to embrace the magic that can happen with parental love and the power of love in any form.

Confirmation

The next day was Saturday and we had our regular shift together at Mama's Restaurant. I arrived at work first and then Dylan, and when he entered the wait staff area, he came right over and gave me a big hug, which brought tears to my eyes. The restaurant then got busy very fast, and we all got to work. When he got a chance, Dylan told me he was to play at Penetang Legion that evening for a total of five songs and asked if I wanted to go watch. At first, I didn't know what to say; he then explained he had a ride and I could just come on my own and watch. I still had no response, as I truly didn't know what to do. What happened in the next five minutes would show me all the confirmation I that I would ever need to know the role I was to play in Dylan's life.

Dylan came back to me with a stunned look on his face. I asked what was wrong, and he said that his ride had just put his car into the ditch and could not pick him up. I was also stunned, and I looked at Dylan with complete dismay as he handed me his cellphone and showed me the text. I was now holding Dylan's phone, and he was sort of behind me looking over my shoulder and looking at the phone as well. I then turned and looked at him; I looked right into his eyes as if I could see right inside of him and right to his heart. I said nothing, gave him his phone, and started walking to the front of the restaurant.

At this time, I started talking to God just as if it were only God and me in the entire restaurant! And this is what I said: "Okay, I get it, I get it. I totally understand that I am to look after this kid—I get it. I then walked directly back to Dylan and said, "I will take you," and he said, "Are you sure?" I said, "Yes, I am sure. I get it—I am to be a part of your life, to take you to your performances, to help you in all areas of your life, support you, watch you play, and just be there for you." We then exchanged a short and powerful hug. I do think that this moment also shook Dylan up as well; I think this was the first time I had seen him realize the power of the universe, as it was right in front of him.

Then Chrissy and I started making plans, and Dylan said, "Well, maybe I shouldn't go," and I said, "Yes, Dylan, you should go." Chrissy chimed in, "Dylan, you listen to Jenny," and Dylan said, "I do; I tell her everything." Chrissy then drove Dylan home while I went home to change, and we were all set. I picked Dylan up just shortly after nine and we were a half-hour later sitting in the Penetang Legion once again waiting for him to perform.

I was happy that some of my friends, Monique and Brian, were there (I had been playing cards with Monique once a month and she had also been at Marilyn's the other night). So we all sat together with good energy, having a drink and listening to the music. This was a serial moment for me as I looked at Dylan all excited to get on stage thinking, how could I have even thought I could let go of this amazing child?

As Dylan took the stage, I had to move so I could see him. Once again, the Dylan Lockstar Fever came over the people as Dylan shined on stage and played even better than before. At this time, I realized he was stepping into his talent more and more during each and every one of his performances. A nice man asked me to dance and said, "Who is this kid? He is stealing the show," and of course I said, "That's my son." Well, I thought the hug I received after Penetang Idol was special, but the hug I received after this performance was something I would cherish for the rest of my life! It was a hug that meant more than just an amazing performance; it was the knowing from both of us that our connection would be there forever, and so it became so!

The night ended with me buying Dylan a sub at Mr. Sub. He asked whether I would be willing to teach him how to grocery shop, and of course, I said yes. Dylan and I were back on track, and all was good.

Life had for sure shown its direction to me, and it was something I was going to embrace instead of fight against. Everything seemed to be in place. I had healed in my life and was strong and living a life full of joy and peace. My mom was living with me, so my caregiving duties were centered right at home, and the financial abundance that resulted from this arrangement was creating an ease in my being able to survive as a single woman. Kate was on her path to graduate in May from Arizona State University as a Civil Engineer, Emily was doing great at Queen's University with her studies in engineering, and Christine was trying again in her relationship with Paul's dad. I was still babysitting baby Paul every Friday and working fifteen hours a week. And so once again it was time to embrace the path that was right in front of me.

Being a Mom

Now that I clearly understood what my position or my role in Dylan's life was going to be—that I was to be a Mom for Dylan—it became apparent that it was now time to be exactly that and get him going with everything he needed. I was standing beside Dylan and for some reason took notice of his coat, and I thought to myself, Dylan, you need a new coat. I am not sure if it was that the colour of grey was off with his black hair or the fact the coat he was wearing looked cold. Or it even might have been just a maternal knowing that he needed a new coat. It was like I looked at him and saw the vision of him in a black coat without a hood, crisp and clean, strong and powerful.

Four days later, I took my mom to get her nails done, and as I was waiting for her I went into the Sport Chek right across the way. There happened to be a coat rack of winter coats on sale, and so I started looking for the right size, thinking Dylan would be a medium to a large. I found this amazing black coat with white trim. It had a tailored collar and was not bulky, but it looked warm. Perfect! By now, a nice young man who worked at the store asked me if I needed any help. I told him I was buying this coat as a gift for a twenty-one-year-old and did he think he would like it. The workers name was Taylor, and he said, yes, it was a beautiful coat and it was on sale, 50 percent off. I said I would take it and headed to the cash register, and I just knew I had the right coat. I could not wait to show it to my mom, and she said immediately that she would pay for half.

Later, we picked up Dylan and took him to my house for the first time. As we settled into the living room, I had a hard time keeping quiet, and so within a few minutes I was presenting Dylan with a gift bag. I can still see the expression of surprise, joy, and love on his face as he realized that whatever was in the bag was something for him. As he looked into the bag and saw it was a beautiful black coat, he closed the bag right away and I could see the shock on his face. Time stopped for a second, and I could tell he didn't know what to do. I then got up and said, "Yes, it's a coat and a belated Christmas gift; let's try it on." He then opened the bag and pulled out the coat and said, "No one has ever bought me a coat." This was a special moment as Dylan tried on the coat and it was absolutely perfect.

We then just sat and talked, my mom and me watching Dylan closely, as he didn't take off the coat. It was a moment I would never forget, a moment of gratitude and a moment of love. Dylan did go outside for a quick smoke and returned saying this was the first time he didn't shiver when he was outside. My mom and I had the knowing that we had just done something amazing for this young man.

We then received a phone call from my friend Stephanie asking if we would like to come for dinner, and Dylan and I accepted. Soon we then were on our way to Stephanie's. Stephanie had a beautiful house on the water, which was always a joy to go to. As we sat watching Stephanie prepare us some of her wonderful pasta, she turned to Dylan and said, "You know, you can take your coat off." And his reply was, "No, I just got this coat, and it feels so great, I can't take it off!"

As we returned to my house, Dylan sat on the couch with his new coat on and I on the Lazy Boy chair, and he began to tell me about some of his childhood and the discovery of his musical talent. Dylan first told me about when he was in grade two and he started running on the cross-country team and found himself running in perfect time—and what was happening in his head at this time was something amazing. He could hear beats and melodies as he was running. It was like his feet were the base drum and the band was playing in his head. I thought to myself, wow, that must have been a little overwhelming, but I said nothing. Dylan said that he wondered if other kids could hear the same thing, but he chose not to tell anyone what was happening in his head when he was running.

Dylan then continued to tell me about his love for the piano, as whenever he entered into a room with a piano, he would be pulled towards it as if it were a magnet. He also told me about when he was five and there was a piano in the basement of the house he lived in, and that with his index finger he taught himself how to play, starting with "Mary Had a Little Lamb" and "Twinkle Twinkle Little Star." I said, "Wow, I should write this down," and he said to me, "You will remember it all," and so I have.

It was at the end of grade eight that Dylan's dad bought him his first keyboard, which to this day was the best gift he had ever received besides the gift of love—as we truly know the best gift in life is the gift of love. He shared that he played this keyboard every day. He started with learning the music that was programed into the keyboard. He would listen to a bit of a song and then he could play it. At that time, he still didn't realize his talent, as he thought that everyone could listen to music and be able to play it. It wasn't until he tried to teach a buddy this procedure that he realized he could do something that most people could not.

One day, Dylan was practicing and his dad came bursting into the room and said, "Now, really Dylan, do you need to hear that Red Hot Chili Peppers song so often?" And Dylan's reply was, "Dad, that's me!" His dad then stood there in dismay, saying, "I thought you were listening to the radio." He walked away thinking, wow that was strange and that Dylan was really good.

It eventually became time for Dylan to go out on his own, around the time when he turned seventeen. He knew that his dad loved him very much, but he felt that the right path for him was to move out and find another place to live. And that is exactly what Dylan did: he moved out and found a room to rent at a buddy's house. This was a very busy time for him maintaining his schoolwork while working at Boston Pizza and learning how to support himself at the age of seventeen.

We Had Started

I remembered back to the fundraiser at the Legion when a couple of people had asked Dylan if he had a business card, and I thought to myself that Dylan did indeed need a business card. I also knew that this coming Friday Dylan had another performance for Garfield at a Lasagna Dinner, and it would be great if he had some business cards to hand out. I contacted Daryl at the Middletown Copy Shoppe and asked him to put something together as a business card for Dylan.

That Thursday, Dylan was working at the hotel that Frank also owned, in addition to Mama's Restaurant. I knew that Dylan needed to see the business card proofs and look at them overnight before he picked the one he liked. So I picked up the proofs and started towards the hotel. I ended up making a pit stop at the Mr. Sub we had stopped at after the Legion performance. I remembered what Dylan had ordered and ordered the same, and then headed to the hotel with lunch and business card proofs in hand. As I arrived at the hotel, I noticed it was very dusty, as they were cleaning up after doing some drywall work. It was like a cloud of dust was everywhere.

Of course, the first person I bumped into was Frank; he asked if I was there to see my son, and I replied yes. I thought how great it was that Frank understood that Dylan was like a son to me—in fact, I felt a large amount of relief. Frank then showed me where Dylan was working, and I had a huge motherly moment, as he had a mask on and was all covered in drywall dust. I knew he was only getting paid minimum wage and that this was not enough for the work he was doing. I then focused on the joy on Dylan's face, as he was so happy to see me and also a little surprised. I first showed him the proofs of the business card, as they were so good that I couldn't wait. Dylan was amazed and loved the proofs right away. I explained that he could look them over that night and pick the one he liked, and I would have fifty printed for the performance the next day. Then I showed him his lunch, and his mouth dropped open and he said thank you and that he hadn't eaten anything yet that day. He then gave me the biggest hug and next started trying to brush off the drywall dust that was now all over me. I said not to worry and I only had a minute, and then we looked at the proofs one more time. He asked, "Are you sure you are not hungry? I could share my sub with you," but I said, "No thanks, that sub is all for you" and went out the door. As I walked out of the hotel, I started to worry about Dylan's voice being in all that drywall dust, but there was nothing I could do about it.

The next morning, I talked with Dylan and then ordered the business card he liked (which happened to be my choice as well), and the cards were set to be picked up in two hours. On my way over, I stopped and bought a great card holder at Staples and then I dropped the first set of cards off at Dylan's house. The excitement was all over his face, as he was delighted with how great they turned out and there is just something special about the feeling when you see your name on your first business card. I said I would see him later, as I was taking my mom to the Lasagna Dinner as well. There were to be three seating's, and I had purchased tickets for the first one. Dylan's dad was taking him to this performance, and all was good.

When my mom and I arrived, we were pleased to see that the business cards were on his keyboard. Dylan was providing the background music and was located just outside the dining hall. There was a nice table there, so Dylan's dad, Mimi, and I sat down for a visit and to enjoy the music. Dylan was doing a fabulous job as always, and I found it hard to carry on a conversation while he was playing, but somehow I managed. We then got some dinner. As the time passed, Mimi and I should have left, but for some reason I couldn't, I just couldn't. It was like I was at my son's volleyball game and I couldn't leave—I just couldn't go. I wondered what the people thought about the three of us who stayed throughout all three seating's.

I finally had the knowing that it was time to go, and as I got up and got the coats, there was Dylan standing right beside me with a huge smile on his face. I just smiled back at him and said how proud I was of him and that he was amazing as always. He told me that he had given out thirty business cards, which immediately brought tears to my eyes. His dad Gary then was by our side, asking if he could help with Mimi to the car, and my reply was yes and thank you very much. Dylan said he was just going to play a few more songs and thanked Mimi and I for coming and hugged us all. As Gary got us to the car, he thanked me for the business cards and I told him it was my pleasure. Then I drove away, and Niagara Falls entered the car as I just completely broke out into a major cry. I couldn't figure out what was happening, but I was having a huge emotional release.

Next I began to notice how very thin Dylan was and I asked him how much he weighed. He said he was not sure, but there was a scale in his house that his landlord Cheryl had and he could weigh himself. I thought great, as we were also on a path to get all his paperwork together and up-to-date, so we needed his weight anyway. I knew that he was six feet tall and had a rough idea about what a good weight would be. Two days later, Dylan told me he had weighed himself and wasn't sure if I would want to hear; he then asked me if I did and I said yes. He told me that he weighed 148 pounds, and I thought, oh boy, time for a trip to Food Basics.

We then got in the car and headed to the grocery store to shop for items that were high fat and contained lots of calories. As we entered the store and picked up a flyer, we both noticed that cookies were on sale, and pasta and bread as well. I remarked to Dylan that they must have known we were coming. We did start with the produce department, as healthy was also part of the plan. We bought apples, salad things, and carrots; then we went to the bread section and bought muffins, nice blueberry ones. We went up and down every aisle, so I could teach Dylan what items went together to make meals and good snacks. We were looking on the higher calorie side, as we needed to put weight onto Dylan bones. When we found the bins of cookies on sale, it was like Christmas, as we bought quite a few packages. We then ended with eggs, milk, and cheese—oh and, of course, we bought peanut butter.

I could see that Dylan was excited to learn about the grocery store. When it came time to check out, I realized that this was Dylan's first large load of food shopping ever. I knew that money was tight for him, so he gave me what he could and I paid the rest. I was happy to do this, as by now he was just one of my kids and this is what he needed.

One of our main goals with Dylan was for him to get his driver's licence and for that we needed a birth certificate. Dylan's dad did have a birth certificate for him at one point, but he had given it to Dylan and somehow it got misplaced. We started gathering all the other information in the meantime, but we soon realized that we needed the birth certificate to get everything else accomplished. It was around the time that we also realized that Dylan would have to contact his birth mother, as we needed some information from her for the application. I know there was a little hesitation on Dylan's part, but I just sat back and let it unfold.

Dylan shared with me that he had sent his birth mom an email asking for the information and also telling her that she would always be his mom, although he now had support in his life and he was happy having this type of support. I can remember looking at Dylan when he told me this and not being able to say a thing, as the emotions I had been experiencing had already been so overwhelming and there was no room for fear.

It did take quite a lot of time to get everything together for the birth certificate. Meanwhile, Dylan was busy studying the driver's handbook that I had lent him from Mimi. I just kept focused, as I had the knowing that it was the birth certificate, then the driver's licence, and finally the passport. I just knew we had to get all these things into place for Dylan!

The next thing that Dylan needed was a new cellphone. Frank at the restaurant had been okay with being the answering service for Dylan, but we all knew that for any large amount of success you needed access to the technology of the times. I talked to Dylan and said we needed to go to the local Rogers store and just ask some questions. So we got in the car and headed to Rogers in Middletown where I had had my cellphone service for the past ten years. We arrived and got in line, and watched the excitement of other customers getting their new phones set up. I had had a cellphone for a very long time and also had a phone for Kate (my ex-husband helped Emily with hers). I had an idea of the questions I was going to ask, mostly concerning what deals were available to add a child to my cellphone line. As I looked at Dylan, I could see the joy in his eyes as it now became our turn.

The young girl was great and explained that I could add another line for a child of mine for only 50 dollars a month more and that we could have free texting and share 400 daytime minutes per month and so many gigabytes of data. This sounded great, so I asked what phone styles were available and how much would they cost? This was a moment of pure joy, as she said Dylan could get an iPhone4 and that the cost was only 50 dollars if I signed up for another three-year contract (she did mention if there was a cancellation, there would be a charge of 400 dollars). I didn't worry too much about the cancellation risk, as I had signed up for so many three-year contracts and I knew that things had been going our way and that this was just more good luck.

I said thank you to the girl, and Dylan and I stepped away to talk about it, as this was the plan from the beginning—that we would look and then talk about it. I asked Dylan what he thought, and he said that the 50 dollars a month would be manageable and that he felt this was okay. He also said he would have 50 dollars next pay cheque to cover the cost of the phone, which I thought was very reasonable. I said, "Well, this is good for me, too; let's do it." Dylan said, "Really?" and I said, "I am good with it as long as you are." We got back in line and the girl took us right away. She then asked Dylan what colour he wanted: white or black. Dylan looked at me and I said nothing and just smiled at him for him to choose. Dylan chose black, and the girl headed to the cupboard. Dylan then looked at me with such happiness and said, "I can't believe I am getting an iPhone4." Once again I just smiled back at him, knowing that to be a rock star he would need Internet, texting, and daytime minutes.

Within twenty minutes, we were on our way back to Dylan's house with the new cellphone in hand. I quickly headed home to get ready for work with a great feeling that Dylan now had a very important tool for success in his business career as a musician.

Boston Pizza

Mimi and I were regulars at the Boston Pizza located in Middletown. We quite enjoyed the food, staff, and atmosphere, and due to the fact we were such wonderful customers, the owner would come over for a visit and talk to us every time he saw us. We would go almost every Monday and Thursday, and so as Dylan became a large part of our life, we started inviting him as well. As he sat at the table, we thought about and missed Emily and Kate, as this was a special spot for all the kids to go.

I always liked to just listen to Dylan, as he was full of great knowledge, especially about music. He also did mention that he worked at this Boston Pizza when he was sixteen and how he had rode his bike from Victoria Harbour (twelve miles away) and back home—and that the ride home at one in the morning was a scary one, as he had to travel Highway 12. I replied that I could imagine. Silently, I wished I could have been there to drive him home. Coincidentally, Kate also worked at the same Boston Pizza at the exact same time as Dylan did.

The Jam Session

Time was passing, we were busy and everything was falling into place. I found myself one Saturday night at a jam session in the lower level of a house just outside of the Middletown area. My first impression of the people was wonderful, as when I entered the room not really knowing anyone, I was greeted by the hostess with an introduction and a warm welcome. One thing I noticed immediately was the diverse age range of the guests. It reminded me of a gathering of family, but these people were there for a reason: they were there for their music and their passion. At first, I had a difficult time finding the right location to sit so I could really be a part of this amazing experience. Then a nice man set me up a chair in a perfect location and encouraged me to move forward and settle in, and this was exactly what I did.

From this perfect spot, I was first of all able to have a clear view of Dylan and his keyboard, which was soothing—just like having a good view of my girls during a waterski competition. I was also able to open up to every detail and every person who was in the room. I can remember thinking how great this was, as I was a people watcher. I could immediately detect their energy and level of consciousness, but most of all, I could feel their love for music. This was the message or the essence of the evening—yes, it became about the love of music!

It was interesting to watch the many musicians search for a song that was familiar to all. I must say, I knew all the songs, and it was funny to see that Dylan did not. I had to remind myself that he was only twenty-one, but his ability to play, pick up lyrics, and so on just showed more brilliance within his musical talent. I was very fortunate to have two wonderful women with wonderful souls sitting on both sides of me. I recognized the woman to my right, Cheryl, as the number-one judge from the Penetang Idol competition, and she remembered me as well. We briefly talked about Dylan and his musical ability, as it was something that we both already knew and it was just understood with very few words.

The Supertramp song "School" became the highlight of the evening. Dylan was giving a mini rundown of the keys and change of cords, this being something he had to learn. He knew how to play the all the music, but to play with other musicians he had to learn the language of music—which was the naming of the cords, which he picked up at a miraculous speed. I was at this time thankful for my musical background, as I understood it all. This song was also the moment when I recognized that the room became one, which made me realize that music made the human race one. Yes, it brought us the people to one, one being, and this was truly the gift of music. I believe that the human race becoming one is necessary to heal the world, and here I saw that music could become a main source of healing. Of course, the song was fabulous, God-like, and amazing, and so was the experience. The musicians were as one. The audience had tambourines and were using spoons as instruments, and the smiles and joy on their faces was raw and yet there was a sense of peace and love within the room.

As time passed, the woman to my left (whose name was Donna) became very apparent to me. She had a beautiful essence within, and her smile was resonating a strong internal love. People in the room were continually encouraging her to take the stage, and I specifically remember the strong support from her daughter, who was about the age of eighteen. Although Donna resisted going forward, I was just watching to see what really was unfolding—and let me tell you, what was unfolding was truly great. I think it was the fourth time she was asked, and a hand was placed in front of Donna that I knew was really the lifeline she so very wanted to receive. The next thing I knew, she was in the center of the stage donning her guitar and preparing to perform. Then I got a good understanding of the true meaning of a jam session: it was the experience of the passion of people for music . . . how fantastic!

Donna's voice was beautiful, magical, and full of love. Her music was like country but with a little opera sense to it. Then the greatest gift appeared: her daughter had moved behind her and was singing as well, and of course this made me warm and fuzzy all over. I never once moved during the two songs they performed, and afterward I felt compelled to give Donna a hug and comment on what a beautiful voice she had and how magical it was to see her daughter singing with her.

I must say, I could have stayed all night and watched the people, the music, and of course Dylan and his magic, but around 1:30 a.m. I had the awareness that it was time to head home. Once again, on the car ride home, Dylan and I exchanged in our regular discussion of the evening, the people, and the music. After I dropped him at home, I didn't feel the need to turn on the radio because the music and the people from the evening were still with me. I know now it was the success, joy, and magic of the evening that was still sitting with me, and the message of this evening was: IT WAS ALL ABOUT THE PEOPLE. On a night of music or art, it is all about the people—as this night truly was—it has the power to once again bring success, love, and most of all the connection of the people as being one. This was, according to my belief system, a miracle in itself.

Mama's Restaurant

Mama's Restaurant actually started to become a difficult place to be for Dylan and me. We noticed that people where watching us and that there was some judgement in the air. The staff members who knew our history understood, although there was judgement in some people's minds, and therefore Dylan and I started to compensate by exuding a completely professional approach to one another. At times it would be funny, because if something happened and we found ourselves in conversation, it was as if no one else was in the room, and when we stopped talking, it was as if everyone was staring at us. Of course, Dylan and I never thought anything of it, as we were just being us. I can remember Frank telling me not to talk to Dylan, and I thought whatever. I tried to just focus on my work, and I was very thankful for Jean and Gerry, loyal customers at Mama's Restaurant, who also had taken in a girl as a daughter at the age of nineteen and understood the relationship completely.

It was a sunny Saturday in early March. I had set up my first small performance for Dylan; I was not completely sure why this performance was taking place, but it was requested and easily set up, and I felt it was just meant to be. I knew that the right people would be there, as this is just the way it always is and how I choose to live my life. I had dropped off a new sweater for Dylan on the Friday before and confirmed I would be there to pick him up at 1:30 p.m. the next day.

As I awoke on Saturday morning, I felt a special excitement within. This excitement was there for many reasons but primarily because I knew that I was going to see Dylan play live. This was becoming one of the most special times in my life and something that was happening on a weekly basis. As the morning progressed, I started wanting to make contact with Dylan to confirm that he was going to be ready and going to bring his keyboard. Although the other side of me was saying to let him be, the business side of me took over around 11:15 a.m. and I sent a text confirming the details of the afternoon, but there was no reply. I waited an hour and a half and then texted him again, asking if he was out there, and still there was no response. I then called him and still nothing.

Now Mama Jenny took over, and it became about finding out whether Dylan was okay. It was getting close to performance time, so I loaded my mom up, as I was dropping her off first to make room for the equipment. It was only one minute into my frantic drive to Dylan's house that I received a text from him, saying he thought it was 2:00 p.m. and he was not ready. I then breathed a sigh of relief and replied, "Glad you're alive," and a follow-up text, "You gave me a heart attack." He replied, "It's okay, Mama Jenny; don't worry, I am okay." I then flashed back to a time when I had to drive frantically to Emily, my youngest daughter, after she called and told me she had hit a deer, which turned out to be a moose.

So I did another errand and got to Dylan's just before 2:00 p.m., and there the answer to all was right in front of me. There was Dylan in his cozy clothes and looking a little green. Now, I knew Dylan was not a drinker and that he got extreme hangovers, but I had never seen Dylan, my wonderful son, in this state until now. I nicely said, "You need to change and put on some nice clothes, and you need your keyboard." There was a surprised look on his face and probably on mine; I was thinking, please give me the right words and let this unfold in a beautiful way. And I must say, it did! We got to Stephanie's, which was like home for all of us, and she quickly got some food into Dylan and the afternoon started to unfold in a very relaxed way.

Dylan's performance was once again amazing. It seemed to me that he got better and better every time he played. This performance in particular was very special because he sang some of his songs, the ones he had written, and they were so very good. He played, "The Killer and the Sin," "She Lost," and my favourite, "Shanti Love." I once again watched the response from the people, and it was like they felt his love and that this love entered into their hearts—it was amazing to see. I spent almost as much time watching the people as I did Dylan as he performed. As we packed up and Dylan sat in the car, his first words were, "Am I ever tired," and this was more confirmation that there was a star sitting beside me. After the performance I had just watched, I knew once again the magnitude of Dylan's talent.

During the ride back to Dylan's and then to work for him (as I was off that night), our relationship moved to a stronger level We started bickering a bit back and forth, and then realized how nice it was to be able to be ourselves and say what was on our minds, knowing it was from a place of love. This was also a moment when Dylan really reminded me of my girls, especially Kate, and the many times we were in the car after a waterski tournament. It felt the same!

The lessons from this afternoon were many on my end—I am sure also for Dylan, but I can only speak from my perspective. Most importantly, this was about having faith and trust that things would unfold, that the right words would come when needed: patience, patience, and more patience. I also learned to trust in my team, that it was okay to be honest and it was wonderful to do this from a place of love. These were all the lessons in my first book and lessons I knew and lived by, but it's always fabulous when you get to apply them to new situations. I also remember thinking that this was just the beginning, that I was going to have many situations where I was going to have to apply my knowledge and consciousness on the journey of Dylan Lockstar, the rock and roll legend!

My Birthday

It was the weekend before my fifty-first birthday, and Anne Marie called and asked if I wanted to join some friends and go dancing in Barrie. My first thought was, yes, I would love to go dancing, as dancing had always been a passion of mine. I could remember enjoying many a year as a young woman and later a mom in dance class. I then thought of Mimi and the money, but somehow I was able to see that I needed some time for me. So I replied to Anne Marie, "Yes, I would love to join you," and plans were set into place.

As I awoke that fine Saturday morning, I had a feeling of excitement within and started to prepare for my evening out. I packed some nice clothes, some snacks, and some wine as well. I touched base with all my kids and Mimi, and headed to Barrie. I arrived in Barrie with a peaceful feeling, as there is nothing like a road trip, even a forty-five minute one. To my surprise Monique was with Anne Marie, and I immediately knew that we were going to have lots of fun. We ordered pizza and started to enjoy the evening.

As we entered the bar, I noticed that it was a little younger crowd, but there was a live band and the music was great. One thing about music and dancing is: it is something where age doesn't matter. You all just become one, and this was what happened. We spent two hours straight on the dance floor, and it was fantastic—I felt fantastic. This was also the moment my dancing shoes came back to life. I think it had been quite a few years since I had placed them back on my feet, but I was grateful to Anne Marie for reopening my love for dancing.

The following Wednesday night, March 14, I was asked to work the Friday night shift for Margaret, which was my actual birthday, March 16. I was already working that Saturday and Sunday night, and this was going to be my night off. Mimi and I had planned to go to Boston Pizza for dinner. I first said no, I couldn't work, and then I heard that Margaret was going to take the night off anyway and that the restaurant would be short-staffed. This was the start of March break for the kids and I knew it would be busy, so I made a call to my manager Dianne and said I would work. I told my mom and Dylan, as he was thinking of joining us for dinner at Boston Pizza, that I now had to work. Emily and Kate were both at school, so it was okay.

I woke up on my birthday a year older and a year better. I had healed, and my life was busy and full of love. Christine called and said that she and Paul wanted to see me that morning and asked if I could come down to her mom's for a visit. I said, sure, I would love that. When I arrived, I was blessed with a beautiful card, a cake, and much love from Christine and Paul. We had a wonderful visit, the cake was fantastic, and the handmade card from Paul to Nana Jenny was very special. I had also received a call from Kate and a call from Emily, and my day was going very well. I then got myself ready for work and headed to the restaurant.

As I arrived at the restaurant, it was already busy with people starting their holidays. When I was ringing in an order, a woman entered the front door of the restaurant holding a bouquet of flowers and asked me directly if I was Jenny. I replied yes, and she handed me the flowers. I placed them to the side and continued to enter the food order. The staff then asked me who were the flowers from, and I said that I was not sure as I had not yet opened the card. When I had time to check the card, I was delighted to see that they were from my daughter Emily. A tear appeared instantly in my eye and the joy of her love entered my spirit. I then told everyone the flowers were from Emily and how blessed I was to have such a considerate daughter. I thought to myself, what a fabulous birthday. After my shift I headed home, as I was tired after all the excitement. I checked my Facebook and received a message from Dylan wishing me a happy birthday. I was grateful for the day, although the surprises were not completely over.

The next morning, Dylan texted and said he had posted a new YouTube video and maybe I would like to check it out. As I was loading his channel, Dylanlockstar, a feeling of joy and love appeared within. I quickly scrolled down to the new posts, and there it was: Styx's "Come Sail Away." I clicked on the video and got ready for the show. I sat and watched Dylan singing one of my favourite songs and a song that now had a history intertwined with this wonderful new son of mine. It became an emotional time for me. I sat with a smile on my face, knowing that this song was for me, and then the tears just started to run down my face, although I had amazing warmth within my heart.

I called Dylan and thanked him for my birthday present and told him what a fabulous job he had done on this YouTube video. Dylan reminded me that he was playing at the Library Restaurant in Middletown for the daytime festivities, as this day was, of course, St. Patrick's Day, March 17. I said, "Oh yes, thank you; I will call a girlfriend and see if she will join me." I arranged for Anne Marie to join me and listen to Dylan for the first time. Dylan had his own transportation and was starting at noon, and I was set to meet Anne Marie at 1:00 p.m. I was excited for this performance, because it was a small-stage performance and Dylan was playing for four hours straight.

I arrived first and got a great seat for Anne Marie and myself. It was so wonderful to see Dylan in this type of venue, and he was shining, which brought so much joy to me. I sat for a few moments and reflected as I watched this young man play the piano and sing. I thought back to one of the movie nights we had recently shared, watching the movie The Blind Side. The storyline was the same as ours, but our story was about music. I remember how this woman said, "That is my son," and I felt the exact way at that moment about Dylan. I went to extreme gratitude for the joy and love that were now in my life. I then came back to the moment and smiled at Dylan, and he smiled back at me. It was as if he saw where I had been, as if he knew what I had been thinking. It was a very strange moment.

Anne Marie arrived with St. Patrick's decorations in hand and a birthday gift as well. We both donned our green leis that she had brought for us and settled in for the show. Anne Marie had not met Dylan, and after a few songs she commented about how talented he was.

Earlier that morning, I had also spoken with Anna Thompson, who was a world-renowned vocal instructor. I was working on setting up vocal lessons for Dylan, and I found myself in a very familiar situation to the many years spent arranging lessons of some sort or another for both of my children. Dylan had sought out Anna two years ago and to no avail, but things were lining up much differently this time. First off, Anna was present during the finals of Penetang Idol, and most important, she had been sitting at the table where Marlene and David were sitting and had the opportunity to meet Dylan. So I was able to arrange the first lesson, which was tentatively booked for March 19. I can still remember the smile on Dylan's face when I told him I had a lesson booked with Anna—just another joyful moment with this wonderful young man.

Anna had been on holidays during the week of March 11 to 16, and so she asked me to call her for confirmation. During this phone call, my heart just about broke in two, as due to poor timing with the local music festival she was not sure if she could take Dylan for his lesson. All I could say to her was that he was so looking forward to this lesson. But the universe had a different idea. As Anna was listening to her radio that morning, she heard that Dylan was the live entertainment for the St. Patrick's Day celebration at the Library Restaurant. She had told me that she called David and Marlene that morning and they were thinking of attending.

As Anne Marie and I were sitting enjoying the music, Marlene and David walked in and I was so very glad to see then. We were now surrounded by family. When I went to greet Marlene, she said that Anna was coming to listen to Dylan. I mentioned that I had spoken with her this morning and I was so happy to hear she was coming for the show.

Dylan did take a short break, where he enjoyed visiting with all the people there, including Cheryl his landlord and some friends from the music world. Dylan then went over to see Marlene and David before he joined Anne Marie and me for a visit. It was nice to introduce Anne Marie to Dylan. I told Dylan that Anna was going to join Marlene and David, and a large smile appeared on Dylan's face. Now, Dylan never sat for very long, as he just loved to play and entertain the people, and therefore it wasn't before long that he was back behind his keyboard getting ready for another set.

About two songs into this next set, Anna appeared at the door and took a seat at the table with Marlene and David. I sent a smile over her way, and Dylan then made the connection and realized Anna was in attendance. It now became very interesting and also a little magical watching Dylan choose the songs that would capture the heart of Anna— and of course, he did! Within thirty minutes, Anna was talking to me and saying 7:30 p.m. was a better time, and then writing her address down on a piece of paper for me. All I could think was, thank goodness I didn't have to tell Dylan about the possibility of the cancellation (and if he is reading this chapter for the first time, he now knows!).

This day had only begun, as after the performance it was time for the both of us to go to Mama's Restaurant for work. We packed up Dylan's equipment and went to work. During the past few weeks, a good friend of Frank's was in the process of reopening a new bar in town. All the staff at Mama's was invited to attend the unplanned opening that night, St. Patrick's Day. I was thinking this would be a good idea, as the local dance bar was closed for renovation and everyone liked to go out for St. Patty's Day. When asked if I was going, I felt a little apprehensive. I thought it would be nice, as it was my birthday weekend and I hadn't really been out (and in two years I hadn't really been out anywhere except with Anne Marie a few weeks ago). I was told it was to be an older crowd, and of course, I had just found my dancing shoes, so I started to lean towards maybe going.

The word at the restaurant was that there would be about eight staff members going, and Frank and his wife would also be attending, so I headed home and found some dancing clothes and then headed back to Middletown. I was happy when I arrived at the bar that Dylan, Nick, and Maryanne were there. Nick was an amazing line cook who worked at Mama's, and he often reminded me of a teddy bear, as he was tall and one of the most peaceful spirits I had ever met. Joe, the bar owner, was very happy to see us and thanked us for the support. I was glad I had made the trip back to Middletown.

The music was great, and I found Nick asking me to dance. I looked to Maryanne his girlfriend and saw that she was very comfortable with Nick dancing with a mom figure. Nick was a very good dancer, and we danced a few dances. I felt that it was almost like being at the cottage or in a family atmosphere or a wedding, where the kids and other parents dance together, although we were in the bar. At that moment, I wondered if all the kids around were missing their parents hanging out with them and if these kids had experienced the joy of family and everyone being together on a Saturday night, as this was what I had experienced for the past fifty years.

I noticed Dylan out on the dance floor and not quite sure how to take his new mom dancing with the kids. I knew that he had probably never even been out with a parent in his twenty-one years of life. I then decided it was maybe time for a break and headed for some water. Dylan came to stand beside me, talking about what a day it has been. I totally agreed and told him that I was going to take a cab home soon. I was glad to have had a dance and given my support to Joe, but it was time for me to go home. I then called a cab, said my goodbyes, and headed to the door, and there was Dylan once again standing beside me, saying, "I will wait until your cab comes." I thought, what a fine young man you are. The cab came very quickly, and Dylan gave me a hug and kiss goodbye and told me he loved me, and I pulled away in the taxi. I then turned to the taxi driver and said, "That is my wonderful son looking after his mother!"

First Vocal Lesson

Around March 19, we had had the most amazing change in the weather. Normally, the temperatures at this time would be around 50 degrees, but this day it was in the 80's. I was excited about Dylan's first vocal lesson, as this was the first lesson of any kind that he had experienced. I almost felt like my mother, as I was a little early to pick him up, and when he approached my car, what I noticed first was that he had the most amazing smile on his face. But next I noticed that he had board shorts and dress shoes on. I, of course, concentrated on the smile and the excitement of the lesson to come as we drove over to Anna's house. I went in as any mother would, and we sat down since Anna had a few questions to go over first (these were the same types of questions I had answered before with Kate and Emily during their many waterskiing and music lessons).

As always, I was so impressed and amazed at the level of communication skills Dylan had and how he was able to handle himself perfectly. Anna asked when he started hearing beats and melodies, and how many songs had he written. I knew Dylan had written at least six songs (as there were six songs on his CD), but his answer was at least fifteen. I thought to myself, wow, that is quite a lot.

As the conversation continued, I started seeing more and more the brilliance within Dylan. He looked over at me a few times, and I just gave him support, as I knew this was what he was looking for: support and stability. It was if he felt safe and this made it okay to open up about his talent. Anna then concentrated on Dylan piano skills. With the level of his ability and skill despite NO lessons at all, just the natural talent, she compared Dylan to Elton John, which I completely agreed with.

Finally, it was time to move to the lesson area, which was in the living room where the piano sat. I took my spot in the kitchen where I was able to see Anna, and Dylan had his back to me, which was perfect. This way, Dylan had the knowing I was there; I could feel his child-like connection at this time. During the next twenty minutes, Dylan learned how to breathe properly and to provide maximum control over his voice using a variation of scales. The most exciting point of this lesson was when Anna let loose her voice, and let me tell you, it was amazing and also like a freight train coming at you. The entire house shook. She commented on how the neighbours could hear her as well, and I immediately thought to myself, I bet they do.

The lesson ended, and Dylan and I found that we needed some time together to reflect on what we just had experienced. So we ended up at Kelsey's having a beer. As I sat there observing the complete joy on Dylan's face and listening to the excitement in his voice, it was almost like being in a movie or in slow motion. Sometimes when events are unfolding in such an amazing way, time stops for just a second, giving you time to savour the moment and the grace of what has unfolded. There are times when I looked at Dylan that the excitement, joy, and gratitude he was expressing was really what I was seeing and experiencing in such an amazing way. It was almost like I wanted time to stop so that I could capture that special and unique moment. And then, within a split-second, I was back in the conversation.

The conversation was fantastic, because this was the very first vocal or instructional lesson Dylan had ever experienced—and this was after playing "Bohemian Rhapsody" during Penetang Idol. Dylan talked about the control of breath, how great Anna was, and the experience itself, and how he was looking forward to practicing the world-renowned vocal warm-ups she had given him. However, the greatest knowledge that had come from this lesson was the brilliance that Anna saw in Dylan. She had said he had a huge talent and that he would make it in the music industry. This was something I completely agreed with and something I was sure she didn't say very often.

I paid the bill, and we headed back to Dylan's house. On the way, Dylan said to me, "Jenny, I have a couple movies I would like you to watch and that I know you will really like." I said, "Okay, Dylan, that would be great." I then asked Dylan if he had any running shoes. He said no, and then I remembered how he had gotten those dress shoes from Frank for serving the buffet and that Dylan and he were the same size, size twelve.

I pulled into the driveway, and Dylan went quickly up to his room to get the movies for me as I stood outside enjoying the warm night. As I heard the porch door open, I turned to see Dylan and he had four movies in his hand and the biggest smile on his face. I looked a little shocked, as I was thinking, four movies to watch. I looked down at them at the same time Dylan said, "They are four Queen movies." I looked up surprised, and Dylan said, "Freddie Mercury is my idol, and you will really enjoy these movies." I said, "Okay, I love music and the group Queen as well." I then gave Dylan a hug goodbye and started on my way home. As I was driving, I thought to myself that I could have never imagined I would have a son, a son I would take to his first vocal lesson at the age of twenty-one and a son who would give me four Queen movies to go home and watch.

It was just after nine when I arrived home, and it was as if the movie on the top of the pile was calling me to watch it. I was aware that I needed my sleep—something that because of having another busy child I had not had much of—but I knew this was my path, so I cuddled up with the movie, which was the history of the musical group Queen. Within a few moments, I knew exactly why I was watching this movie, as it gave me such insight into the music world and the talent of Freddie. I also saw the same talent in Dylan, and I knew this was why I had been drawn to watch it, as Dylan was gifted just like Freddie. I then thought, wow, how strange that must have been seeing a legend like Freddie and being able to play the piano and sing with the same range as Freddie. Then all of a sudden all the events of the day gelled together and it was like a brick wall had just hit me. I realized I needed to watch and learn as much as I could from this movie and that one day this would all make sense to me.

The next day, I woke with the knowing that I needed to make another trip to the Sport Chek in Middletown, and so this was exactly what I did. As I entered the store and headed to the running shoe section, Taylor must have seen me. As I was looking at the many different types of men's running shoes and thinking that this might be a little more difficult than I thought, I realized that Taylor was standing there asking me if I needed help. I said, "Yes, thank you; I now need a pair of running shoes. And by the way, Dylan loved the coat and it was perfect." Taylor then helped me pick out some Nike running shoes, black and white, and said that I could return them if Dylan didn't like them. On my way to the cash register, I found pair of nice men's flip-flops as well.

I left the store feeling great and somehow managed to enter the Zellers and found myself in the men's department looking at walking shorts, t-shirts, jeans, and a nice black shirt for summer performances. I was having so much fun that I ended up at the cash register with some of each. I then thought, well, Dylan will be surprised. He was at this time working at Mama's Restaurant, so I decided to just leave the bags on the porch and text him saying I just left a couple things for him at home.

A couple hours later I received a text from him saying, "OMG, thank you! The running shoes are perfect!" I then said, "You are welcome; Mimi and I went together on some early birthday presents." I asked about the t-shirts, and Dylan said that they might be a little too big. I thought maybe some mediums would be better, and Dylan thought this was a fabulous idea. I said I would pick him up the next day and we would go to Zellers and get the right size.

I did exactly that: I picked him up at 3:00 p.m. and we were on our way to Zellers. As we entered the store, we went to the customer service area to return the shirts. Dylan was wearing the flip-flops, as it was still very hot outside. I handed the bag to the clerk and said that the t-shirts were too big and we were going to get some smaller ones. She said no problem and started to make the return, and then pointed out that all the tags were off. I shot Dylan a surprised look and no words were exchanged; I just looked at the girl and said, "Sorry, next time we will remember to leave the tags on."

Then Dylan and I went to the men's section and started looking for some nice medium-sized shirts. We found a few black ones. I also picked out a red one and Dylan said nothing, but a few minutes later he pulled it out of my hand and placed it back on the shelf. I just smiled and we kept on looking. Then Dylan said to me that this was the first time ever in his life that he had been shopping with a mom. I looked at him and just wanted to hug him, but I smiled and said nothing. We then went through the cash, and for some reason, I took Dylan into the Sport Chek so he could see where I had bought his running shoes and coat. As we were looking around, there was Taylor once again standing beside me. I said, "Hi, Taylor; this is Dylan." Taylor and Dylan started talking, which was nice.

I then all of a sudden noticed a great sale on some skater shoes and found Dylan beside me saying, "Yes, these are really nice shoes." And of course, there was a size twelve pair sitting right on the top. I thought, well, then Dylan would be complete: three pairs of shoes, shorts, t-shirts, and a shirt for his summer performances. As I was paying for the shoes, Dylan just stood beside me enjoying his first-ever shopping spree. Life was good!

Second Vocal Lesson

Now it was time to really be the mom and pick Dylan up, take him to his lesson, drop him off, and pick him back up in forty-five minutes. Dylan was so cute when he said, "Are you sure you don't want to come in?" I reinforced how important it was for him to develop a relationship with his teacher and that I knew it would not be the same with me in the room, that Anna would be different with me sitting there. I also told him about the many lessons I had taken the girls to and that I had taken them and picked them back up as well. So he hugged me, told me he loved me, and went towards the door. As he entered, he turned back to wave at me and I waved back and smiled, knowing he was going to have a fantastic lesson. This was quite the moment for me, as when I pulled out of the driveway I could feel my heart flip-flopping all over the place. I felt like I had just left my kid at the door of his first-grade classroom. I then thought to myself how blessed I was and to have Dylan in my life!

I next went to the library and started writing more of this book, and I realized that the story I was really writing was the story of Dylan and myself, of our connection, and the amazing parental love that existed between us. This was the story I was to write for the people for inspiration, hope, and proof of love (which is spirituality). But most of all, it was to be about the love between a mother and a child and the power of it; it was all tied together and I got it. I completely got it!

I was watching the time very closely, as I didn't want to be late to pick Dylan up from this second vocal lesson and first time being dropped off by himself. This feeling was something I had experienced many a time with my girls, and once again it felt like I had taken him to his first grade-one class and it was time to pick him up. I somehow managed to get there right on time and pulled into the driveway at 8:15 p.m. sharp. I just sat and waited for him to finish talking with Anna as he headed towards the door. I could hear their conversation and it was about the talent that was within Dylan, and I could see Anna's excitement.

Dylan then said his goodbyes and got into the car with a musical score in his hand. I asked him how his lesson was. He said great and then, "Guess what?" I said, "What Dylan?" He said, "I can sing in Italian!" I exclaimed, "Really?" He explained, "Yes, Anna gave me this music to sing that was in Italian and I could sing it!" I said, "Wow, that's great." I then thought, the talent within this kid is endless. And then we just smiled at each other and I drove Dylan home.

A Wonderful Surprise

The following Friday, Christine called and asked what I had planned for dinner and would I like some company. I agreed that yes, of course I would love to see her and Paul for dinner. I then jumped into my car and headed towards Foodland to get fixings for a wonderful dinner for Christine, Paul, Mimi, and myself. Christine arrived early, and we enjoyed great conversation while we prepared dinner together. I notice during this conversation that Christine was developing a stronger inner self which made me very happy. As I turned to get the salad fixings, I heard the front door crack open very slowly. I immediately stopped in my tracks and thought, who would be coming in my front door, and then my daughter Emily appeared! I looked at Christine, as I now understood why I was cooking this nice dinner—Christine knew all the time that Emily was on her way! So then, of course, I gave Christine a big hug, too.

It was so great to have Emily in the house. She didn't come home very often, as the university she attended was a four-hour drive (far, but I guess better than a five-hour plane flight to Arizona). Emily was also happy to be home as I could sense her happiness the moment she walked in the door. We enjoyed more great conversation and a nice dinner as well. As we were cleaning up the kitchen, I remembered, "Oh, I am supposed to meet Marilyn and her family at the Legion for drinks." Emily said, "Oh, I will join you and drive as well." I thought, wow, this is fantastic to have Emily home and a night of family.

Christine and Paul left, and Emily and I got ready and headed to the Legion in Middletown. Marilyn was happy and surprised to see Emily, and I explained the nice surprise. We all then settled down at a large table full of friends and family. There was Marilyn, John, Rebecca and some close friends. I had a little chuckle as Marilyn and Rebecca were dressed almost like twins, probably not the greatest for a daughter but they we so similar in character. Yes, they were both very strong willed, determined and full of love. The table then filled with laughter and fun. A little bit later, I noticed I had a text from Dylan asking what I was up to. When I told him, he asked if he could join us. Of course, I said it was fine, and he agreed to be there in five minutes or so as he lived just up the street. And so within five minutes there was Dylan walking towards our table and then sitting between Emily and me.

This became quite interesting, as Emily and Dylan had been friends since high school and I was sure they never imagined they would look to the same woman as a common support. This was a very special moment for me, and the best part was watching Emily and Dylan's relationship transform from friendship to siblings. I could even hear them sharing experiences they had had with me. It was very strange and good at the same time. This also ended up being a nice opportunity to introduce Dylan to Marilyn and her family, and Marilyn's special friend Barb, who was in the middle of a separation within her marriage—a marriage that had been intact for a very long time. I could see at this time that some pain was still with Barb as I was too familiar with this situation and thankful that I had healed from it. I also knew it was just a matter of time that Barb would also heal from the pain of her past.

Dylan, Emily, and I then decided to go over to Hugels Bar, the one that had just opened on St. Paddy's Day. I was at this time thinking to myself, well, you just never know how things are going to unfold. Hugels was busy, and Emily enjoyed talking with some friends from high school while I hung out enjoying the music, swaying a bit to the beat. The next thing I knew, Emily was beside me saying, "Mom, no dancing in the aisle." My first thought was, good thing you weren't here at the opening, as I was actually dancing on the dance floor and kids, why do they judge us parents.

We enjoyed just hanging out until it got late and was time to go home. As we dropped Dylan off at his house on our way home, I thought to myself how much joy of family had been brought into our lives and how very blessed we were. The next day, we made plans to have a movie night at our house with Dylan, Emily, and myself that turned into a relaxing time of snacks and treats while watching Blood Diamond. Most of all, it was family time for all of us, and it was nice, very nice.

It was two weeks later that Dylan was asked to play at the Legion in Middletown for Junior's birthday party. Junior being one of the drummers present at the jam session and the announcer at Penetang Idol. Dylan was happy to do this and it also provide at time for Marilyn, Barb, Kim and family to come and watch Dylan play. As I arrived I was happy to see everyone especially Kim as she had experienced the loss of her husband and was healing as well. Everyone seemed very happy and over the top excited. I especially saw a shine coming from Barb that I had not seen in a long time. I was smiling at Barb and thinking how fantastic and Kim leaned over and said, "You won't believe what happened on the way over." She then explained that this nice man was getting into his car at The Boat House Eatery and she stopped him and said, "You would be perfect for my friend Barb and why don't you join us as we are going to the Legion to listen to some live music." Ron then introduced himself and explained that is was his first time in Middletown. Also that he had just bought a cottage in the area and that he would love to join them. Kim then pointed to Ron and starting introductions with Ron and I. Well this was sure an "ah-ha" moment as I now knew why Barb was glowing. I then looked at both of them and it was amazing as if you could see the love. The moment was interrupted with an announcement that Dylan Lock was taking the stage. Dylan was fantastic as always and it was wonderful that my friends and family were now a part of the Dylan Lockstar fever.

It was one week later that Marilyn told me that Ron and Barb were dating and that they were both grateful to have found each other. This brought goose bumps, warmed my heart and placed a large smile on my face.

New Opportunities

Another week passed, and Dylan began to encounter different types of musical opportunities; he was also enjoying practicing with a female singer, and they were set to perform at a coffeehouse located at the Aboriginal center in Middletown. I loved this place so much, as I believed in the Aboriginal beliefs of community and the respect of Mother Nature. Dylan had asked me if I would come and watch, and of course, my reply was yes. I had also mentioned this event to Christine and was encouraging her to attend to meet Dylan and listen to the music.

As the night started to unfold, I received a text from Christine saying she was planning to attend with her good friend Laurie, whom I was very fond of. I said this was great and gave her the start time and location. I then received a text from Dylan saying that something had happened to his co-singer and he was now going to the performance by himself and could I possibly pick him up. I said of course and that I was on my way.

As I was driving to get Dylan, I thought to myself, wow, I am once again where I am supposed to be, driving Dylan to a performance. We got there right on time, but what I soon learned about coffeehouses was that they were similar to jam sessions—just in a public place. Therefore, there were many other musicians also waiting their turn, which was fine. This extra time gave Dylan and me a chance for reflection, and as we stood outside waiting, we started to talk about life, business, and girls—basically everything. At this time I could also see the growth happening within Dylan. We then decided it was time to sit and watch some of the performers. As we were enjoying the show, Christine texted and said she was there. I quickly went out to meet her and help her find us, as it was a little dark in the stage area. As I returned with Christine and Laurie, Dylan came up to greet us. It was kind of funny, introducing Christine and Dylan, as they were both like my children—

children I hadn't gave birth to but who were in my heart. I could see the delight on both their faces at this moment of beginning, and this felt very good. We all then settled in to watch the entertainment, with Dylan to the right of me and Christine to the left. I could sort of feel them checking each other out with me in the middle, and this was fine, as Christine was a very attractive young woman and, well, Dylan was just handsome in all ways.

Then the woman in charge told Dylan he would be up next; we checked the time and realized we had been waiting an hour and a half. Although there were only twenty people in the audience at the time, this was just fine—no matter how big his career got, Dylan was still going to perform at small, cozy functions just like this one. Moreover, he was building his fan base and so it didn't matter how many people were there.

When Dylan finally took the stage, he was amazing as always; he was continually stepping into his talent and into the hearts of the people. Christine then whispered into my ear, "Is Dylan really like a brother to me?" Now, the only answer for me to give at this time was, yes, he was like a brother, although Christine and I exchanged a loving smile between us. Dylan played a couple songs on his own and also a few with the other musicians. He also felt the urge to jump behind the drum set and play for a song, which I knew he enjoyed very much.

When Dylan was finished, we all sat back at the table deciding on plans for the rest of the evening. Dylan then whispered in my ear and asked me if Christine was really like a sister to him, and time stopped for a second as I thought, Christine just asked me the same question a few minutes ago. No words came out; I just nodded my head yes.

Well, once again we ended up at Hugels, and let me tell you, I could start to feel the judgement as soon as I walked in, and I thought to myself, this is the last time I am coming here. Rather than worry about it, I focused on the good, which was that I was with Christine and Dylan, two of my wonderful kids, and Laurie as well. Christine,

Laurie and I had no problem dancing in the aisles, and I remembered Emily with a smile on my face. The music was a little loud and Dylan was saying something; I couldn't hear him, so I leaned a little closer and caught that he just was saying, "I love you." I looked at him with a smile and gave him a hug and told him I loved him, too. I knew he was so enjoying a sense of family, a sense of belonging, and a sense of love—and this was what it was all about.

Christine and I then hit the dance floor and Dylan joined us, enjoying dancing with Christine. I was starting to feel a little tired and returned to our table. A few minutes later, I noticed Dylan outside and then I noticed Christine dancing with a man who was closer to a grandfather figure, and I knew that this was Christine just being Christine, loving and non-judgmental. I thought to myself how nice, as I remembered that Christine had grown up at the cottage where it was all about family and everyone danced together.

Soon it was almost closing time and time for us to leave. I was thankful Laurie was with us and was doing the driving. I rounded everyone up and said it was time to go. Christine immediately went and got her coat, although Dylan had a strange look on his face. He said, "I am fine. I am twenty-one, and I am staying." I then got a stranger look on my face and said, "We came together as a family; we usually leave together as a family." I then gathered up the coats and we started towards the car. Dylan was with us, but he was still complaining. When we got to the car, I said we would just take him home and I put him and Christine in the backseat and started giving directions to Laurie for Dylan's house. In the backseat, Dylan was still saying, "I am twenty-one, and I am going to run back to the bar." This was so strange for me, as I really didn't know what to say, but the words did come out: "Okay, well, at least I will know you got home safe once this night." We then pulled into his driveway, and I got out and let Dylan out, and we stood in the driveway having a talk.

We first established the fact that we were like mother and son and that we were in each other's hearts and that at times it was a little strange for both of us—which was probably the first time we actually talked about this, even though I knew we felt it many times. Next, I start to cry! Then the talking was over and just hugs as the tears were rolling down my face. I ended it by just saying to Dylan, "Do whatever you feel is right; we are on our way home," and I get back in the car. Christine then said she wanted to go to Tim Horton's, the local coffee shop, and so we all headed back downtown: us in the car and Dylan on foot.

The next morning, I did hear from Dylan saying what a great night he had and that he really enjoyed meeting Christine and Laurie and going out with us. He also asked a bit about Christine, and I explained that she was trying again with the father of Paul and we just left it at that.

On Track

A few days passed, and Dylan and I found ourselves at the local Tim Horton's having our first business meeting, as it just seemed like a natural progression. We had completed the birth certificate application and it was on its way. Dylan had all the things he needed to be a businessman: cards, phone, clothes (I must say, he was looking fantastic). He was eating well and gaining weight, writing songs, and networking. He was adding more YouTube videos and doing the vocal warm-ups every day that Anna assigned him, and his voice was stronger because of this. I had also gotten a calendar, as the gigs were starting to come in, which was fantastic. We were setting goals and they were happening; everything was going fantastically.

During this conversation, we decided that Dylan needed to get into another studio, and so this was the next thing put on the list. We were both focusing a lot on the power of attraction, and it was working. We were always paying attention and following up on any leads, and the leads just kept coming. We were also very thankful for Garfield, as he had been a great support for Dylan. Now was the time for the business side of Dylan's life as a musician to start to come forth.

Garfield had set up a performance for Dylan to play at the Hart House, which was located on the grounds of the University of Toronto. Dylan had also talked to me about the possibility of going to a university or college, so Mama Jenny started arranging a trip that included exposure to two universities. I then contacted Emily, as the performance was on a Tuesday in Toronto and she was driving home on that Thursday since it was also Easter weekend. I thought that after the performance I could put Dylan on a bus to Kingston and he could check out Queen's University as well. Emily thought this was a great idea, and she actually set up the bus ticket and paid for it. Once again, everything was falling into place. Of course, I had to check with Dylan first (as I always let him be in control of his life), and he thought it was great. He said he hadn't been out of the Middletown area too much and so a road trip would be fabulous. I booked one day off work for Dylan from Mama's Restaurant, and we were all set.

The next day, Dylan called me and said that he thought he had found someone who had a studio who might be able to help. I said that that was fantastic and asked how it unfolded. Dylan said it was kind of strange: he was working at the restaurant bussing tables and he heard this man talking about owning a recording studio in Penetang. Dylan explained that this man was a regular customer and his name was Dan and he seemed like a real nice guy. Dylan said he gave Dan his business card with his YouTube channel on it and told him to check it out. I said, "That's fantastic; good for you." A thank you came forth with a smile behind it. So once again things were falling into place just the way they should be.

A few days later, Dylan received a call from Dan saying that he had checked out his YouTube videos and that he could see the talent in Dylan. Dan also said that would be willing to help him out with some recording at his studio and that he understood that Dylan didn't have the resources to pay for anything at the moment. Dan explained to Dylan that his studio was just a side thing and that he owned a door business, which was his career. Dylan was very thankful and they set up a time for the first session. I must say, when the call came from Dylan and he knew he could start recording again with his own ideas, it was easy to detect the excitement in his voice.

Last Trip to the Bar

Everything was going fantastic! There was a studio for recording, gigs were being set up for the summer, and Dylan was looking healthy. Things were good. On a Saturday night, we were finishing up at work and everyone made plans for an after-work trip to Hugels. Dylan asked me if I was going to join them and my response was, no thank you. I loved dancing; I just knew that it was just not the place for me that evening. Dylan always respected my decisions and just said okay.

It was about an hour later that I received a text from Anne Marie asking if I was in the mood for dancing and that she and a girlfriend were going to Hugels. I also responded that I didn't think I was going there tonight. She texted me back an unhappy face and a "please could you come." I responded that I would think about it. I then overheard the kids at Mama's talking about meeting at Nick's for some pre drinking and some drinking games before going to the bar. After a bit, I mentioned to Dylan that I might be going to the bar after all and he was happy about that—he even invited me to Nick's, but I said that I didn't think this was the right path for me. I knew by now that Dylan just loved going places with a parent, and to me it was normal, as within my family we spent so much time together.

After work, I dropped Dylan off at Nick's still undecided about my plans for the evening. I arrived home and was sitting quietly thinking what to do when a text came through from Anne Marie once again asking please for me to join her. I thought, okay, I am going. I replied to Anne Marie and said I was on my way. I then sent Dylan a text saying the same thing, and the response was the same from both: "Yay!"

As I was driving to Middletown, I thought to myself that there must be some reason I was on my way to the bar, as I always believe you are always in the right spot at the right time. When I arrived, I found Anne Marie and her girlfriend Donna and felt the familiar happiness that I always did as soon as we were together. I so enjoyed Anne Marie's energy and friendship. It was also nice at the bar at that time, as not too many people were there and the dance floor was kind of empty. I found myself in a conversation with the owners, and I could see the stress they were going through, as they were my age and the late-night bar life was starting to take a toll on them.

Anne Marie, Donna, and I were enjoying the music and having fun on the dance floor, and so I didn't notice that it was starting to fill up. We were enjoying some conversation in our seats when I saw that the staff from Mama's had arrived and they were heading towards our table: Chrissy, Dylan, Nick, and Maryanne. Chrissy looked so cute and young (and because of this, she was still constantly being asked for ID), but there was also something special about her. Chrissy just had a shine about her that was easy to see. I could see the smile on Dylan's face, although I noticed something was off with him as his eyes seemed strange. He then gave me a big hug, and it was as if he hadn't seen me in a week when I had only dropped him off ninety minutes ago. He also said hello to Anne Marie and I introduced him to her girlfriend Donna.

It was then time for some dancing. I found myself just not quite in the mood for the bar scene, as I really truly felt I should be at home, and yet there I was dancing. Chrissy, Nick, and Dylan were more in the middle and really seemed to be enjoying themselves, which was good. I then noticed that Maryanne was not up there dancing, and I tried to get her to join Anne Marie, Donna, and me. She was resisting and I felt it was best just to let her be, although Anne Marie had a much different idea and she somehow managed to get Maryanne on the dance floor with Nick dancing right beside her. It was a magical moment, it was wonderful, it was family, and I felt all warm all over. I did take note of Dylan. Something was not right, I just knew it, but I wasn't sure what it was. I simply knew he was not himself, and I became worried—another new place for me

Gradually, our group became larger and larger, as there were friends of friends joining in. I was at this time keeping a close eye on Dylan, and

I also became aware of the many different types of sexuality that were being shown on the dance floor. Understand that I have no judgement in this area whatsoever; to me, as long as a relationship is healthy and full of respect, kindness, and loyalty, then it doesn't matter if they are gay or lesbian. And then something happened! I saw an inappropriate situation unfolding around Dylan with him in the middle of it, and Mama Bear came to life like you wouldn't believe. I actually flew across the dance floor, grabbed Dylan, pulled him out of the situation, and then continued to hold on to him. He just looked at me and said, "Oh, that wasn't very good," and I said, "You're darn well right."

I then took a real good look into Dylan's eyes and I knew what was wrong. The kids had been talking about drinking games before the bar and clearly he had joined in. Plus, even though Dylan was gaining weight, he was still so thin, with no meat to absorb the alcohol. It only took five minutes for Dylan to regroup, pull himself together, and head outside for a smoke. I found myself quite upset and talked with Anne Marie for support. She also talked about the many different types of sexuality choices on the dance floor and said to not be upset, as Dylan was beautiful. I protested that this didn't make it any better. I knew I was also upset about the feeling of wanting to protect Dylan, as he was truly twenty-one and had survived most of his life without a mother. These times of reacting like a mother bear to Dylan really were hard for me, as I still at times couldn't believe I had a son and it was such unknown territory.

I went for a walk. It seemed like there were fires happening everywhere within the walls of this bar with many of the young adults. I watched a young woman fall to the ground and managed to help pick her up and place my business card in her purse. I then started looking at the people and, of course, into them, meaning reading their energy. I thought, wow, there were a lot of drinking games before the bar, and tried to remember in my youth if we drank that much. I thought, well, I was lucky, as I was busy. I was in marching band and a lifeguard, and I drank, but shooters were not around. I then thought about family: were all these kids missing family and active parents in their lives? This started to feel like the answer. I then had a tug at my heart, and Dylan was back in my awareness and I started looking for him. I found him on the dance floor and chose to keep my distance, as one rescue by your mother was probably enough for one evening. I thought I should probably go home but for some reason I couldn't go.

I found a spot near Anne Marie on the dance floor and started once again dancing to the music and trying to enjoy myself. Time passed and the lights came on, and there was Dylan asking me if I had seen his coat, and I thought, oh boy. I then remembered he didn't have it on when he came into the bar so it must be in the coat check, and I headed that way. For some reason, I looked into the back room and found this beautiful coat I had bought him in a pile on the floor. I picked it up, dusted it off, and took it to Dylan. It was as if I had presented him with a thousand dollars, he was so happy I found his coat. I then said my goodbyes to Anne Marie and Dylan, and headed out to get a cab.

On the way home, I thought, wow; guess I was in the right spot—what a night! I also thought about the different sexualities and that the kids of today were experimenting with the openness and availability. Plus that there was a lot of turmoil within our youth of today and they were numbing the pain with alcohol and most likely a lot of other types of things. This made me sad and brought the need to assist our youth and bring more family activities into existence with our youth.

Hart House

I picked Dylan up, and we first made a few pit stops before we left Middletown: one being Mama's Restaurant for his skater shoes for the Kingston part of his trip and the other being the music store for a cord for his performance. We then headed down the highway, and I was thrilled to realize that I finally had a kid who liked to listen to AC/DC just like I did. We stopped for a burger at the service center just at the top of the city of Toronto.

We had lots of time and were excited to walk around the University of Toronto. As we arrived, we found a great parking spot right in front of the Hart House where Dylan's performance was to take place. We were looking forward to a tour of the Hart House, as it just happened to also be the music building at the University of Toronto. As Dylan opened his car door, we could hear someone playing the piano and it was beautiful. As I watched Dylan, it was as if his ears and his body became alert to this music, and I knew we had to find out where it was coming from. We went in and then found ourselves in the cafeteria area of the building, which was about half full of university students. Dylan looked into the hall and we actually lost the sound of the piano, so we headed back out to where we had started and soon realized that the music was coming from the top floor window.

We headed to the main doors and started up the stairs, trying to keep track of this beautiful classical music. Fortunately, Dylan's ears were like a tracking device. As we walked down the second-floor hall, the music started to get louder. Dylan looked at me as if to say "we are almost there." We then turned into a wonderful music room. The windows were large and open, and there was seating for an audience, although there was only one person in this room and she was playing the piano. I was not sure what piece she was playing, but it was simply beautiful. Her hands were moving back and forth all over the keys in fine detail.

I found myself standing along the side wall across from this wonderful musician and watching Dylan take a much closer look. He actually was standing right beside her but just back enough so she didn't see him. It was like God was in the room, as the sun was shining in the windows and Dylan and this pianist were glowing. I thought to myself that she was going to sense his presence behind her and I chose to just watch, as it was a very special moment. Of course, a few seconds later she did sense his presence and she jumped a bit on her piano bench. Dylan started apologising, saying that he didn't mean to scare her and that she was wonderful and that he played the piano as well. He then asked her to continue, as he was enjoying this very much. A smile appeared on her face, as she could see how kind Dylan was, his energy so loving, and I could tell she thought he was cute as well. Still standing against the wall, I exchanged a smile with both of them and then sat down in one of the chairs to listen to the rest of the performance.

When the girl was finished playing, Dylan started to ask her a few question and they started to talk about the piano and her life as a musician. She told us she had been playing and studying at the Conservatory of Music for the past fourteen years and that she was a business student as well at the university. She also shared that she was performing in this room in a few weeks. Dylan started talking about his piano skills and saying that he could also play classical piano, and he also shared some of the music he had played. He then said he was at the university looking at the option of maybe being a part of the music program. Dylan thanked her for letting us listen, and I could tell she was happy to have had an audience. Up until this moment of thanks, I had said nothing, as I knew my role in Dylan's life was just to be there and that was exactly what I had done.

After we left, we began to rehash what had just happened. Dylan started talking about his love for classical music and shared that he had even written a classical piece two years ago. I replied that I would really love to hear that piece sometime. He then said that he could probably play the piece we had just heard in about a month if he had the time to practice.

At the end of the hall, we saw the sign for the event Dylan was scheduled to play at, so we decided to see where he was to perform and we continued down the beautiful halls of this building. It was wonderful to see Garfield and his wife Jane, as they were truly special people. Garfield explained the venue for the evening and where Dylan was to set up, and we thought to set up the equipment first and then tour the campus a bit. We did just that, enjoying the feeling of being on campus and the fresh air as well.

I was happy to discover that I knew some of the people, since my deli had been in the same building as Garfield's office. As I was enjoying the show, listening to Dylan play, this lovely woman Heather sat down beside me. She mentioned that she worked at the Orillia office for Garfield and then started to ask me some questions about Dylan. She mentioned that just as she had arrived he was finishing "Hallelujah," and did I think that he might play it again. I first thought, well, most musicians don't like to play anything twice. However, this same thing had just happened with another song at another performance, and we had talked about it and decided that due to this person's disappointment, it would have been best to just play it again. I said to Heather, "I will ask him for you."

A few minutes later, Dylan took a break and headed for the men's room. When he returned, I greeted him and mentioned that Heather wanted to hear "Hallelujah" again. I was interested in Dylan's response, and he just said, "Of course, I will." I was quite happy about this, and Dylan returned to his keyboard and played "Hallelujah" beautifully. Then the gift came. Heather revealed that she was an announcer at an Internet radio station located in Orillia. She then gave me her card and said that when Dylan had a CD of his original songs, she would be happy to play it for him on this Internet station. I thanked her and said that, yes, we would be in contact with her.

As the performance was reaching its end, I began receiving texts from Emily, who was excited for Dylan's visit. She had been to the grocery store and was baking some cinnamon buns for Dylan, which were his favourite, and all was set to meet the bus when it arrived in Kingston. Yes, Dylan was set to stay with Emily, who lived with four other university students—all girls. Emily lived on the top floor with her friend Heather and was giving Dylan her room for the two nights he was staying there. Emily would stay in Heather's room, and there was a bathroom for the three of them. Emily had also planned a tour of the campus and downtown Kingston as well. When I checked the time, I realized that it was actually getting close to the departure time of the bus. I knew it was only a few minutes' drive, although I wasn't exactly sure where the bus station was located, but Garfield helped with that. So Dylan finished and the evening was a great success, and we all helped with the equipment. Garfield thanked me for bringing Dylan with a wonderful surprise of some gas money, which I was thankful for, and then he said the most wonderful thing. He said, "I can tell when there are true feelings, and I can tell they exist with you and Dylan." I just smiled and said thank you.

We only had fifteen minutes to get to the bus, so we hurried. I was excited for Dylan, although I knew I would miss him as well. Dylan had his iPhone going with a map, which worked out great. As I pulled up at the bus station, I had a feeling of excitement for Dylan. We quickly fixed his bag and organized a snack for the bus, and then Dylan gave me a hug and a kiss, and walked over to the doors of the bus. I just stood and waited for him to get on the bus. I watched him give his ticket and then just before he walked up the stairs, he turned and gave me a wave and a smile, and he was gone.

I quickly got into my car with all his equipment in the back and headed towards Lake Ontario and the highway. I didn't mind driving in Toronto but knew that the highway was the best option for me. It was probably longer, but I could go at a faster speed and it was less stressful. When I reached the top of the city heading north, the vision of Dylan getting on the bus really hit me and once again the tears of joy rolled down my face. I also thought, wow, I am crying a lot these days, and they are always tears of joy around my experiences with Dylan. I then realized that it was twenty years of a kid's life of joy that I had experienced within a seven-month span, and it was wonderful and overwhelming at the same time.

I arrived home and got into bed and waited for the text from Emily to say she had Dylan with her. I did hear from Dylan only a few times, as his phone was losing battery. There was also someone else he was getting close to and was probably busy texting—the possibility of a new girlfriend, which made me very happy. It had been a healing process after parting from his last relationship, and I wanted him to be happy.

Kingston

Dylan and Emily were having a fantastic time. She took him around the campus and the town itself. I would receive texts from both of them separately talking about the trip; it was nice and cute at the same time. They talked about shopping and going dancing, and Dylan told me about this new melody that happened in his head and that he was grateful he could record this on his iPhone. I was busy working and enjoying the tales from their trip. I was also excited for both of them to return home, as it was Easter weekend and I had been shopping for some Easter baskets.

Emily texted me the next day and said they had just left Kingston and would be home in four hours. I was very happy they were on their way and knew I would be relieved when they pulled into the driveway. About three hours later, I received a text from Dylan saying he missed me and that he had bought me something on his trip. I replied thank you and that this was very nice of him. I must say, the next hour was very long and I kept watching the clock and checking the driveway. The car was full with three other kids coming home for Easter, so there were also three other sets of parents waiting for them all to return. When the car finally pulled up, I felt instant relief and went and gave Emily a hug and then Dylan, of course. I was so happy they were all home safe.

My house became a little busy, but Dylan was jumping at the opportunity to give me the gift he had bought for me and so he placed a gift bag in my hand. Before I opened this gift bag, I gave him another big hug and told him I missed him and that I loved him very much. I then opened the bag and there was a wall hanging that read "Family" at the top and underneath it read "The love of a family is life's greatest gift." Of course, I started to tear up, but a smile appeared on my face as well. I thanked Dylan and said how perfect a gift this was. He then said that there was something else in the bag for me. Surprised, I looked into the bag and there was a DVD called The Doors and L.A. Woman.

Dylan remembered how much I loved the Doors and most of all that "L.A. Woman" was one of my favourite songs. I gave Dylan another big hug and said that I couldn't wait to watch it.

Finally, it was time to unload and talk about the trip. Maggie (a young woman I have talked about before who had a cottage near the lake that I lived in during the breakup of my marriage and who was also a fabulous singer) had come for a visit and to meet Dylan as well. We all sat around the island in my kitchen talking about old times and the path of these two musicians' careers. It was wonderful mixing all these wonderful kids together: kids with tremendous goals. Dylan then asked to talk to me in the other room for a minute, and I said sure. He confided that while he was enjoying visiting with everyone, there was this girl who wanted to hang out with him later that night. I said no problem and that I would drive him home right away. As we returned to the room, I announced that Dylan had to go to Middletown and Maggie all of a sudden said she would drive him. I thought, wow, this is great! I kissed both Maggie and Dylan goodbye and headed to bed.

I didn't hear too much from Dylan the next day but on Saturday morning he texted me a happy face. He asked if we were still all going to Stephanie's after work for an Easter dinner and confirmed that he was going to play for a few hours at the fire. I replied yes, that they were expecting us. Dylan then asked if he could bring this girl, and I said of course, that this was family and everyone was welcome. He also asked if I could pick him up for work, and of course I said yes. I thought I would stop at Wal-Mart for some extra Easter treats; it would be nice to have a little gift bag for the new girlfriend, as I had big gift baskets for Dylan, Emily, and Christine.

The night was beautiful, the stars were amazing, and there was family sitting around the fire listening to Dylan. However, there was a little turmoil at this particular fire, as Emily was not ready to make a commitment to Brandon and thus Brandon had a new girlfriend— although it was plain to see that Brandon couldn't keep his eyes off of Emily. There was a special smile on Dylan's face with his new girlfriend beside him. Maggie had also come to watch the show, and it was turning into a very special night. As I watched Dylan, I had this knowing that things were pretty complete in his life.

When it was time to go, we chose to stop in at my place, as I wanted to give the Easter baskets out to the kids. So we loaded up the equipment and headed to my house: Dylan, Emily, and me, as well as Dylan's new girl Lauren. We sat for a minute in the kitchen and then it was time to open the Easter baskets. I placed the bags in front of each of them. Lauren and Emily both started to open theirs, and all was good. I was watching Dylan closely, as he had told me he could not remember getting anything for Easter in a very long time. We also had had a bit of wine at dinner and I was starting to feel the emotion bubble up within him. I was at this time very in tune with how Dylan was feeling and in sensing his emotional state, as I somehow truly felt that he was my son.

When it was Dylan's turn to open his Easter basket, there were two cards and he opened them: one from Mimi with a fifty-dollar cheque and twenty-five in cash with a lovely card from me. Then there was also gum, almonds, chocolate, deodorant, socks, and much more, as I had loaded it up just like a Christmas stocking. Dylan said thank you and put his head down on the table. I thought it might be time for some snacks and enough of the Easter stuff.

As we started clearing the table and pulling out some food, I noticed Dylan was standing by the front door with his head down. I went directly to him and noticed he was having a hard time with everything. I said nothing and just hugged him for a minute. He then said, "This is wonderful. This is the happiest day of my life."

On Monday, I cooked my turkey dinner and we had a full table: Mimi, Christine, Paul, Emily, Dylan, and me. We were missing Kate, but I wasn't too sad. I knew I was going to Arizona for five days for her graduation in approximately three weeks and that she would be home for five weeks after that before she moved to California to start her full-time job.

The Birth Certificate

It was a wonderful moment when I received the call from Dylan that his birth certificate was in. Now we could move on to the next thing, this being the driver's licence, which to me was so important for Dylan in so many ways. For one, the experience of driving is great and the independence that comes with it is a major part of anyone's life. Also, a driver's licence provides an important form of identification. We then picked a day for a trip to Barrie so he could take the G1 driver's test. We choose a Thursday and set a time, as I needed to go to the Barrie mall as well. We also needed to find a parking lot for Dylan's first driver's lesson and then make it back to Middletown to pick up Mimi.

I awoke that morning with a sense of gratitude, as the weather was beautiful—a perfect day for a trip. I had everything in place for the day: the car all gassed up and everything scheduled just right. I texted Dylan to confirm the pickup time, and he texted me back asking if we could leave an hour later, as something else had come up. I thought for a few minutes, and my reply was that I didn't think we would have enough time to complete everything and I didn't think this would work. Dylan's response was, "Okay, we can go to Barrie another time," and I just said okay.

I must say that I was disappointed and was just trying to grasp the fact that we were not going. I sat quietly for a few minutes, and then a call came in from Christine asking what I was doing for the day. I said I had planned to go to Barrie with Dylan for his G1 and for some reason it didn't unfold, and I was just at home. Christine then said she would love to go to Barrie, as she needed a new dress for an upcoming party this weekend. I said great, as I still needed to go to the mall in Barrie as well. Before I knew it, I found myself on my way to Christine's house to pick up her and Paul.

It was a great drive to Barrie. But although I found myself with people I loved and Christine found a beautiful dress for the party on

Saturday, I was feeling the loss of connection with Dylan. As I entered a store looking for a pair of jeans for myself, I pulled out my cellphone hoping for a message from Dylan and nothing appeared. But I was really feeling the loss so I chose to enter his YouTube channel and choose a new post. Not even realizing what I was doing, I chose the post "Stand by Me."

I think I only made it through a few seconds of the song and the message was right in front of me and I could see the light and it was shining all around me. I then found myself looking around to see if anyone was watching or noticing this light that was around me and the smile on my face, and then walked out of the store, opened my messages, and sent a text to Dylan. It was a text of connection, and that was all that was needed. Of course, there was a quick response because we always know when we truly need each other. At this moment, I started to close the door on the fear and the doubt and the disappointment that I had experienced throughout my day.

I then returned back to Middletown to Boston Pizza for my regular Thursday night dinner with my mom. With the help of a glass a wine, I realized I was still a little upset with the outcome of the day. My disappointment was beginning to come out in my texts, as it was still sitting with me but I was having a hard time expressing it. So I ended up saying how I believed Dylan should have had his G1 today, which was the first step in getting his driver's licence in Canada. I must say I loved his response: "Should?" Knowing that I had written in my first book the concept that "should" is a word of judgement and that judgement is a dysfunctional place, a smile appeared on my face. We bickered back and forth for a bit, and then I let go of the disappointment and sent my love. Knowing this was the first night Dylan was going to Dan's studio to record, I sent a message saying, "Sing your heart out xo," and the reply came through, "Okay, I will xo!"

The next day, I was set to pick up Dylan to do some errands, and as I sat in his driveway waiting for him, I had a bit of uneasiness about the previous day's events—although I was very excited to hear how the night at the studio went. I then saw Dylan heading towards me with the biggest smile on his face and a CD in his hand. He got in the car and started talking about what a great time he had at the studio with Dan and that he was so happy he finally had some music recorded that was just him. He popped the CD into the car stereo and I could feel his excitement. I sort of settled in for the moment and got ready for the show. I could have never imagined the first song that would come out of that stereo—it was "Bohemian Rhapsody." Within a few seconds, I was completely engulfed in Dylan playing the beautiful introduction on his piano and with his new developing voice belting out the word, "Mama!" I became frozen in time, completely frozen, and as I looked at Dylan, the tears of joy started rolling down my face and all I could do was to search for my sunglasses, which were between the seats, and place them on my face. It was as if he was telling me something with this song, and really all I could do at this moment was hold back the tears.

We sat in the driveway for a while listening to the music with the sun streaming in. I was still in awe that the first song was "Bohemian Rhapsody" and over hearing this young man, whom I felt was a son to me, belt out the word "Mama" with so much passion and love. This was followed up by some of Dylan's songs that he had written with only him playing, and this I knew was a special moment for him. I now had my breath back and found myself saying how great it was. Dylan responded with, "Well, you told me to sing my heart out." He then said, "You know I can do better," and I looked over at him and it was if I could see him hearing something different with his songs, his music. It was like watching a genius mind in action.

Once again, this wonderful CD ended up being a gift to me as when I dropped Dylan off and went to eject the CD, he told me it was for me. This brought me to a place of happiness. I was so full of joy and love—and maybe disappointment in myself that I had felt the disappointment with Dylan the previous day.

Back on Track

Life was busy, and we were back on track. Dylan had attended a few more vocal lessons and I drove him. He was really enjoying the experience and Anna's tremendous expertise. Anna felt that Dylan also had the ability to be a fabulous opera singer and reinforced that his musical gift was at the genius level. We were now working on securing a passport and waiting for the right time to go for the beginning driver's licence test.

We visited the high school looking for special teachers who had touched Dylan's life during his high school years to be his references on his renewal of his passport application. It was interesting walking the halls of the high school and listening to the stories that came about Dylan. These stories basically all had the same message: these teachers had seen the light in Dylan and felt compelled to tell him so. We talked about one teacher who had called the house he was living in at the time because he was late for an important math test; this teacher offered to pay for the cab to get him to school so Dylan wouldn't lose the credit. I thought to myself, wow, that was nice of him. As we were walking the halls, I took note of the kids. The hair and the dress were maybe a little different than I could remember, but the spirit within was still the same.

With that errand complete, all the information was gathered and we were now set to send in the passport application.

"Come Sail Away"

As I reflect back on the many times this song has entered into Dylan's and my history together (and my own personal history as well), I see the power of memory that can come from a song. I first heard this song in high school with my first boyfriend Jeff, excited to watch my first live concert. Hearing it again takes me back to being sixteen and my love for music. When I hear this song, I am likewise brought back to the very first time I heard Dylan perform this song live. It was at the performance that Garfield had set up and the first time I watched Dylan live.

The next time I heard him perform this song, it was also live—it was at Stephanie's during the first performance I had arranged. Then too I found myself in the very same situation as the tears started welling up immediately once Dylan started to sing, and then my entire body started to react to this strong and amazing state of emotion. At subsequent performances, Dylan would always play "Come Sail Away" for me and I got better at embracing the feelings of emotion that came over me and learned to simply enjoy the moment of this wonderful young man singing this special song.

On the Saturday following Dylan's second visit to the studio, I picked him up for work and he appeared with another new CD with some new cover songs (songs written by other groups). The CD started with a few Elton John songs, which were fabulous, and I could tell that Dylan's voice was getting stronger and stronger. I felt quite content, as we were almost at the restaurant and ready for our Saturday night shift. I can remember it being a warm, sunny day and just feeling the peacefulness of this special moment. Then "Come Sail Away" came on. I had my sunglasses on, so it wasn't until the single tear started rolling down my cheek that Dylan realized I was once again having an emotional moment.. He knew it was a moment of happiness, and before I had a chance to say anything, there was this "Aw" that came from Dylan and then a kiss to my cheek. Then we found ourselves in the parking lot of the restaurant and going into work. I can remember leaving my sunglasses on and hugging Dylan in the kitchen, unable to say much. At this time, I had also begun to notice more judgement forming from some of the staff, as I was now most of the time arriving to work with Dylan.

Dylan once again gave me the CD, and I found that every time I would hear Dylan singing "Come Sail Away," I would have the same reaction. I can remember thinking to myself, "I don't have this reaction when he sings out 'Mama'; I just smile like crazy. As I sat quietly later this evening I realized that it was the gift of music that Dylan was giving me as this was his way of showing his thanks for everything I had done for him. I realized that I found all of this quite wonderful although it was also very overwhelming for me but I started to understand why I was getting so emotional as what I was experiencing at this time in my life was truly extraordinary.

All My Kids

I was feeling very grateful at this time and full of joy because of the wonderful contact I was having with all my kids. Kate was in San Diego at a waterski tournament with her new amazing jump skies. She sent me a picture of herself with the new skies, and both she and the skis were absolutely beautiful. Her voice was full of excitement after she skied her first set on these well-crafted, state-of-the-art jump skies, and this excitement and joy in itself was worth more than words could give justice to. Emily was busy in Kingston studying, although she had just been to the movie theatre to watch Titanic in 3D. She called to tell me how fantastic the movie was and what an epic story it was—and moreover, how she had cried during the movie due to the passion of the love story, which reflected her own life (which is the magic of movies and music as well).

I was sorry I had to work that Sunday night, as I was unable to see Christine's shining in the new dress she had bought on our trip to Barrie. However, I could imagine her amongst the people, glowing and spreading her joy all around. I could even see baby Paul following her around and wanting her undivided attention from a place of motherly love. Then there was Dylan, who was home having a night of reflection, rest, and creating more music and enjoying a special gift of the ability to sing in Italian.

This special time of connection with all my children brought me to a place of reflection on the strength that was a part of each and every one of them. I reflected on Kate, Emily, Christine, and Dylan, as they all had many identical characteristics. Yes, I could see the love within all of them: their strength, their passion, and most of all, their happiness. This gave me a tranquil and peaceful feeling within my entire essence, which then took me to a place of extreme gratitude for all of them in my life.

Dylan Lockstar Fever

Dylan Lockstar Fever was everywhere, and it was a wonderful thing to experience, as Dylan was really getting into the hearts of the people. I at this time also became aware that Dylan Lockstar Fever was a twenty-four-hour state of being for me. I would at times feel overwhelmed or exhausted, as we were busy and I had become a point of contact for the people who were concerned with Dylan's progress. I could actually start my day with Dylan Lockstar Fever and end my day with Dylan Lockstar Fever.

While this was great, I started to notice my life disappearing a little bit more and more each day. I still knew I was on the right path, doing the right thing, but I would start to flounder because I was either overtired or frustrated. But then I would notice that Dylan would provide me with the answers I needed to hear within a song that he would record. At this time, I felt as if the words were speaking directly to me, which brings me back to the power of music. In fact, it was at this time in our journey that the song that came to me was "Lean on Me." It was exactly what I needed to hear and exactly the motivation I needed to keep going.

The Doors

I think I was twenty when I first heard the band The Doors, and I instantly fell in love with the song "L.A. Woman." For some reason, throughout the next thirty years of my life, this song would remain one of my most favourite songs to listen to. As I went about my daily duties, I kept looking at the DVD of The Doors that Dylan had bought me for Easter wondering when the perfect time would appear for us to watch it.

It was a beautiful warm Monday, a day to put on your shorts and enjoy the change in temperature—as where I lived, the temperature could change drastically quite quickly. On this day, I was figuring out how to burn Dylan's latest CD on my laptop: a new over-the-top CD that Dylan had just recorded. As I was working, I noticed a text on my phone from Dylan. It read, "I have a cold, been blowing nose and sniffling nonstop." And the next text said, "Maybe we could just relax tonight and reflect?" First, I went to the place of being a mom and thought that I'd better make some chicken soup. Then I sent a return text stating that I would call Anna, as it was vocal night, and cancel his lesson. He sent a happy face in return.

I then went and got the ingredients to make chicken soup and had a great conversation with Anna, who wanted Dylan to drop off a copy of the new CD that I was burning. I relayed the message to Dylan and got a return text with a thank-you and a suggestion that maybe we could watch a movie tonight. I instantly knew it would be the Doors DVD about the making and history behind "L.A. Woman," and I thought, how fabulous.

When I picked up Dylan, he asked if we could stop by his dad's house and pick up some movies, as his dad just happened to live around the corner from me, and I said of course. At this moment, I thought to myself, well, maybe it is not the night for The Doors and "L.A. Woman," and whatever movie we watch, it will be perfect. As we pulled into the driveway at Dylan's dad's house and we approached the door, I could sense the happy feeling Dylan had of being home. Gary was quick to greet us, as Gary and I got along fabulously—although I knew, of course, that we would because we had something that was very important and special together: supporting Dylan. Gary was also a fantastic craftsman and he was happy showing me his work around the house. I could also see the love Dylan had for the beautiful Labrador that had been the family pet for the past thirteen years. Dylan went over to the movie cabinet and started to pick out a few movies, while Gary and I continued our conversation. Within a few minutes, Dylan appeared with three movies and we were on our way.

When we arrived at my house—it was time for some homemade chicken soup and pizza from BP. Next, we had a business discussion on the plans for the week and some necessary return calls that had to be made, as well as a time to reflect on his new songs. This was all perfect and something I so enjoyed sharing with Dylan. Next, it was time to pick the movie, and to my surprise, The Doors movie was the one Dylan picked. I was so over-the-top excited and quickly opened up the movie and placed it into the DVD player.

Instantly, a smile appeared within, as the background music was "L.A. Woman." Then we settled in as mother and son to watch The Doors and the history of the song that actually brought us to this very moment. I must say, it was like God was sitting in the room with us; it was a magical moment that lasted one and a half hours. The story and the history of the band The Doors was amazing; truly Jim Morrison had the gift of a genius, and the sadness of the loss of such a talented man came into my awareness. I then focused on his attributes, as he was a poet and the words in his songs were of consciousness; I could see in his eyes the frustration over the dysfunction of society. I truly believed this was really what killed him; it was the negativity of the world itself.

But there was much more to this movie: the talent of all the members of the band, how they wrote their music, the performances . . . it was all so great. I particularly loved the history of the song "Riders on the Storm." It followed "L.A. Woman" in the movie and was another favourite of mine, as it brought back the memories of a wonderful woman, Margaret who had touched my life and who I missed very much, as she lost her fight with cancer ten years ago.

However, the highlight was watching Dylan and how he responded to the information and the music throughout the movie. His comments blew me away, as he always heard music from his place of genius. My greatest gift to him was that I could understand and see in the music what he was telling me. I knew that he was learning all this information to assist him with his writing and his future career as a rock star.

The movie ended, and we were both full of inspiration, music, and the need to listen to "L.A. Woman" in its entirety. It was also time to take Dylan home. So we jumped into Mimi's car and I placed my L.A. Woman CD into the player, Dylan took over with the volume, and we were on our way. This next eight minutes were simply wonderful; Dylan and I were separate in our own space, letting the music fill every ounce of our souls. We never spoke one word during this ride home to Dylan's house, as we had long been able to just be when we were together. For me, I kept feeling the gratitude for this kid I could sit and listen to "L.A. Woman" with and who was actually enjoying it as much as I was.

I dropped him off and, due to the fact he had lost his house key, I watched him scale the side of the house and do a swan dive into his bedroom window and then come back to the car for his soup, mirror, and copy of his CD that I had burned. I could once again see the love in his eyes and I also felt the love in my heart as I gave him a hug good night.

My ride home was good, as I immediately placed Dylan's music into the car stereo and listened to his voice, which was simply fantastic. However, it wasn't until the next morning that I stated to reflect on the evening, my past experiences, my book, and the music, and I found myself frozen in time. Yes, this was the moment when everything came together and I truly understood the uniqueness and the special gift of our unique relationship. I then realized that this was a story to share, a story for inspiration, and a story for the world: to share the joy that can come from helping a youth in need, for taking the risk. I had heard the other day the phrase "risk equals faith," and I thought, that's for sure. There doesn't have to be a blood connection to feel love for a child; there is greatness in adoption. And there are so many kids who need families and parents—parents who are active and willing to be part of these kids' lives. The greatest gift you can give to kids or anyone you love is the gift of time.

I couldn't get my laptop up and running fast enough, as I had found the direction I had been asking for. It was right in front of me, and so was the completion of this book with all its beauty. It was just a matter of getting it into black and white!

This Girl

Dylan returned from a session at the studio with Dan and called me to tell me that he had a couple new songs on a CD and he couldn't wait for me to hear them. He explained that he had taken the melody he had heard in his head and had recorded back when he was in Kingston, and the words had just come forth—and he was over-the-top excited for me to hear them. I said, "Okay, I am on my way."

So once again, we sat in Dylan's driveway and a CD was inserted into the car stereo. The melody was great and the song was great; it was inspired by the new girl in Dylan's life. I immediately fell in love with the melody of this new song and felt the greatness of Dylan's song-writing ability. There was a break in the music and another song began with a different beat. The amazing thing about this next song was Dylan's ability or the gift he has to "scat," which I had never heard him do before. It was fantastic and amazing in itself. He then explained that he had written this song five years ago. I once again was in awe, still not believing my life or the amazing experiences that seemed to be happening to me on a daily basis. I then offered to take the CD home and burn some copies for Dylan, this girl, and his friends and family.

As another week unfolded, we were busy burning CDs and booking gigs. My thoughts kept coming back to Dylan's next night at the studio. I mentioned it to Dylan, saying that I had this feeling I was to go with him to the studio. I was thankful for the wonderful spirit in this kid, as he was completely open to me attending a recording session at the studio. So the plan was set into motion for Thursday, April 19 around 6:00 p.m. We planned to do passport pictures that same day as well.

As we were walking around Wal-Mart waiting for the pictures to be ready, Dylan brought up the studio. He mentioned that I may not be able to hear anything, as he wasn't sure if earphones were available. He also for the very first time gave me some direction, which was very strange for me. He said, "You can't slow us down." I said, "No, I won't," and thought to myself that all I planned to do was take in the very moment of it.

After Wal-Mart, I ended up at Marlene's for a visit and I relayed that I was unsure if I was going to the studio and that I would have faith in the universe and just let it unfold. I did send a text to Dylan saying, "All is good, whether I attend the studio or not." A smile was returned, along with the message, "I will keep you posted." I ended up back at home in bed for a much-needed nap, as work had been busy for the past few days. I woke up around 6:00 p.m. and looked to my phone and there was no message, so I lay back down. Around 6:45 p.m., I started to send Dylan a text asking what was up when the house phone stated to ring and there was Dylan. He sounded so excited and said that everything was set for the studio and could I pick him up at 7:20 p.m.? He also mentioned he had a buddy with him coming to the studio and asked if I could also run his girlfriend home, and of course I replied yes to all of it.

Twenty minutes later, I found myself on my way to pick up Dylan for the studio, knowing this was exactly where I was supposed to be. As I pulled up, all three of them came out of the house. I got out of the car to open the hatch for Dylan's keyboard and I made eye contact with him, and he looked a little taken aback. After a few seconds passed, I said, "Where's your keyboard?" He replied, "OMG, it's a good thing you're my mom; I almost forgot my keyboard." Then his friend Donald and he returned to the house to get it.

We arrive at Dan's house excited for an amazing night at the studio. Dylan had already been there a few times, and it was an experience he was enjoying with all his essence. Dylan introduced his friend Donald and me to Dan. Dan's energy was very open and he seemed to have a very kind spirit. Dylan explained that I was like a mom to him and that he wanted Donald to play a little acoustic guitar in one of his songs. Dan was very hospitable and was wonderful with setting Donald and me both up with earphones so we could be included in the recording session. At one point, Dylan looked at me and a smile appeared on his face, as he was happy I had a set of earphones. Another thing I noticed right away was the view I had of Dylan. I was now experiencing him playing from his perspective, as Donald and I were sitting behind him. Right away during the first song, I noticed his piano skills, as I could watch him playing behind his keyboard.

Dylan was still suffering from the effects of his cold during the first hour of recording. As time passed, Donald realized he probably should head home to the family. Donald asked if I could give him a ride home, and I immediately said yes and then asked where he lived. Donald said that he lived back in Middletown, which was fine with me. I could see the uneasiness appear within Dylan as he said, "Well, I guess I could finish now too," knowing he had just started. It was time for the motherly look that he understood so perfectly. It was like an understanding between us with no words being spoken—such a gift. Before we left, I needed to use the ladies room and asked Dan where it was. Of course, it was in the house. Nightfall had set in, and the honourable young man stopped recording to walk me down to the house—such a gentleman!

Donald and I then got into my car and start talking about how Dylan and I had found each other, our amazing story of being always placed together during his performances, and the fact that I felt Dylan and I had to have been mother and son in a previous life. Then, all of a sudden, I had the awareness that the conversation needed to be about Donald, and that was exactly what happened.

Donald had already shown himself to me to be a caring, smart, loving young man, although as we started talking, it became apparent that, like most kids, he had had some difficulties during his youth. As we talked, he became quite open about his childhood and his history of being ADD and the fact that he had to live with the stigma that came with being labeled with ADD. I then started to explain my beliefs about ADD—this being that boys are busier, have more energy, and need much more activity than girls, and that boys are expected to sit quietly in the classroom as the girls do, and if they can't then they are labeled as ADD and given medication. Then I shared my belief that these boys are just normal boys, as I saw this with baby Paul—he was so different than having a girl, so busy. I then turned to Donald and said, "Let it go. You are just a guy, one who has lots of energy, is busy. Put that energy into something you love to do and, most of all, let go of the labeling that I personally don't believe in it. You, Donald, are just a normal guy with lots of energy. We are all different, and that's just fine!"

As I look over at Donald, I could actually see the negative energy leaving his body. I dropped him off knowing there was a new peace within him. Then I headed back to the studio.

When I arrived, I could see that Dan and Dylan had such easiness within their relationship, which made me very happy. I could see that Dan let Dylan be Dylan, which allowed his genius talent to come to the surface. Dan was wonderful to me as well, setting me up with the earphones once again and leaving his beautiful house open for me to use when I needed a washroom. Dylan at this time was working on the song "She's Lost," which was about his sister: as she was a normal girl with a normal life, and then she was lost. Dylan explained this to me that his sister left the house they were living at during the beginning of her teenage years. He said, "She was there and then all of a sudden she was gone." It also contained the line "But I am still the same," this being exactly what happened in his life.

I just enjoyed every second of this experience, watching Dylan play the piano and harmonize a section of the song eight different times while remembering the different cords needed to complete what he was hearing in his head. Dan handled the recording with such patience. I was so thankful for this amazing event in my life.

I also felt part of things, as Dylan would frequently ask me my opinion, realizing the gift of a fine-tuned ear (I can even hear when he is off so ever slightly). That night, a team was established, which consisted of Dylan, Dan, and myself. We were busy, and we got a lot done. We also took time to sit and reflect and enjoy conversation, which was fabulous and happened with such ease among the three of us. In addition, we got to listen to and enjoy Dylan's songs that were recorded just the way he heard it in his head, with Dylan in complete control of his music thanks to Dan. I even got to dance around a little. At one point, Dylan gave me a hug and said, "You are so my mom!" Then Dan picked up his acoustic guitar that was sitting off to the side and started playing it.

It was nice, as Dan was a musician as well; he actually was a drummer, but his love for music was very apparent. I looked over at Dylan sitting to the far side of the room and exchanged a smile with him, and then it was like he faded out of the room and it was just Dan and me in the moment. I was not exactly sure what was happening in this moment, but I embraced it and it was very nice. As I dropped off Dylan and then headed home, I noticed that something had changed and that I was feeling a type of warmth within.

The next day, I asked Dylan to send my contact info to Donald, as I believe when you have awareness opened, it is essential to be able to contact the source. It was only a few hours later that I did hear from Donald, who said that things were going well and that it had been a great night. I responded that I was glad to hear it and that it sure was.

Two days later, I heard from Donald again and turmoil had re-entered his life. He explained that the ups of life were great but that they were followed with the extreme downs of life, and that these were difficult times to deal with. I told him it was good that he was seeing the pattern and that this was what life was all about: to be aware that this was going to happen again and to prepare for the downs to come. I told him that when he prepared with his family on board and recognized his triggers, this would be much easier to deal with when the bad times did happen. Donald, being so smart, understood completely, and a thank-you was given, and this was the end of our connection.

Time

As we continued to follow the path and direction shown to us, I started to notice how strange it felt to be at Mama's Restaurant going through the motions. Many times before I had this similar feeling, but nothing compared to the Saturday night following that Thursday night at the studio.

However, this Saturday became different, as Tyler in the kitchen had left his iPod at home and so Dylan's first CD became the music on the radio in the kitchen for the night. It was as if these two different worlds were colliding, and the power of Dylan's world took over my being, which became amazing and weird at the same time. It was also fun because Nick and some of the other staff and I were all singing the words and loving it. I looked over at Dylan numerous times trying to sense his feelings, his energy, his essence, and he was the same.

It didn't really hit me until I was signing out and I said to Dylan—who was waiting to enjoy a family night with Emily, me, and a movie—that our days seemed to go from one extreme to another: that one day we were at the studio recording and in the heat of amazing music and the next working at Mama's Restaurant waitressing and washing dishes. I then shared that at that moment, that particular moment, it felt so unnatural to be there at Mama's Restaurant. Dylan understood exactly what I was saying and agreed with a smile, and that was that!

As another movie and family night unfolded with Dylan, Emily, and myself, it brought me to a place of family and my gratitude for a home that was filled with love. We enjoyed watching a science fiction movie with snacks and treats in a magical way once again. I reflected at this time on the power of the universe and the power of living each day, paying attention and embracing whatever comes your way. I thought back to a year and a half ago when I surrendered and the power that lay within this, as now I was living my life by letting it unfold, living in faith, and paying attention.

Another Day of Fun

I picked Dylan up for another day of errands. He had asked me to bring the CDs, and of course I thought he meant his CDs, but I was wrong: he meant the ones his dad had just given to us on Monday. I felt bad for a split moment and then remembered that everything happened for a reason. I could see the disappointment on Dylan's face while he said the words, "That's okay," and I smiled at the kindness of his essence. Then all of a sudden he said, "Someone just gave me this CD to listen to; I will go get it." And back into the house he went.

I had no idea what he would return with, and to my surprise it was a Burton Cummings Greatest Hits, and at this moment I knew that this was the CD we were to listen to. We talked a bit first, as we always took time to reflect on everything that was happening around us. Then Dylan had the CD in his hand and into the stereo it went. He immediately went to song three and turned up the volume. I must say, this was one of my favourite things, driving around with fabulous music playing and Dylan and I just enjoying it—it was an amazing experience. Just imagine pulling up beside a small Toyota sitting at a stoplight with the music very loud, a mom and her son beating to the music, and the son singing at the same time. I must say, the entire car shook too.

Anyway, it was song seven that really was perfect for Dylan: "'Cause I got my own way to rock, I got my own way to roll." We pulled into a gas station to get gas, and I could even hear the music in the pay booth. When I got back in the car, Dylan said, "This is how I learn the music. I can listen to it once or twice and then play it." I thought to myself, you are so amazing, so amazing, and a smile was exchanged between us.

Over the next few hours, we focused on getting things done. We first went to a new restaurant and Dylan received a booking for paid gig. We then took a visit to the grocery store, stocking up on great food, as Dylan was gaining weight and looking healthier every day. The next stop really put a smile on my face. We decided to go to a nice restaurant by the water for a pint of beer: The Boat House.

As we were sitting there enjoying the view of the water and relaxing, an idea came to Dylan to give out his business card, as this would be another place for live entertainment for the upcoming summer. When a manager entered the bar area and came close to us, Dylan took this opportunity to introduce himself. As this was taking place, another distinguished gentleman entered the bar area as well. I actually caught a smile from this man, and I could tell that he was enjoying talking to the customers. The man who was talking to Dylan then said that the owner was right there and passed the business card over to this distinguished man. Dylan and this man exchanged pleasantries, and Dylan actually said out loud, "You look familiar—where do I know you from?"

Then a great conversation came forward, a conversation of the history of music, the business of music, and different people in the music industry. Dylan was busy taking notes and being such a wonderful businessman. I just sat there with a big smile on my face, watching him interact with this man. I then caught a glimpse of this gentleman's watch, I realized I was now late to pick up my mom, but I had the knowing I was to sit still, as it was time for Dylan to make his pitch for being the summer entertainment at this establishment. Dylan did a fabulous job of doing exactly this, and as we were leaving, we both had a feeling something good was going to happen.

As we got to the car, I was in a state of "Ah" because this event furthered my theory of letting things unfold and the power of the universe. I also marveled at the power of our team and the energy we put out together as a team and the amount of fun we had together—it was simply a gift and amazing. I quickly dropped off Dylan, got Mimi, and headed to work. I completely enjoyed listening to Burton Cummings once again on the way.

That night was a good night at work, as Chrissy and Meghan were working and the three of us always had lots of fun together. The highlight of the evening was when Meghan got into my car as I was driving her home and she noticed the Burton Cummings CD case, picked it up, and said, "This guy looks like he would have a speedo on." There was silence for a moment, and then I looked at her and started to laugh and said, "You are right; he does look like he would have a speedo on. This is Burton Cummings; let's listen to his music on the way home." Meghan said okay, and it was now Meghan and I singing and beating to the music in my little Toyota.

Driver's Licence

We had a date for the G1! Garfield had called me and said he had set up an interview for Dylan in Orillia at this great restaurant called Era 67. Garfield was very fond of the owners and had passed on the message that he knew of a new entertainer. As I mentioned the interview to Dylan, I said that we could make this a great trip, as they also had a driver's test center in Orillia. Dylan was very excited about this and said that he would get out the driver's book and review it.

On Wednesday, April 25, and we headed to Orillia: me driving and Dylan busy reviewing the driver's book. We also had business cards with us and were set to attend the interview at Era 67 after the driving test.

As we arrived at the driver's test center, I could see and feel the nervousness within Dylan. I also was a little nervous but so happy just to be there, as I could remember my excitement when I took my beginners driver's licence test. Driving was just so important to have established in one's life. We both approached the counter and I stood just to the side and back a bit from Dylan as he did all the talking, only looking once or twice towards me. The woman filling out the information was great and understood that I was just the mom standing behind. However, it was funny when this woman asked Dylan about his postal code and he looked at me and I had no idea at all. She asked, "Isn't it the same as your Mom's?" and we looked at each other and said nothing. Then Dylan said, "I have had so many postal codes I can't remember the one I have now." There was silence for a second and then Dylan realized he could call Cheryl his landlord and ask her—which he did, and then everything was finished.

Dylan then moved into the area to write the test, and I sat in the waiting room with a clear view of him. He was busy writing the test but looked at me a few times and I smiled back at him. About twenty minutes later, the woman said to Dylan, "Congratulations, you have passed your G1 license." I wanted to jump up and down, but Dylan was quite quiet and so I went with that. As we were leaving the building, I told him congratulations with a big smile on my face. Dylan replied, "Thanks, but I am twenty-one, almost twenty-two, and it feels sort of sad that it has taken me this long to get my G1." I looked at him and say nothing, just gave him a gentle smile, and I thought to myself, I guess this is exactly what a bittersweet moment is. I then said, "Let's go to the interview, and then we are going to head to the old Wal-Mart parking lot for your first driver's lesson with me being the instructor." We smiled at each other and got into the car.

The interview was great, and Dylan was soon booked for the May long weekend, which he was very excited about. I then headed for the parking lot, which was perfect because they had just moved the Wal-Mart and the old building's very large parking lot was empty. I parked the car and got out, and Dylan did the same, and we traded spots, with Dylan in the driver's seat. I quickly explained the mirrors, the seat location, and the workings of the car, and then it was time for Dylan to put the car in forward and start driving around. I just let him figure out how much gas to give, how the brakes worked, and just how the car moved around, and sure enough, he did. The best part was the smile that was on his face the entire time—this made it all worth it. I could also tell in the first fifteen minutes that Dylan was going to be a good driver, as he already had the feeling of the car. I then said to him, "I think you should drive back to Middletown," as the road was just a small two-lane highway and one that he could drive on with a driver in the passenger seat. Dylan said, "No way, really?" and I said, "Really."

Dylan then drove to the next parking lot to practice a bit more, as it was full of cars, and then we headed onto Highway 12 towards Middletown. Dylan did a very good job keeping the car in the center of the lane and learning to maintain a constant speed, and I could tell that he was loving every minute of it. He did say it was a little challenging being on the highway and that he was glad he was a little older than most brand-new drivers. I reinforced that if he were sixteen years of age, I probably wouldn't have put him directly on a two-lane highway but that I knew he was ready. We enjoyed a wonderful drive back to Middletown, and we were both happy.

Getting Ready for Kate's Graduation

It was now five days before I was to leave to Arizona for Kate's graduation. I was very excited for the graduation itself, as it had been four years of determination, hard work, and a lot of money. Kate had always wanted to attend Arizona State University and ski on the waterski team; it was an extreme bonus that she was graduating as a civil engineer with a high grade-point average.

I was to arrive on the Monday before to take care of the pre-grad arrangements, and my ex-husband was going to get there on the following Wednesday (the ceremony was Thursday). I was set to fly out of Arizona on that next Friday morning. I felt bad for Kate—as I knew it was hard to have parents who were divorced and stressful to try to keep us all happy—but this was just another fact of life. Emily was going to start her new job, so she was going to drive me to the airport and pick me up, which was a treat for me, and I was very excited about this. Christine was going to stay with Mimi for the four nights and drive her to her activities, and thank God for family.

I had one loose end to tie up before I left on my trip. The plan was to complete this fantastic new song called "This Girl." I remembered Heather from the Hart House and said I thought it would be important to get a copy from the studio this week that we could actually send to her. Dylan also thought this was a great idea. As we arrive at the studio, Dylan discussed the plan with Dan and revealed that he had written an ending to the song and felt this would complete the song and have one final song called "This Girl." Dan said that was great, and we got to work. The song started off with a slow section with the new melody and the words: "I got this girl for me." Then it went to, "There's a problem," and ends with, "I got these fantasies." The song was good, and Dylan started to add in some harmonies. It was so amazing to watch him sing and create his music. Plus, Dan was very good with him, as Dylan instructed Dan often to stop and start again, and it was all good. After quite a few hours, we start to pack up with "This Girl" on a separate CD and another CD with some originals that we had been working on over the past few weeks.

We got into the car, and Dylan turned to me and said, "I am happy!" I replied, "Dylan, that's great; I am glad that you are happy." Dylan then said, "No Jenny, you don't understand—I have never been happy." I turned to Dylan as I was driving with a look of shock on my face, and he saw that I didn't know what to say. He smiled at me and I then smiled back at him.

As I looked to the road, my mind repeated what Dylan has just said—"I have never been happy"—and I was frozen once again. I thought about this twenty-one-year-old boy who was sitting beside me and the joy that was in his life and the joy that was in mine. I thought of all the years he went without maternal parental love, and I wished once again I had been there for him. I was thankful that he was now sitting beside me and happy.

I then looked over to him to find him sound asleep, and I smiled once again because here was this kid who always told me he had such a hard time falling asleep, yet this kid seemed to fall asleep every time he was with me. I thought how strange that truly was and then marveled at how peaceful he was asleep in the passenger seat. He woke up just as I was pulling into his driveway, thankful that he was home. I said good night and promised that I would burn some copies of the CD and drop one off with a note to Garfield's office in Middletown for delivery to Heather, who worked for Garfield out of the Orillia office.

As I was making the final preparations for my trip, I experienced a strange anxiety about leaving Dylan, as if he were four and I had to go on a business trip and I was worried about my kid. It was such an unusual place for me, and I felt that it was going to be the same for him, that he was going to miss me just as much.

A Graduation to Remember

I was so thankful that Emily was able to drive me to the airport, and as I sat beside her, I started reflecting on how thankful I was to have her in my life. I thought to myself that she probably didn't know or realize how very special she was to me and that she was my rock. Emily was also the one who sometimes had been left out of the drama of life; I was not sure if she realized what a great thing this really was, as we know the meek are to inherit the Earth. I was at this time thankful to have bought her this car and that I was able to help her with some of her expenses while she was in university. Her life at this moment was wonderful, as her relationship with Brandon was again intact, happy, and healthy. She was also set to start her first business-orientated job in her field of engineering that very day. As we pulled up to the departure area, I hugged her and told her how very proud I was of her and that I loved her very much.

As I waited at the gate, I texted all four of my kids and said my final goodbyes, still experiencing the first separation pains from leaving Dylan. My flight was good, and Kate was there to pick me up. We enjoyed reuniting and headed to her house, where she lived with two other girls: one I had known for years and both whom I was very fond of. As I settle into Kate's room, she told me she had a class to attend and that one of the boys on the waterski team lived at a condo with a great pool and I could spend the afternoon there. This made me very happy, and then we made plans with a couple of Kate's friends to go for drinks at a margarita bar later and then for dinner at Chili's, one of my favourite places to eat.

Later, Kate and I were joined at the margarita bar by her friends Jeremy and Sandra, and we enjoyed lots of laughs and a couple of wonderful margaritas, too. I was happy at this time, enjoying the kids and feeling their excitement to be graduating in a couple days. They talked about their friends, families, and future plans, as the real world awaited them very soon. We also enjoyed a fabulous dinner at Chili's. On Tuesday, I spent another day at the pool and a quiet night, as there was one big party scheduled to happen at Kate's house the next day and my ex-husband was to arrive for some of it.

As Wednesday unfolded, Kate and I enjoyed a large trip to Wal-Mart to get all the party fixings; we even got cake mix for me to bake a graduation cake from scratch. Kate then went off to attend her last class of university, and Mom, being me, broke out into a cry. I felt at this time so many different emotions: happiness, sadness, and those of a job well done. I then got myself together and started preparing all the fixings for this graduation party that was going to take place in a few hours. I was over-the-top excited, as I loved hanging out with the kids; the conversation was always good and they were lots of fun. I found that I was also a little nervous about seeing Kate's dad, as time had passed and we were healing, but there still was a little uneasiness. Matt, Kate's boyfriend, was also due to arrive for the celebration, and this was a great thing for Kate.

The girls of the house presented Kate with a huge wall frame full of different pictures of her and her friends over the past four years. This was a very special moment for Kate, and I knew it meant a lot to her. As the house filled up with twenty one-year-olds, the fun started. Some of the guys sat in the kitchen playing a card game, where you placed a card onto your head and tried to guess what the card was. I got a kick out of one of the boys bringing a case of Canadian beer, as Kate is Canadian. I also noticed that the food was a hit and disappeared quickly.

Then it was time for Kate to run over to the airport, which was only ten minutes away, to pick up her dad, half-sister, and niece. When they arrived, I noticed a coolness from Kate's dad and I just accepted it for what it was. We all managed to enjoy the celebration around the cake, and this was important for Kate. Kate's dad and family then took Kate's car to their hotel, and the party turned into a small dance party. At this time, one of the boys from the ski team, Ozzy, went to turn up the music and looked at me, and I just smiled and said, "Turn it up!" The look on his face was so funny, and Kate just said, "Yep, that's my mom!"

After a while, it was time to head to the bar, as it was dollar drink night at one of the university campus bars. Someone asked Kate if I was going to join them, and she said of course. I truly at this time hadn't decided if I was going to go, and I thought, well, I guess I am. (I still believe at times that down deep the kids like us to hang around them.) Cars were loaded up, as we had enough designated drivers to get us to the bar. As I entered the doors of the bar, the head bouncer asked, "Do you have a graduate?" and I replied yes, and then the red carpet was laid out, which made me feel great. I also noticed there was a bit of an older crowd—not quite as old as me, but I felt comfortable. The line for the drinks was quite long, as they were only a dollar, and Ozzy said he was buying for me and most of the gang, which was also very nice. I sat back and enjoyed watching the kids dancing and thought, no dancing for me, as this night was about Kate. That was just great, and we all had a lot of fun.

The next day was Thursday, my last day there and Kate's graduation. We didn't get much sleep and we had had a bit to drink, which probably was a good thing for me as I had to spend at least four hours with my ex-husband. There were actually 30,000 people there with graduates, friends, and family, and I was so very proud of Kate. I was thankful that Matt's parents and brother, whom I was also fond of, were in attendance, even though there had been some turmoil in Matt and Kate's relationship.

Kate looked amazing in her gown, and her smile was worth all of it. The guest speaker was very good, as one of his messages was that when he stopped chasing the money, the money came to him—that when he made it about what he loved and the people, success was all around him. At this moment I smiled, as there was a book that was almost finished called, "The Business Side of things." Pictures were taken and all was good. Matt's family headed home and we then proceeded to dinner. We went to a fun restaurant where Hannah (Kate's niece) almost fell asleep in her dinner, but she did very well through everything, given that she was only three. As we dropped off Kate's dad, I had the knowing that I had made the right decision to move on with my life.

We arrived back at Kate's, and I snuggled into the couch and took a few minutes to reflect on the day. I was so happy and proud of Kate. I was also okay with being a single woman on my own at the graduation, and I reflected on the fun that I had with Kate over the past four days. It's like there comes a time when the rewards start to come forward after all the time, effort, and investment that you place into your kids. I could remember many a time wondering how I was to get through this motherhood responsibility (as it is full-time twenty-four-hour, seven-days-a-week job). It's like always being on call, and the emotion, love, hurt, and pain are all part of it.

As Kate dropped me off at the airport the next day, I was totally at peace with the knowing that she was going to be home for five weeks before she moved to California to start her career as a civil engineer. As I kissed her goodbye, the love within the child and me connected, as a thank-you for all the love that had been given over the years was said. I then boarded the plane knowing that as a mother I had done what I was supposed to do.

Home

As I landed, I texted Emily that I had arrived, and I was grateful to receive a text from her saying she was already outside the airport waiting for me—what a great kid! I then texted Christine and said I would be home soon to take over Mimi duty and thanked her once again. Finally, I texted Dylan, who was so happy to hear I was back in the country. He asked if Emily and I could pick him up on the way home from the airport so he could hang out with us tonight. I said yes, of course, and we then headed to Dylan's house. While driving, Emily told me all about her new job and all the excitement of her week. Emily had had a fabulous week, and she was excited about being in the research department developing new techniques for making foam. She talked about the traffic, the people, and how her day went at work. I once again did most of the listening.

When we arrived at Dylan's house, there he was outside waiting for us with his laundry bag in hand, as I had been doing his laundry for the past four months, which he really enjoyed. I gave him a hug and it was as if he didn't want to let go, which I held on tight to, as I had missed him, too. We then all drove to my house.

Emily saw that Dylan needed some mom time, so I found myself sitting at the kitchen island listening to Dylan and hearing all about his week. This stretched into a two-hour conversation, and then it was time to show him all the great clothes Kate and I had picked out for him. He was over-the-top excited, and everything looked great and things felt normal again. When it was time to take Dylan home, as we were walking out the front door he said to me, "Don't ever leave me again!" I said nothing and just hugged him and told him, "I will always be with you, Dylan, always."

Staying the Course!

In the weeks that followed my return from Arizona and Kate's graduation, my role with Dylan changed dramatically. The positive thing was that our mother-and-son relationship was solid and completely in place; it actually was so strong that Dylan and I started texting the same words to each other during our conversations. But now things became more about business and I became mom and manager. The mom part was solid, but I had to learn the role of manager and this became very overwhelming for me.

The first aspect for me was controlling Mama Bear when business affairs came forward. When some people saw Dylan and realized his talent, they wanted a piece of him. I did believe this was just a dysfunction of life that had been carried through time, and I also saw it as excitement within the people.

Dylan was becoming a great driver, as every time we drove somewhere, he was now in the driver's seat and thus getting tons of practice. Although I did start to notice more judgement and concern with this, as we were always arriving places together with people not realizing that a pre-driving lesson was on the agenda first. Wherever we arrived, Dylan would be in the driver's seat and I in the passenger seat, and we would have to change spots, and of course there was always a hug between us as well. I knew that if Dylan were ten there would be no judgement of the showing of affection, but it was hard to explain to everyone that he had never had a mom to take him anywhere, ever, and never in the past eighteen years had he felt love for a mom, despite that he was such a loving person.

Thus, I found I needed support of my own, which made me once again pick up my phone and call Rosie. Now, Rosie had been in my life since 1998, and I could not imagine a day without knowing she was a telephone call, a Facebook message, an email, or a twenty-minute drive away. She was a true older sister, and I was so very grateful to have Rosie in my life.

So this Wednesday night I found myself picking up the phone to call Rosie, and as we talked about how our families were, we moved quickly to Dylan and I had an "Ah-ha" moment as I realized that Rosie was my support with the miraculous situation that I found myself in with a new son and a brilliant one at that. Moreover, I realized that I had called Rosie often for many reasons: one, I trusted her because I knew she loved me; two, her belief system was the same as mine, as she also lived in faith; and three, she was full of consciousness. I knew I could always call her when I was not sure of my path with Dylan and was experiencing doubt or fear.

I told Rosie about the people, the studio, and my role changing towards business: booking gigs and becoming like a manager for Dylan. Her first response was, "You are great at business. You ran the deli, the building, a large restaurant in Mississauga—you are fabulous in business." I thought, you're right, although I could hear myself saying over and over again that it was so overwhelming. Rosie then went to faith, which is what I needed: a reminder of faith. And her final words were just what I needed to hear—"Stay the course"—and I got it! Yes, this was all I had to do, to have faith and stay the course, and so the stress lifted from my essence immediately.

Next, I found myself all cuddled up in bed, organizing the following day and contacting Dylan, as this was already a nightly occurrence. And then I had the most amazing sleep: a sleep without fear, a sleep with peace.

Mother's Day

As our first Mother's Day was quickly approaching, I could see that this would be a day full of different emotions and a day where the outcome was completely up to the universe. Firstly, I was aware of the slight feeling of confusion within Dylan concerning who exactly his mother was—although during a conversation where Dylan talked and I listened, I think he sorted this out for himself and the answers were known yet unsaid.

There was another situation that had strongly taken hold, a situation that I had been aware of for quite some time. Lauren, Dylan's girlfriend, had lost her mother five years ago. So here it was the very first Mother's Day that Dylan had a real mother—meaning a mom who was in his life on a daily basis, knowing his needs, supporting him, and loving him. Therefore, on the one hand it was going to be a day of complete celebration, and on the other hand, for someone who was important to him, it would be a day of sadness and loss. Dylan and I briefly talked about it, and I completely turned to faith, believing the correct passage would take place. Moreover, I had learned years ago that Mother's Day would always unfold perfectly and that I should have no expectations of my children, simply knowing they would act from a place of love and that this was to me the greatest gift of Mother's Day.

As the day got closer, we also realized that Dylan was working the day shift and I was working the night shift at Mama's Restaurant. Dylan tried to switch his shift but to no avail, so the fact that he was working all day and I was working all night soon became the reality, and this was okay. Stephanie had invited us for a wonderful brunch, and this felt very good, as it was a time for me to spend with my mom and also with Emily, Christine, and baby Paul. Dylan and I discussed the fact that Lauren would spend the evening with him, and then I would pick him up and have a visit after I finished work. So the plans were set and all was good. The night before we had found ourselves at a campfire with

Dylan and his keyboard, and to me, listening to Dylan play live was the best Mother's Day gift I could ask for anyway. But I could not have imagined the joy that this Mother's Day had in store for me.

As I awoke this beautiful Mother's Day, I received a text from Kate that read, "Happy Mother's Day! Thank you for everything you have done for me. I don't know what I would do without you! We will have lots of fun while I am home! I love you!" This was a very special text from Kate, and it made me feel warm and fuzzy all over. Then I could hear the pitter-patter of feet heading downstairs to my bedroom, and there was Emily wishing me a Happy Mother's Day, shining and full of love. I said thank you and that I was very happy she was home. Next, it was time for me to wish my mom a Happy Mother's Day and present her with her favourite bottle of wine. Then Emily headed out to Stephanie's and I found myself making some coffee. Mom and I sat and enjoyed our coffee and a piece of toast. We at this time reflected how very blessed we were.

Emily soon texted and said she would be back to pick us up, which was perfect timing. Thirty minutes later, we found ourselves on Stephanie's beautiful deck enjoying a Caesar and basking in the sun. Christine and Paul were there, too. I enjoyed a moment of reflection on the importance of family and women, and a moment of gratitude. The brunch was fantastic, and Bryan (Stephanie's husband) was the perfect host. We then moved down to the waterfront to enjoy the afternoon. It was great watching Christine with Paul, as she was a marvellous mother, and once again being with family and a representation of four generations.

As late afternoon approached, I realized a nap before work would be a good idea, as the night was going to be a late one. Therefore, Mimi and I headed home. I had a marvellous nap and awoke looking for a text from Dylan and there it was. He said the restaurant was so busy and that he had just got off work, as well as "Happy Mother's Day!" I replied thank you. I knew that the evening would be a wonderful time to celebrate. Emily had told me that Dylan was holding onto my Mother's Day present, but this was not important to me because I had the gift of love from my four children and this was all the present I needed.

I confirmed with Dylan I would text him before I left the restaurant. As I sent this text, a text came in from Dylan saying, "So tonight is completely your night, Mom ☺. I'm excited to just be with you ☺ xoxo. Would Lauren be allowed? She sounded interested to just be a part of what we have, but be completely honest if you just want your son ☺. And I have a poem for you and something else ☺!!" My reply was, "Hey, family, it's all about family, and everyone is always welcome. Lauren is always welcome xoxo. And you are right: what we have as mom and son is very special!"

After work, I picked up Dylan and Lauren, and by the time we got to the house, Emily and Brandon were already there. A gift appeared, along with many smiles on my children's faces. I opened the bag, and to my surprise, inside was an iPod full of music I loved and, of course, music played by Dylan. I could see the joy on Emily and Dylan's face, and I quickly called Kate as well to thank her. At this time, I realized we had some hungry people and dinner was then started. I knew that there was a poem on the way and the timing would be perfect.

As Emily headed to bed due to an early-morning drive to Toronto, I saw Dylan slip over to the front door and pick up a book he had hidden under his coat. I took a deep breath, knowing myself to be an emotional person—a person who wears her heart on her sleeve. I could see the pride and smile on Dylan's face, and the room then became magical. He told me that this poem had just flowed out of him and that maybe it could be a song. He also said that in time he could see his song-writing skills becoming amazing, as he felt he was just beginning to tap into his talent with words and writing. As he prepared to read this poem to me, I started to brace myself. I looked over at Lauren and all was good. Then Dylan started to read this poem for me, a poem called "Mom!! :)" (a poem written for all mothers on this Mother's Day).

Mom!! xoxo

For who I have become,
for how I've grown to feel,
for why I now have faith,
for love I truly feel.

For lessons, for discoveries,
for days I fall apart,
for showing me myself,
and finding me my heart.

For pain that's far diminished,
for smiles that don't frown,
for setting the example,
of standing on ones ground.

For running on our journey,
for breathing by my side,
for opening my spirit,
for understanding pride.

For shifting my own energy,
for hearing the unheard,
for actively surrendering,
to people you have cured.

For being my bright angel,
my mom and my best friend,
for finding my beginning,
while waiting at the end.

For tolerance, for patience,
for happiness to come,
I thank you for your consciousness
and for being my Mom!!

xoxoxo

Your son Dylan Lock xoxo

Happy Mother's Day

As Dylan read the first four lines, I started to have an out-of-body experience, which I would like to describe as a magical moment. The lights in the room were glowing, and I was doing everything in my power to keep it together. I would also like to add that this was one of the most amazing moments in my life. When Dylan finished, the tears started to run down my face, and he hugged me and Lauren got the kleenex and I thanked him for the poem. I know for sure that he knew I was doing everything I could to maintain my composure, and this was really good, as he started talking about our journey and how he thought maybe the word "walking" was a possibility in the poem, but then he had to change it to "running" which seemed to be the proper word.

We sat for a half-hour just talking about the wonderful experiences that had led to this amazing Mother's Day poem, and then Dylan said, "I will read it to you any time you like," and I said, "Could you read it one more time?" as I was not sure if I really heard all of it. And so he started again, and this time I was able to listen to each and every word, and it was magical and so perfect. He said it all and in the most amazing way. By the time he got to the "best friends" part, the tears were flowing down my face again, and of course there he was holding on to me and a little in awe. I managed to pull it together, and Dylan returned to his chair and he said, "I think I am going to cry, too," and no more words were spoken. I looked over at Lauren hoping she was okay and knowing that this must have been hard for her with everything happening that day in her life, but I was glad she was there to understand the mother-and-son relationship that existed between Dylan and myself.

Then it was time to drive them home and return home to read my poem alone. I had the feeling to keep it private, as Emily had been so wonderful that day and I didn't want it to be all about this poem (she had even cut the grass for me). As I lay on my bed and reread the poem to myself, I could hear Dylan's voice saying the words. I also at this time could see the depth in every line, as every line had a true message: a message of love, hope, and commitment, and the presence of a mother figure for the first time in his life. And so my Mother's Day ended in my room alone with a magical poem from a new son that once again brought me to tears, and I thought to myself how very blessed I was!

When I woke the next morning, I had the knowing that it was time to share this poem. I texted Marilyn and talked about the existence of this beautiful poem and the awareness started flowing forward: that while this poem was written for me, it was meant for the world, it was meant for everyone and all mothers. I knew that it was to be shared, and I also knew the path would unfold, and so I started slowly.

When Stephanie came over for a visit, I started sharing the poem and all she could say was, "Wow." Next, I had to share it with Rosie, and her response was beautiful and magical. Later, I found myself at my laptop writing this last chapter, and then I finally felt it was time to share it with my girls and to savour this magical poem Dylan had written for me.

The Opening of the Hotel

The hotel that Frank was building was finally ready to open, which was great for all us employees at Mama's Restaurant, as we were still waiting to have our Christmas party (which had been promised to be held at the new hotel). We were all quite excited about the party and the get-together for all the staff and family. I did notice a sign posted with news that the famous Dylan Lock was going to be the entertainment, which I had already heard about. I was so over-the-top excited for Dylan, as this would be a time for him to show his true abilities to Frank. I thought about the time I found Dylan covered in drywall dust cleaning the very room he was now going to perform in. I knew he needed a new shirt, as the ones I had bought in Arizona were much too big for him, so I headed off to Mark's Work Wearhouse to find a dress shirt for Dylan for the party.

It took only a minute to find the perfect shirt and it was even on sale. I returned home, ironed it, and then went back and picked him up from work, as he was hosting at the front door that day. I took him home to get ready and returned back home to get myself ready. I wished at the time I had a date, a man in my life, but I knew this would be coming soon.

As I arrived to pick up Dylan, he looked very handsome in his blue shirt. It was as if he were going to his high school graduation. I was also happy Lauren was going to attend the party after her shift at work was finished. We arrived early with all of Dylan's equipment, and while Dylan was setting up, I enjoyed a guided tour of the hotel with Frank. I could see how very proud Frank was of the craftsmanship and design of his hotel. When I returned to the dining room, Dylan informed me he forgot a cord and we needed to return to his house to get it. I just smiled at him and pulled out the keys and told everyone we would be right back. On our way back to Dylan's, we talked about the hotel and how great it looked. He then ran in and got the cord, and we headed back, this time talking about how an equipment checklist on the dash of my car might be a good idea.

By the time we returned, many more people had arrived and Frank seemed to have experienced a shift in energy. He turned to Dylan in front of everyone and said, "Wow, look at how you have changed. I can remember what you looked like when I hired you, and I can't believe you are the same kid." I thought to myself that he did look fantastic in this blue shirt, and I felt very proud. Dylan then said to Frank, "That's because I have a mom now." Frank got a funny look on his face, and I then added to the conversation, "Yes, he came to Mom's Restaurant and found a mom."

I then turned and realized that the room was now filled with our staff from the restaurant, as well as their friends and family. I saw Chrissy, who was a little sad, as she was on her own because she had recently removed herself from an unhealthy relationship and was waiting for the right man to enter into her life. I also saw Nick busy in the kitchen cooking for us; I didn't think this was fair, although I knew he liked cooking for us all. Maryanne, Nick's girlfriend, was there as well, missing Nick too. Joanna was also single and came over to sit with me. Meghan came in with her boyfriend, very excited to see Dylan and watch him play live. The rest of the staff was with their other halves, and there were also a couple close friends of Frank and Sandra's in attendance.

The food, the hospitality, and the people (as we were like a small family) were all great. Everyone seemed to relax, enjoy the food that Nick had been busy preparing, and simply enjoy each other. Lauren soon arrived, and all was well. I could see that Dylan was so excited in anticipation of showing off his talent, which warmed my heart. He was twenty-one at this time, an age that I remembered all too well, but I could also see the boy in him wanting approval from the people—which he seemed to receive with flying colours, and I was happy for him, as he deserved every bit of it.

As he got up and began to play, I could see the reaction from the people as they began to realize the scope of his talent. The night ended on a great note, "Bohemian Rhapsody," and of course, love was all around us once again. I just embraced it as always and remembered the gifts of life. Frank was very generous to all of us this evening and to Dylan for his performance as well.

Spring

Spring was now upon us, and Frank was in some need of yard work both at his home and around the hotel, and he wanted Dylan to do the job. I was at this time controlling every ounce of my Mama Bear. Dylan was so fast and an amazing worker, but the gardening work was only for minimum wage. But only Dylan could set boundaries in his life. Two days after the Christmas party, I receive a text from Dylan stating that he was at Frank's house and not dressed well, and he was cold. I immediately said I was on my way and found some sweatshirts and coats that would be suitable for a male. I then stopped at Tim Horton's and picked up coffee, water, orange juice, two chicken wraps, and a cinnamon bun for dessert, as Dylan did not like donuts. I texted Dylan and told him I would be in Frank's driveway in five minutes.

As I pulled up, I saw Dylan heading towards me, and the mother in me turned up the heat in the car as I could tell he was very cold. He got into the car and gave me a hug and a kiss and started trying to warm up his hands. I then turned the heat up to full blast and noticed that his precise hands were all covered in dirt. He sensed my feelings, but no words were exchanged, just a look of "I know my hands are covered in dirt." I then showed him all the treats I got him, and he was so happy and excited. We started to talk while he warmed up his hands and enjoyed his lunch. We talked about family, the restaurant, boundaries, music, and more about my trip, as it wasn't that long ago. We both then realized it had been a forty-five minute lunch break (although with the hourly wage, I believed it should have been an hour lunch break). But by this time, Dylan was warm, full, and happy.

He got out of the car and I did as well with the many coats and sweatshirts I had brought for him. He was happy that most of them were black, even though a little small. I then start helping him with the layers, and he looked so cute with the hood of Emily' s sweatshirt up. It was if he were now dressed for snow, which it almost felt like, even though the calendar read May. Once again, there was a hug from Dylan, and then he disappeared to the back of the house.

Rainbows

For some reason, for the past few years of my life I have seemed to continually experience sightings of rainbows. I actually started to take note of this a couple of years ago when I was staying at a friend's farm while waiting for my divorce settlement to come forth. The location of this farm seemed to be on holy ground of some kind, because as soon as I would drive on the property I felt a sense of relief, strength, and the knowing that everything was going to okay. It was during the second sighting of a rainbow that I found myself outside with my iPhone taking a few pictures. This rainbow was unique, as it was like a goblet coming out of the Earth. It was very early morning and the sun was beside it, and it was an amazing sight. I called the owner of the house and told her I had had another rainbow sighting and how beautiful it was.

Six months later, I was driving with Stephanie and Christine, and we encountered the most amazing sighting of a double rainbow that was right on the road directly in front of us. Stephanie was so excited, saying that she had never experienced anything like this in her entire life. I once again took a picture with my iPhone, and Christine also enjoyed the beautiful display of nature.

Now today I was at Mama's Restaurant, and I noticed that the people coming in the door were all lit up and talking about the amazing double rainbow that was right outside in the parking lot. I immediately stopped what I was doing and had a look out the window. "Wow," I said and then I headed out the front door with my iPhone in hand. I felt a sense of excitement all over, as this was the clearest double rainbow I had ever seen and it was directly in front on me. It was almost like I was standing in it. There were other people in the parking lot as well taking in the excitement of this rainbow. I took a few pictures of this fantastic sight and then realized I'd better return to the restaurant and get back to my duties. At this time, I felt a very strange feeling all over my body, like I was bubbling inside.

"It's Lonely at the Top"

The line "It's lonely at the top" was beginning to feel so real to me because I felt lonely during this part of my journey and I truly didn't think anyone understood what it took to support a gifted child. Some of the things it entailed included daily planning, lots of errands, knocking on a lot of doors, time in the studio, lessons, and more. Then there was the massive amount of judgement I was encountering. Maybe this would have been less if I had actually given birth to Dylan and was his biological mother. Yes, I believe this statement to be true, as when someone heard that I was Dylan's mom and they didn't know that I had only been his mom for eight months, they were so supportive. But most who knew that I was not his biological mother and had only known him for a short period of time had so much judgement towards me that their energy actually hurt me.

I thought back to The Blind Side and felt for the people involved when the controversy was taking place concerning which college team Michael was to play for and the integrity and judgement of the family. This family clothed this young man, taught him to drive, brought him into their family, loved him, and gave him opportunity. Yet still people thought the worst. I could feel this energy as well, not from everyone but from a lot of people, and it hurt—it just plain hurt.

Even my own children were having a hard time with it, and I would at times wonder, how did I get here, knowing I would never change a thing and I didn't care if Dylan was a rock star or a dishwasher—I loved him either way. Moreover, I knew there was so much more to what was happening than Dylan becoming a rock star. I knew it was bigger than Dylan and I, and still it was Dylan and I—just Dylan and I. It was like others just wanted something from Dylan and all I felt I ever did was give to Dylan and that was okay, because I knew what he needed at all times, which freaked me out. But it was lonely and sad at times.

However, I knew I had to stay the course, not for just Dylan but for all the other kids in the world who needed someone to stand by them and give them that little boost in life that they needed. Yes, this story was about all the kids, not just about Dylan and I; it was about everyone, and I needed to focus on the kids and the parents, too. I also knew it was very important to get the message out about how important parental love was and the power that comes with it, and that there were so many kids who only had one parent and at times no parental guidance in their lives at all. Most of all, these kids needed love, unconditional love, love with boundaries, love with lessons, love with respect (meaning both ways), and love from friendship.

Within the span of three days, confirmation came forth that I was on the right path. Six more children came into my world who were missing a parent and some who didn't have any parents at all. I thought to myself, oh my, it is everywhere; the awareness of our kids in need is everywhere. I then found myself at a craft show with three other women vendors, and the story of Dylan came forth. One woman asked me how old Dylan was, and I said twenty-one. This woman said, "That makes sense," and I looked at her with a puzzled look on my face. Then she started to tell me that she and her husband were going to adopt and that there was such a need for kids, especially boys, between the ages of sixteen and nineteen for adoption. I was surprised that there would even be kids at that age on the roaster for adoption, and then I thought, wow, what a need and what a message to get to the people. All I could think of was, I understand, I totally understand.

Boundaries

It was one week later that Dylan called and told me about the conversation he had just had with Frank about the gardening at Frank's home, the restaurant, and the hotel. Dylan said to Frank that he was not hired to be a gardener but that he was available for any hours at the restaurant. To that, Frank replied, "If you can't do what I want you to do, then you don't have a job." Dylan said, "Are you sure?" And Frank said, "Yes, do not show up for any more shifts."

As Dylan was telling me all this, I was thinking quite quickly. First I thought, good for you for setting your boundaries and I am so proud of you. Then I thought about the loss of income, as he did need to pay rent. I knew the gigs were starting within the next week, and there was already a concern on how he was going to get all the time off work that was needed. However, the next few sentences that came from Dylan brought peace to me. He said, "There is no fear; this must just be the time for me to move forward in my life."

As I listened, I also felt the exact same thing for Dylan. I did feel sad, as there would be no more Dylan at work, and I reflected on all the funny times that had taken place there: like him talking on his cellphone too much and the time he took two motion sickness pills before work when we had been busy doing errands most of the day and I couldn't understand what had happened to him at work. Then giving him the advice not to do that again as he became quite sluggish during his shift. I remembered fondly the smile he always had for the customers, him joking in the back with Nick, and the essence of his strength and the shine that was all around him. This would be something that would be greatly missed at Mama's Restaurant.

I was then okay about it, because I knew he was on his way and I was already such a large part of his life outside the restaurant. But I was still a little sad that we weren't leaving Mama's Restaurant together.

Internet Radio

Dylan received an email from Heather about his song "This Girl," and they set up a time for a live interview. We were both so over-the-top excited about it. It was to be a Thursday night, a night we usually would have been going to the studio to see Dan, but instead we would be taking a trip to Orillia for a live Internet radio interview. Our path was continuing to unfold perfectly, and life seemed great. Kate was now home, which was wonderful. Emily was working hard and enjoying her new job and learning how to deal with the city traffic. However, Christine was once again experiencing turmoil within her relationship with baby Paul's father. I was praying for her every day that something great would happen in her life, as she so deserved it.

That Thursday we headed to the radio station with Dylan driving, of course. I looked out the window many a time taking in the beautiful scenery, realizing how blessed we were and how excited I was about the interview. As we arrived at the house where the Internet station was located, we were greeted with such enthusiasm and excitement. We sat with one of the staff and he explained what was going to happen and that there would be a chair for mom. He also said that I might be asked a question. I immediately said no, thank you, that I didn't want to say anything, and I looked to Dylan and he knew that I was only there as support for him.

As we were shown into the room where the recording was to take place, I enjoyed a visit with Heather. She was excited Dylan was there and said that she really liked the new song. I smiled at Dylan and settled in a chair right beside him, which was not hard to arrange as the room was very small. Dylan was himself, all cool and collected—I don't think I have ever seen him nervous at all. However, I could feel my heart beating outside of my body. The interview started first, and there were quite a few questions on the history of Dylan. I guess because I was sitting right beside him that he felt it was okay to say how I had inspired him and he mentioned my book. Frank even got a plug for us meeting at Mama's Restaurant. I felt a little uncomfortable and wasn't sure if this was the right path, although there we were and this is what had unfolded. Dylan also talked about his dad, teachers who had helped him, the artists who had influenced him, and all about his talent.

As we were leaving, there was a sense of greatness within all of us. We enjoyed a fun ride home and had a beer on the porch of his house, where we started talking more about his childhood and his youth.

Dylan started to tell me about his strong athletic ability and that he thought at one time he was going to be in the NBA. He was also told at one point that he could probably make it at the college level as a volleyball player. However, it was his love for music that returned to him when he finished high school, and that first year he had practiced five hours a day every day redeveloping his love for music. He also told me about when he worked at pizza places, about how very good he was at making pizza and very fast. I could see him twirling the dough and singing his heart out at the same time. He then told me that he had returned to his dad's two months before he started working at Mama's Restaurant to regroup and to return to his music, as he had stopped playing for a while and felt that he was basically lost in some way.

He told me that there was some dis-ease between the two of them and he was not sure of how things were going to unfold with his dad. But one night, there had been an explosion between he and his dad that actually brought them both to tears, and that this was the start of some healing that needed to take place for both of them.

Dylan also told me about one night when there was a tremendous rainstorm and the ceiling above his keyboard started leaking and covered the keyboard with water. He had wiped it off and tried to plug it in, but it did not work. This was a moment of truth for him, as the thought of losing his keyboard was like losing his life. He was told to let it sit for a few days, let it dry out, and see what happened—he then told me that these were the two longest days of his life, as the thought of losing his keyboard was a place he did not want to go. Two days later, he plugged in his keyboard and it worked once again, and the joy that Dylan felt was something amazing. The funny thing was that the ceiling had never leaked before in that very spot and it had never leaked there again. Dylan then started playing his piano again and two weeks later he moved to Middletown and started working at Mama's Restaurant.

After we finished our beers, I headed home. A half-hour later I received a strange text from Dylan stating that I was standing too close to him and that I was preventing others from standing beside him. All I could feel was the knife cutting my heart in two. I thought for a second but not long enough, and I began to react from complete woundedness. It was like I threw everything into the fire and was willing to give it all up and back completely away. And then of course the tears started flowing down my face like Niagara Falls.

I knew there must be some truth to this, so I looked to the place of figuring out what I was doing wrong. I thought to Penetang Idol when no one was there to stand beside him or drive him or help him at all. I thought of all the things that Dylan needed and how I just did them. I thought about how I didn't know how to be half a mom and do half a job. I then said, "Fine, I just won't stand beside you anymore." It was as simple as that.

Dis-ease within the Heart.

All relationships go through turmoil, and Dylan's and my relationship was no different. And so the turmoil set in within this new relationship of mother and son. We were going through growing pains in finding our way in terms of boundaries and responsibilities, and our love did take a time to grow, but when it was fully developed, it never altered. I then started to think about this amazing power of parental love and wonder why it came with pain. Why did life come with pain and suffering? Were we afraid to love because it came with pain? Was it to make us stronger, make us value the love and respect each other more? So what was the message, that we all were to suffer like Jesus did and to have faith that something amazing would come in return? I truly knew and understood that it was important to feel whatever I was feeling, and so once again I knew to sit with the pain of dis-ease with Dylan that I was experiencing at that moment.

And so I sat in the pain and eventually it passed and I felt at peace once again. I was thankful and grateful for the ability given to me by my faith. However, I did have to step back a bit from Dylan; I would have to say that this was challenging, but I had to step back from him as life was just unfolding in this way. I knew there was growth happening for both of us, although my heart was hurting in a way that was difficult to take. I also immediately had the knowing that I would not change one thing that had happened in my life with Dylan, because the gifts, love, and joy were worth it. I realized it was also overwhelming that I had only had Dylan as a full-time son in my life for six months, as we had been through so very much and I loved him. But I had to step back (just like the saying "Let them go and they will grow").

Moreover, I still had to maintain my connection, support, and love and not act anymore from woundedness—a place most people go to and a place I was all too familiar with. If I didn't already have the teaching and awareness, I probably would have stayed in this behaviour. I also wasn't sure how strong the power of parental love was. But my only choice was to have faith in the strength of parental love and most of all the strength of maternal parental love!

It didn't take much time before Dylan and I were back on track. It was as if things just kept happening that caused our connection to stay intact. I had pulled back a bit, which was good for both of us, but things were getting busier and maybe a little more exhaustion was setting in. And I found myself once again in a place of doubt.

Now, this doubt did not concern the love I had for my newly acquired son but rather was about whether this was really what I wanted to be doing in my life. I knew that I was to help heal the people, especially the women and the kids. I was also aware of this wonderful youth program I had created that sat on my laptop. But most of all, there was my book and the knowing that I was to teach the world to have faith. However, if someone asked me how my week was, all I could refer to were events involving helping Dylan become a rock star. I wondered what had happened to my life's purpose and basically my life in a nutshell. Although I wouldn't change a thing, at that time Dylan involved late nights, society's judgement, and frankly drama from some people, and I could feel the weight of it all on my shoulders.

So there came another time of questioning my direction and questioning my purpose, and all I kept feeling was that I wanted to get out. I also knew that when this was happening to me—and thank God, it wasn't very often—and Dylan sensed it, he would give me the needed space at the beginning and then the reassurance I needed at the end. Moreover, I would only last about twelve hours with the thought of "maybe I should let go of Dylan completely," and then of course my heart would ache. And so I felt recommitted to supporting Dylan, but something was different, something had changed this time. I was now questioning my life's purpose and looking for the answer.

After a few days passed, the answer was strongly placed right in front of my face. It first started with an unexpected movie night for

Dylan, Kate, and myself, with Dylan bringing the movie August Rush. For me, the message Dylan wanted me to hear was of the need for this boy to find his parents and the love of his family; within the first few minutes of the movie, I understood exactly why we were watching it. Plus, the musical gift within this boy was of course the same as Dylan's. The last scene of the movie put me right over the edge and brought the waterworks on again. As August was on stage playing and his mom and dad were making their way to the stage, I tried really hard to hide my emotions, but I could feel Dylan watching me and knowing that this moment was ripping my heart apart. I also realize that this was Dylan's way of telling me something. He was telling me that he needed me in his life. Somehow, I managed to get through the last scene with some composure and drove Dylan home without saying too much. Yes I must say, it was a quiet ride home filled with music from my iPod.

Once again, I sat with the knowing of me being Dylan's mom and the love of family. I felt better, although I was still wrestling with how I was to touch the lives of the other kids. The next day was vocals, and I received more answers. Dylan was telling me that a boy who had been visiting at his house and had helped us load for a recent gig had returned to visit him that afternoon, and that one of the things he had talked about was me. I looked puzzled at Dylan, and he continued to tell me that this young man had asked, "Who is the woman who was helping you?" Dylan said he explained that I was like a mom to him and the story of our journey. Then Dylan told this young man how I had written an inspirational book, which then led to an advanced level of conversation, and that this young man had taken my book home to read. Time then stopped for me and I completely got it. I thought of Donald and now this young man and how I had met both through Dylan. And so I was still helping the kids, and this felt good.

The next day, I drove Dylan to a jam session, and as we were unloading, the parents of the musicians greeted us with such love and enthusiasm it was truly wonderful. I then went off to work, only to return in a few hours to pick up Dylan, and this was when all the pieces started to fit together for me. I was sitting with the mother of the house, and she said how Dylan had told her how I was helping him and that I was a mom to him and that I was his angel. I smiled and thought of the poem, and then recited the line he had written: "My bright angel, my mom, and my best friend," and I could see the joy and love in this woman's entire essence. When Dylan and I left and reflected about his evening on the way home, I started to understand the answer to my question of purpose. When I arrived home, it all came together for me and I sent this text to Dylan: "Home. Great day and thank u. I love being your mom and good comes from conflict, as two days ago I was in question of my purpose and I now know to embrace what a wonderful gift it is to be your mom and our relationship. Setting the example IS helping all the kids and the parents too. Sometimes I need reassurance because we are all human, and I plan to be by your side as your mom forever. Sleep well. Love you. xo." Of course, a beautiful reply came: "Omg, love you too forever. xoxox ;-) ❤."

I got it and understood completely that I was to be Dylan's mom and that our relationship would set the example of the power of parental love, which would in turn help the kids, parents, and the entire world. And then I had the complete knowing that I was in the right spot doing the right thing and fulfilling my life's purpose, as well as helping Dylan embrace his gift of music!

We Settled in Once Again

It was now time to focus on the good, the joy, and business. So we worked on the paperwork, the music, and family once more. We were mailing copies of Dylan's music for copyright purposes and sitting in on jam sessions with the kids—which I must say was my favourite part of my role to Dylan. I just absolutely loved watching him play live, and I still thought he got better every time I heard him. We also spent a lot of time driving around in the car and listening to music, and I truly believed we could do that most of the day.

I also really started to realize the power of parental love and the maternal love in itself, and I thought to myself that I had opened my heart to a son and that this was a commitment that I could not just give up on and it was also something that I could not even imagine being without for a minute. I could really see how Dylan had been strengthened by experiencing maternal love, and I also saw that without it he floundered and that without Dylan I floundered, too. But the situation was different, as he was a gifted child—something I needed to be aware of. But I knew that this must be my path, that Dylan must have been placed into my care for a reason. This I truly believed, and this was what I decided to put my complete faith in.

Family

Our worlds then started to collide. We were becoming a family, we were becoming one, and we were having a lot of fun doing it. It now became about Kate, Emily, Dylan, Christine, Paul, Mimi, and myself. One day, Kate, Dylan, and I packed up the car and headed to the waterski lake, as Kate needed to practice with her coach Ryan. I packed the cooler, lunch, and a few chairs, and we headed to the lake. I sat in the back of the car, as it was time for Kate and Dylan to start to develop more of a friendship. I found it quite interesting listening to them, as to me they were very similar. They both were gifted, both passionate about their talent, and both strong-willed, determined, and sensitive all at the same time.

As we arrived at the lake, I was not sure who was more excited for Dylan to ride in the ski boat and watch Kate slalom: Dylan or me. We first spent some time visiting with people, as the waterski world was small and like a family unit. Kate wanted to ride her new jump skies, and another boy Stevie, who was at Kate's level, also wanted to ride his jump skies. Now, Stevie and Kate had been very close in their waterskiing journey over the past fifteen years, experiencing ups and downs in their relationship, but now all was good. The interesting thing was, they both had experienced a large jump crash at the end of the last season, which had brought them back to the fear of the jump ramp. I personally could not understand why they wanted to be boomeranged towards a jump ramp in the middle of the lake and soar through the air in the first place.

As Dylan and I watched from the shore, it was easy for me to see the fear that both Kate and Stevie had to work through. I thought about how great it was that playing the piano and singing was not a life-threatening occupation. Dylan was in a complete awe watching the sport of water-jump skiing, and he was taking all of it in. As Kate came off the water, she was really not so happy knowing that she was skiing like she had five years ago, but Dylan greeted her with such enthusiasm about watching her ski. She did say, "My slalom skiing will be better."

Kate then changed her ski while I introduced Dylan to Ryan, and then we prepared the boat for a slalom set. Dylan and I were seated facing Kate, with Ryan driving the boat. I explained to Dylan about the course, the gates, the rope length, and the goal to ski around all six buoys. It was great to see everyone's excitement, as Kate was one of the most beautiful slalom skiers in the world! Dylan enjoyed taking lots of pictures, and fun was had by all.

Then it was time to head back to Middletown. Once again I enjoyed the back seat while watching Dylan and Kate talk. During the drive, we planned a kayak ride to take place over the next few days.

A few days later, we pulled into Stephanie's driveway and started to prepare for the kayak ride. Stephanie was getting her hair done, so we headed directly down to the water's edge to collect our lifejackets, kayaks, and paddles. Kate and I both noticed it was a little rough, but we were both okay with the thrill of the water. When we were all set, we started walking with our kayaks until we could board the boats, as the water was quite shallow. We then headed out into Georgian Bay. I was out in the front, then Kate, and then Dylan. I was keeping a close eye on then both. As we started to enter the open water, we found it quite difficult to gain any distance because of the wind.

I at this moment felt a great sense of freedom, as there was nothing like the power of the water. As I returned back to reality, I could hear Kate having a little chuckle and I looked back to see a frightful sight. Dylan had fallen out of his kayak and seemed to be struggling, and he looked at me with his eyes popping out of his head. He yelled to me, "What should I do?!" and I replied, "Stand up!" Dylan was able to stand up, which was a good thing; although I knew he was a good swimmer, he was out of his comfort zone. I then decided it was too rough and we should head back to shore. Dylan was able to secure his lifejacket and reboard his kayak.

As we got back to shore, Dylan was extremely cold and shook up but still trying to be the man in front of Kate. We put the boats away and went to the car. I told Dylan I would drive, and he replied, "NO, I am fine." When we arrived back at my house, I start the kettle for hot chocolate and brought out some snacks. I could still see that Dylan was a little off, and I felt so very bad; I knew I would have jumped in and saved him no matter what. Dylan enjoyed his hot chocolate and then cozied up on the couch for a nap, and I covered him up with a couple blankets. Kate felt bad as well, as she didn't realize that he was not sure of what to do. Dylan awoke a half-hour later feeling much better!

For our next adventure, Christine, Paul, Emily, Dylan, and I headed off to a friend's cottage for the day. We were very fortunate to have such wonderful friends who had a great spot for swimming only a half-hour away. I packed the car and the cooler once again, and we were back on the road. As we arrived at the lake, it was as if we had been a family forever. Everyone was helping to bring our supplies to the lake, playing with Paul, and just being together as one. I at this moment felt so very blessed to have such wonderful children in my life and felt the fullness of their essence.

We sat for a while enjoying the sunshine and then we all headed for a swim out towards the raft. Christine and I were taking turns with Paul; in my youth, I was a swimming instructor and thus really enjoyed swimming with Paul. Dylan dove in and swam towards Paul and me, and I could feel the connection of him sensing the love, joy, and fun that Paul and I were having (I was asking Paul to blow bubbles and kick his feet, which he did with a large smile on his face). I looked at Dylan and wished I had had him when he was two and had taught him to swim as well. We all enjoyed a great afternoon of fun on the water and then headed back to my house for dinner, after which Dylan and I went off to two small performances.

Gossip, Drama, and Fame

Our situation then all of a sudden started to change, and the stories that were making their way to me were a little different than what I was used to. The people at Mama's Restaurant were experiencing situations around Dylan that they were feeling hurt and upset about. It was if they were not important anymore. I down-deep understood where it was coming from, and while at first I chose to ignore them, those same stories became more and more frequent and I realized I had no choice but to bring them forward. I knew I was taking a chance and that there would be great risk, but these people all had the same emotional feelings—they were hurt. It was a long conversation that I had with Dylan that led to just bringing out the facts, and unfortunately the results were not in my favour. There once again came the statement that I was too close and too involved with Dylan, which was completely true, but it was where our journey had led us. I also felt like I was just the messenger, passing on the information that was coming to me, and that I must have been getting this information for a reason, so I was just paying attention. Moreover, I believe everything happens for a reason and there is always a lesson within. We just have to be open and pay attention to the lessons. Now this was once again a new spot for Dylan and me, and it was not going so well.

The basic repercussion of this new situation of turmoil that I found myself in with Dylan was actually causing me to lose my faith. Yes, I actually was starting to lose my faith within and my faith with the people. I thought about how people managed to deal with fame, as there was so much judgement around it. I then tried to concentrate on the positive—the good energy and the people—without judgement, as they were also around, but the underling negativity of society was starting to take over. I began to once again think, "Why me? Why do I have this ability to detect this kind of energy from the people?" I found myself sleeping with my Bible and praying for the faith that was such a large part of my essence, a faith that I believed in. However, I could see myself losing ground every day as I started to feel like I had been guiding in a wrong manner, or helping incorrectly and feeling like I had done something wrong.

I then remembered helping this young boy when I was thirteen and a young lifeguard to learn to love the water and then the many kid's lives that I had touched in a positive way and I knew down deep that I was to assist the people. Moreover, many people had called me an angel, but now my angel light was out. Yes, I actually felt for the first time in my life that my light or purpose with the people was over. I tried to go into gratitude and think of how many people I had helped, so that if I were to stop now and that part of my life were to be over, I would be okay with it because I had helped so many. Then I thought that perhaps this was a lesson about not getting too involved with the people who had entered into my life. I was hurt again and in pain, and I just had to wait it out and just be. The timing was perfect, as Emily was suffering from a sore throat and wanted to have a movie weekend, and she had the marvellous idea to watch the Harry Potter movies, so we started. We spent time watching the movies, hanging out, and just being away from the drama.

As the weekend ended, Dylan and I started talking through Facebook messages and trying to figure out why I was hurt and why he was upset with me what had happened between us and how to get back on track. I then received a phone call from Garfield to set up arrangements for a performance at Georgian College in Orillia. This performance was to take place in one week, and I knew I was to take Dylan. Plans started to unfold perfectly, and a pickup time was set into place. I felt peace come over me and a reassurance of faith once again.

It was a week later and the morning of the performance, I enjoyed a wonderful walk with Stephanie and started to feel excited to see Dylan. It was the same feeling I had had when it was time to pick Kate up from the airport to reunite mom and child. As I pulled into the driveway, I could sense the feeling of joy enter into my awareness and I could see Dylan at the door ready with his equipment. I got out of the car and opened the trunk to load his keyboard and there he was. I hugged him, and he said how he missed me and I said I missed him too and that I loved him, and he said the same. And then time just went back to normal, or the way it always was, as if there had never been any uneasiness. It had always just felt normal between us. I placed the keys to the car into Dylan's hands and saw the smile on his face and the excitement as he pulled out of the driveway.

The drive became a time of listening for me and a time of talking for the Dylan—it was a forty-minute drive altogether. During the drive, Dylan actually said, "It's good to be home." I looked at him and could see his eyes full of emotion and love, and my eyes also filled with emotion and love. Then it was time for the music to go on and to have fun just being together. We used the iPhone to find the directions to the campus.

Since we arrived early, it was time for a little rebel action as we sat in the car and had a Corona before we began to unload the equipment... As we started to set up the equipment, we discovered that there was a bonus in the area Dylan was to play in: an upright piano. Dylan immediate checked to see if it was tuned, and of course, it was. After he had set up his equipment and keyboard, he cozied up at the piano. It was a wonderful moment, as I had never seen him play a real piano, and of course he was fantastic. He played "Titanic," the "Cottage Song," and his classical piece. People responded to him playing the piano just as they did when he was playing his keyboard and singing. This response from the people was absolutely amazing, and something I had never gotten used to (and I hope I never will, as seeing joy and excitement is what music is all about). After a half-hour, Dylan then took his place behind his keyboard and the room came to life once again.

Garfield then appeared at the door with a man he had just been talking about that would be a great connection for Dylan and he had just bumped into him in the hallway. Dylan stopped playing for some introductions and this lead to an incredible opportunity. I did mention to Dylan that it was important that we were in good communication because at this time we were caught without any business cards, and this I did not like, as I was also being portrayed to the people as a businesswoman. We also talked about not letting anything come between us ever again, as we were a team.

Dylan then started to play again, and I needed to make a trip to the loo. As I headed to the door, I heard Dylan start to play "Bohemian Rhapsody" and I couldn't believe my ears. I thought, that is strange, as now I could not leave the room. I started talking to a few people who were excited he was playing the song. But then I noticed there was something very wrong; it did not sound like Dylan and he was struggling with the song. This was something I had never heard and I didn't know what to do. Within a few seconds, I moved back to the top of the room where I had been seated so Dylan could see me. I waited for him to finish the song, but there was no strength behind it. I then felt sick inside, as I knew the message was: don't ever leave me.

I finally went to the washroom, and when I returned, Dylan asked if I thought it was okay if he was done and I said yes. There were some snacks there and Dylan filled up on a few and we started to load the car. The first thing I realized was that we needed to talk again and get things completely on track, and this was what we did. We talked about the gossip, drama, what came with fame, and that we had to have a tight team, and this was agreed on by both of us. As Dylan climbed into the passenger seat, I saw this six-foot-tall young man turn into Jell-O right in front of me. I wished at this time that Dylan was four so I could pick him up and rock him to sleep, and this was sort of what happened. He put his feet up on the dash and put his head under the seatbelt, and it was if he were snuggling beside me as if he really were four. I didn't move, and next thing I knew, he was asleep.

I turned on The Doors' "Riders on the Storm" at a low volume and realized now that Dylan had finally experience for the first time a full time mother like influence in his life and that it would be something he would need forever—how wonderful and how powerful! Yes, I thought to myself, the power of parental love—and I must say, maternal love—to a son was more powerful than I ever could have imagined. Moreover, at this moment I understood why I was there and that my role was plain as day. Even though most didn't see it, I did, and this was okay.

As the next few days unfolded, Dylan and I spent quite a bit of time together and things were good but I still had one last moment of doubt and I was unsure once again what I was too be doing. I couldn't understand what was happening to me, but I was still floundering. As I turned to others for support, I wasn't quite sure why I once again felt like I wanted to get myself the heck out of the situation that I found myself in. Once again, I sent Dylan a message of my doubt—although this time it was different, as I was unsure of my role in his business career but certain of my role of his mother (which I guess was an improvement, as before I kept giving up on everything). While Dylan loved me as a son, the businessman came forth and he asked me to make a decision: was I in or out?

As I sat contemplating the situation, I was taken back to how easy, fun, and wonderful the beginning performances were when it was just Dylan and me. Now it was getting bigger and involved more people, and with more people frankly came more unconsciousness and, as I called it, more drama. I knew that I was to be like a mom, but I also knew I was not to be his manager. Yet at this time I was sort of both, and it was taking a toll on me. I would think back to how simple my life was months and months ago, and I would wonder once again how I ever got here. I then remembered a time in my marriage when I was in a similar position and that when dealing with drama I ran the other way as quick as I could. Thus, I started to realize that it was time to learn how to deal with the negativity in the world and not run the other way, as this time I would be running away from Dylan who was very important to me.

I then thought back to that past Sunday and the sermon I had watched on TV where the message had been about letting the negativity of life roll off your back like a duck's back in water. At that moment, I had an amazing awareness: I realized it was time to learn (as we are always learning right up until the end) and it was time to not give up on what was important to me because of the negativity that was such a part of society. I got it and thought to myself how very strong I would be after I learned this new skill of not changing my path or what was important to me because there were obstacles in the way.

So I replied to Dylan and said, "I am IN, and I am going to learn to deal with these obstacles and not let them affect me." Even though my gift was to know, sense, and detect this energy, my new mission was to leave their energy with them. I almost saw myself with a plastic coating around me stopping the negativity from entering my atmosphere, and this was wonderful. So there was no more living in the story, no more complaining about the negativity, and no more taking ownership of it. It was now time to stay on my path and do what was important to me.

Also, during this time I had an awareness that while it was time to be there for Dylan, it was also time to let go, and once again the saying "Let them go and they will grow" came forward. So I changed the setup and let Dylan know that I loved him very much and was grateful to be in his life, but I was going to put him in charge of the plans and he needed to tell me what he needed me to help him with and when he needed me to take him places. I guess I actually turned his business career over to him and went to faith, which brought so much peace to both of us.

I could remember doing the same thing with Kate and her waterskiing around the age of eighteen. However, with Kate I had been with her for eighteen years and so it was a natural progression, and I was thankful I realized it, as I had seen parents hold onto their kids and never let them be in control of their own lives. I think this message was reinforced in the movie August Rush with the overprotective man who acted like a father. Nothing much changed with Dylan and me with the amount of time we spent together and worked on moving forward on his career, but there was a dramatic shift in the energy and ease around it. I actually received a text a few days later from Dylan saying thank you for the space, and my response was you're welcome and it was good for both of us.

A couple days later, I heard there was going to be a Middletown Idol competition held on July 1 at Little Lake Park. I immediately texted Dylan and told him about it, and he replied, "Oh, that would be great." I then said I would pick up the information and registration form at the Rec Centre and drop it off for him to look at, and this was exactly what I did. The next day, we chose to fill out the forms and register for the event. Dylan decided to make it a singing competition and wanted to perform without his keyboard, and I thought this was a fantastic idea.

We later hit the Middletown Library, as at this time we were renting out movies on a weekly basis to share and learn from. We were enjoying all types of music documentaries, one of my favourites being about Celine Dion. I was completely in "ah-ha" about her for many reasons: one being her strength as a woman, another being her love for the people as well as her fans, and also her values concerning husband and family, as well as her sense of humour and her natural gift of music. We also rented Eckhart Tolle's enlightenment video, which had been a lifeline for me a few years ago and he was still my mentor.

As Dylan was picking the movies that afternoon, he showed me a very special one and one that I knew the timing was perfect for: This Is It with Michael Jackson (a movie I had already seen twice). I said that it would be great to watch for the upcoming Middletown Idol competition, and a smile appeared on Dylan's face. He then picked a few other movies and we had our regular visit with the librarian Sue, who had been a great customer at my former deli. Sue had a wonderful spirit, and her son was also a writer who was moving forward with his writing career.

Two days later, Dylan told me he had watched This Is It twice and how great it was, and then he gave it to me to watch, which I did for the third time in my life!

Father's Day

Father's Day was now upon us, and Dylan was set to perform at the Barrie Blues Festival which was the opportunity we had received from the function with Garfield and we were all excited for the event. I was going to pick up Dylan's dad and the equipment, Lauren and Dylan were travelling together, and Lauren's dad was heading down with Lauren's younger sister and their aunt. A lunch date with the gang was planned for after the performance.

I had met Dylan's dad quite a few times so the ride down to the event was comfortable, and of course, we talked about Dylan. As Gary was talking, I had the knowing that he had done the best he could for both Dylan and his sister Amber. He talked about the times he had walked them both to school and picked them up as well. He talked about how one day he was late to pick them up and Dylan was in tears, and that he made sure he was never late again. He also spoke about the people in the area where they lived who were much more fortunate than he was and that he felt that he could lose his son because of that. This was one of the reasons he moved his family to a small town north of Barrie. He also talked about working a lot and making sure he read a story to his kids before bed and the fun times they had going camping as a small family. Gary also worried about the outcome of his and Dylan's relationship, and I thought to myself that Dylan would love him forever. I knew from Dylan that in his early teen years there was an obstacle that came between him and his dad (the song "Killer and the Sin" described this time in Dylan's life).

The setup was great at the Barrie Blues Festival; it was very well-done, although there were only a few people enjoying the waterfront festival. Dylan was amazing as always, and it was good for him to be around a group of family supporters. After the performance, we then headed up the street to a restaurant for lunch. The dads and I ended up on one side, with me at the end, and the rest on the other side of the table. It was great watching and being a part of this Father's Day lunch. Gary was over-the-top excited, as this was the first time Dylan had had the resources to celebrate Father's Day (Lauren and Dylan split on the bill and I left the tip). The food was good, and we enjoyed great conversation throughout the lunch. As we were leaving the restaurant, Dylan and I had a small talk about upcoming business. We all then said our farewells, with Lauren's dad heading home, Dylan and Lauren heading to Toronto, and me and Dylan's dad returning to Victoria Harbour.

As we were driving home, the conversation turned to a "thank you for helping my son" and a note of knowing that I was also important to Dylan, a part of his heart. I just smiled and said that Dylan was very important to me and also a large part of my heart as well. Then there was a moment of silence, followed by a very strong message from Gary. He said to me, "Don't ever leave him!" I just smiled and said, "I won't."

Just Being There

The doors continued to open for Dylan. A woman actually said to me, "The universe is opening up for Dylan," and I thought to myself, yes, and it is because we have not tried to control it. We have let the universe do its thing, and we have paid attention, followed every lead, and followed our gut.

It was now time for the grand opening of the Middletown Cultural Centre, and Dylan was a guest performer. I thought that Anna had something to do with this performance, and we were very grateful. Dylan had received a call from the lady in charge to attend the private opening and that he would be able to play some background music during this event. Dylan called me and was very excited for the opportunity, and he started to prepare for the event immediately.

Four hours later, my phone rang and there was an excited voice on the other end as Dylan started to tell me about his evening and how it had unfolded. He ended up giving a private concert to the founders and developers of the Middletown Cultural Centre, and their reaction to his talent was amazing. He mentioned one name in particular: Greg Hacker. Greg was a wonderful man: a man of community and a man whom I respected very much. It was also a joy to hear the excitement in Dylan's voice.

Dylan had another performance booked for 10:00 p.m., and as it unfolded, I found myself putting on my makeup and heading into town to pick Dylan up—which was once again one of my favourite things to do. After the performance, we went for a snack and realized that the Dylan Lockstar Fever had already reached the people we now were encountering. It was simply amazing! It always took us back a bit, but it only took a smile between us to quickly move forward and remain in the moment.

As the Dylan Lockstar Fever started to get bigger and was making its way to more people, the excitement started to make its way back to me. I next ended up in a conversation at Marilyn's house concerning what was happening as more and more were becoming aware of his talent. I found myself talking about my role as a new parent or mother to Dylan, and the words just popped out of my mouth that I was "just being there" for Dylan, just as I had been for many other children as well. That was the moment Marilyn said, "That's the title for your book!"

Five days later, I thought about this as a title of this book. I liked it and it felt good! But I wanted to get some feedback. Of course, I started with Dylan and the response was, "Oh, that is good!!!" I thought, okay, this is good, but I still felt unsure. I then texted Anne Marie and received what I needed to hear. She said, "I like it. Your last book was A Woman's Passage to Freedom. This would link you as an author to your next book being about the next stage of your life and what you've come to learn about kids." I then replied, "Yes, for sure: "Just Being There" Once again Anne Marie replied with amazing insight; she said, "It says a lot, and it's the mantra of parenting! Sometimes we have to shut up, stay out, and watch them crash, and it's enough for them to know that our JUST BEING THERE will get them through with LOVE." I then asked Anne Marie if I could quote her, and this was the reply: "Ha! 4 sure! Congrats on the title! And put in brackets at the end of the quote [even if it kills us!]." And so it became official that this book had a name, a fantastic name: "Just Being There."

It now became time to share this name with the people in my circle: basically with friends, family, and the people I worked with. It became very interesting hearing the feedback. One comment became predominate among all of them: it was, "That says a lot." I realized everyone was saying the same comment, and I would reply, "Yes, you're right; it sure does." Then I could see the people going to a place in their memory when someone was there for them, meaning present in their lives when they needed someone, and then joy was apparent within. And all I could think of was, wow, how very powerful. This was definitely going to be the title! (PS: Thank you, Marilyn.)

All the Kids

Kate was doing great. She was experiencing a wonderful time at home, although that was coming to an end in another two weeks. She was skiing well, and she was getting ready to start her full-time job in California. Emily was also great. She and Brandon were settled in a healthy relationship. This was good for both of them, because when you are in a healthy relationship, this allows you to be successful in all other areas of life.

However, at this time Christine was still in turmoil, and I was aware of it. I was doing the best I could to help her and I had the knowing that something was going to shift within her life. I wished for happiness for Christine, as she was such a wonderful girl: a smart, caring, loving, and conscious girl, and a fantastic mother. Yet still she was in turmoil in her life and still stuck in the drama, if you want to call it that (or still in the high school unhealthy days), and she deserved better. I knew that it was difficult for Christine to decide what was best for her, and I believed that it was faith that I was to teach her—and this was what I continually said to her. I did offer for her to move into my house if she felt like she had no other choice. Baby Paul was growing and talking up a storm, and I just loved it when he followed me around saying "Nana Jenny."

Around this time, I was checking my email and noticed an email from Quantum Distributors, which stopped me in my tracks. I remembered the name immediately, as it was the company I had sent my book to: A Woman's Passage to Freedom. At this very moment, I could feel numbness come over me and I opened the email and noticed the attachment, which read "distribution agreement." Then a sheer joyful panic came over me, and it was very hard to stay centered, which was just fine. As I realized the depth of meaning of this email and that it could be a passage to get my books to the people, I then found myself lying flat on my bed with tears of joy running down my face. Not long after, I fell fast asleep on my bed. I awoke shortly, wondering what had happened. And then I began to figure out how this was going to work and where I was going to find a supplier. I contacted my special people and family to share my great news, and the response was fabulous—and I must say it felt really good, yes, really good. However, I was not quite sure how to move forward with the contract and therefore found myself at a bit of a standstill, which I must admit I did not quite understand at this moment in time.

Life then started moving at a very fast pace with Dylan, which I think was also part of the time of year that we were entering: summertime. It was interesting, because we first printed 50 business cards, then 100 business cards, and now 250 were being printed. We also had a fabulous, productive and professional time once again at the studio. I must say, it was actually my favourite and most enjoyable time being in the music business because Dan, Dylan, and me experienced such ease during our time together. Two amazing things happened during this particular visit. First, we were able to fine-tune and complete a demo CD with five original songs that was ready for sale—and the most important part of this CD was it was all Dylan. Yes, it was just Dylan, and it was just how he wanted it and how he heard it in his head. Second, we were able to film "This Girl" and "Shanti Love" in the studio for YouTube. This was a big step, as Dylan had previously been filming in his bedroom, which at this time in his life was the only space that was completely his own and a place he felt comfortable in. At the time, there were lots of critics on this, but at least he was on YouTube and this was a milestone on its own. Now we now had demo CD to sell and professional original songs on YouTube, so we were making headway and moving forward.

It was now time to say goodbye to Kate, as she was ready to enter into the real world and start her full-time job in California. This moment in my life was certainly bittersweet, because it was great to see her start another chapter of her life and it was sad to see her moving so very far away. I found this to be quite an emotional day, but it was okay, as it was just fine for me to be human, to love, miss, and just plain have emotions. So I cried and felt the loss of my beautiful daughter.

A Busy Time

I really had little time to mourn Kate, as that following day Dylan and I were entering into the busiest four days of performances that we had yet to experience. It was Thursday, June 28, 2012, and we were loading up my truck and heading to the Boat House for a three-hour performance. The Boat House was located in Middletown, on the water in Middletown harbour, and I would have to say that the patio was one of the nicest patios I had ever seen. It was a very hot night, and as Dylan started to play I found myself searching for shade, which I found as well as the company of some wonderful regular customers.

The night started to unfold beautifully. The people loved Dylan's performance, and a breeze picked up to cool us off. I was completely enjoying the people around me as well as the music, and I would have to say that this evening was turning into a magical moment. I was sitting off to the right-hand side and quite a distance away from Dylan, and I found it very interesting and wonderful to watch the people and how they were reacting to Dylan and his music. On this particular evening, he was experiencing feedback from a wide range of ages, and most of the young women were taking note of this good-looking singer and piano player, which for some reason brought a wonderful smile to my face and to Dylan's as well.

The evening ended with another booking at this great establishment and a beer and nachos at Cellarman's up the street. It was Dylan's treat, which felt good for both of us. As we entered this small, friendly establishment, we were greeted with enthusiasm, which Dylan could take all the credit for. This also became a moment in history, as Dylan sold his first two CDs and with a tip included. I then dropped him off and we set up a pickup time for Friday morning's performance at 10:35 p.m. On my way home, I enjoyed reflecting on what we had experienced this evening.

It was now Friday morning, and first I had to get my mother all set for the day, with coffee and toast, and a packed lunch, and then she was off to Balm Beach for an afternoon of bridge. I then had to take my camera to the Copy Shoppe to have a picture lifted for a poster for the Surf Restaurant. I actually made it to Dylan's five minutes late, which for me was unusual. At this moment I looked back to the times I had made Dylan learn to be punctual with a little apprehension, and then the mother came out in me: "Well, that really won't hurt him."

We finally arrived at the Bayfield Retirement Home located in Penetang and started preparing for an early Canada Day celebration. At this time there was a man that was in the music business that just happened to show up at this performance. He was asking me a lot of questions about Dylan and I felt a little uncomfortable giving all this personal information about Dylan without his permission. I did say to this man that I would mention to Dylan that he was interested in Dylan's musical history and that if he wanted to set up a meeting with Dylan he was welcome to do that. Dylan then started to play and compensated with his extremely large repertoire of covers and originals to the crowd at hand. He immediately captured the audience with Roy Orbison and some piano tunes, and then used his amazing ability for insight and to feel the energy of the people as he moved to some Elvis tunes. The next thing we knew, one lady had pulled up a chair right in front of him and another two women were up on their feet dancing. It was great to see, and I noticed the smiles appear on everyone faces, starting with the women dancing, then the people watching, then the staff, the administration, and Dylan and me too. It reminded me of the joy that music can bring to our hearts.

At this moment, an older man sitting quite close to us, who had been joking with Dylan throughout his performance, now said to me, "There must be a lot of joy in your house due to the amount of music," and my reply was, "Yes, there is!" Dylan played for three hours and then announced he was going to play his final song; it was the Guess Who song called "These Eyes." Only a few seconds into this song, this man who had just made the comment about the joy in our lives started to have what I call an emotional release: he started to cry and he was crying quite hard. I froze and immediately looked for Dylan's response, and the first thing I heard was a weakness in Dylan's voice, but he continued to play and sing. Dylan's emotions were also very exposed, and his eyes filled with tears, without a single tear running down his cheek. Dylan managed to compose himself, and then shortly after, the man did as well. It was a special moment, one I was thankful and privileged to have witnessed and experienced. I looked over at Dylan and thought how very proud I was of him.

After the performance, we enjoyed some much needed lunch, visited with the people, and took our time packing up. We then returned to Dylan's place for reflection, refreshment, and regrouping, as the posters needed to be checked, printed, and delivered to Balm Beach and the Surf Restaurant. We both approved the proof, and then I was off to Balm Beach and then home for a short rest and visit with Emily.

Later that day, I headed back to Dylan's to pick him up for a performance at Neil's retirement party. Many a time over the past few days, I had questioned how this was actually going to unfold knowing there was a slight amount of turmoil still between Neil and Dylan. I also had the knowing it was all about credits, which basically is the money and we defiantly know what happens when we make it about the money. As we walked into the Penetang Legion, memories of the many times we had been there for performances quickly flooded back. I could see Dylan standing on stage playing "Mama" and the crowd getting to their feet, and then I could see him playing the night everything came together and his ride went in the ditch. I looked at Dylan and saw his ease and enjoyment as he and Neil exchanged a hello and spent some time catching up. As I was watching, I could see that both of them had healed and that both of them were leaving the past in the past. Moreover, it was at this very moment that I realized why we were in that very room: it was to heal the past. It all made sense and it was truly perfect.

We did have to wait an hour or so for Dylan to take the stage, and it was a bittersweet moment as he jumped on stage and started singing Led Zeppelin without warming up his voice; his excitement and love for music were definitely the driving force, as Dylan was giving it his all. He played a few songs with the guys on stage, and I must say that these men and Dylan gelled very well together and the people were up dancing and enjoying the ease of these musicians.

Next, it was time for Dylan and his young band to take the stage and play some of his originals. There was Alex on the drums, Taylor on the sax, and Guy on bass. It was their first performance as a band and it was very special for Neil, as they were all musicians who had touched his life in some way. I could see Neil off to the side with a smile on his face, enjoying Dylans originals with Dylan at the helm. This night became a wonderful night of friends, family, and music as Dylan and the boys touched the heart of the people as well.

I enjoyed a great conversation with one of Dylan's previous math teachers; he spoke of seeing the light in Dylan in grade nine. I then found Dylan standing beside me reminding me about the story he had told me about a teacher who taught him one morning about the concept of thinking: that your mind is a like a computer and sometimes you have to turn it on and hit the delete button and clear away some files. I remembered the story very well, as I thought at the time what a great way it was to describe letting go of the past. The teacher also talked about The X Factor and that Dylan would win and what an amazing talent he had.

As a new group of musicians took the stage, Dylan had the opportunity to dance a little, and he was enjoying dancing with the people. I was standing near the back, and a woman came up to me and said, "You must be Dylan's mom. I know because when he was playing his originals you were standing at the back of the room watching him and singing all the words, and only a mom would know all the words to his original songs." A very large smile came upon my face as I thought, was I singing? She then mentioned how talented he was and that she had one of his first CDs that Neil had recorded. I said thank you and that I was very proud of him.

I spent the rest of the evening just hanging out with the people, dancing a bit, and being with family. Around midnight, I dropped Dylan off as Lauren had just finished her shift at work as well. I then arranged to pick him up for Saturday's performance at 1:15 p.m. As I drove to my house, I started to reflect on the past twenty-four hours and how amazing they had been. Then it was time for a midnight snack, which I must say was becoming a regular event and truly not the best for my waistline. But I thought to myself, oh well, it just is!

I am still not sure how I managed to be perfectly on time, but I did and this time Dylan was a little behind. He said, "I am not ready; going to be another half-hour." Five years ago, I would have gone to fear, but thank goodness I knew now to just go with the flow and believe that I was always in the right spot at the right time. I also remembered that I had the papers for my book distribution ready to give to Marlene and David for their opinion, and so it became a time to run a much-needed errand and get a Tim Horton's Coffee. I actually returned to Dylan's house thirty-five minutes later and he was totally ready, and we started moving quickly, as it was getting close to the start time.

When we arrived, the timing was, of course, perfect as always, and the owner and his wife were fabulous and commented that all musicians were late. I thought, yes, you are right, and poor Dylan has to put up with me always being on time and right to the second most times. This place was a special, cozy little venue full of beautiful art. Dylan's girlfriend Lauren worked here part-time preparing lovely snacks for the guests and acting like a mini hostess. Lauren's dad, aunt, and a few family friends were also in attendance, and so we settled in for the show.

Immediately, I could hear how great the sound was in this room, and Dylan's performance became special. It was kind of a strange feeling for me, as Lauren had a lot of family support and for Dylan's family it was just me in attendance. Dylan played songs for everyone: "This Girl" for Lauren and "Tiny Dancer" for Lauren's dad. And he ended his performance with "Bohemian Rhapsody," which still warmed my heart.

As the concert ended, I noticed that all the CDs had sold and I found myself running out to my car to see if I had any other copies available. As I was looking around, I heard this wonderful voice say, "MOM, what are you doing?" I turned and started walking fast towards Dylan explaining that I was looking for some more CDs, and he was at this time walking fast towards me. We just ended up in the biggest hug, and I looked at him and said, "You were magnificent." Then I had to go, as I was going to be late for work. He thanked me again for being there for him As I opened the door of my car, I looked to the porch and there was Dylan watching me. He waved to me with his wonderful smile, and I waved back, thinking how blessed I was.

The next day was Middletown Idol, and Dylan asked me to pick up his dad. He was okay with his equipment, as it was still at the Art Gallery and he had a way to get it to Little Lake Park. I told him I would see him there. I then packed up the chairs and headed over to get Gary. Stephanie, Bryan, and Bryan's kids were also on their way, as were Christine, Emily, and Paul.

We all met at the park and found a great spot to watch the show. I was having a bit of a hard time dealing with the emotion of worry, as it was getting close to performance time and people were starting to ask me where Dylan was. I said I was sure he was on his way and started to sit on my hands so I wouldn't text him. Christine, Emily, and Paul decided to go for a walk and check out the vendor booths that were located on the grounds.

Ten minutes later, they came back and Christine had a very special gift, a gift of family. Christine then presented Stephanie and me with special handmade bracelets with very special names on them. Stephanie received hers first with "Nana" written on it, and it was beautiful.

Christine then presented me with mine, which said "Nana Jenny." Emily then showed me hers, which said "Auntie Emily." Christine also had one with "Mommy" and finally Paul had one too with "Baby Paul"! I saw at this time that Christine was bursting with pride of family and she was shining throughout. We all place our bracelets on, and the strength and love that came with family warmed all our hearts. Emily then leaned over and told me that Ron gave Christine $30 to spend on Paul at the celebration of our great country (that being the only money she truly had), and Christine wanted to show the love from Paul to all of us. This moment made me feel very loved.

Fifteen minutes later, I couldn't stand waiting any longer and I texted Dylan saying, "Where are you?" He replied right away, "Just loading the equipment and we will be there soon." I said, "K, thanks," and then smiled at Gary, trying not to let him know that I was almost jumping out of my skin.

Dylan finally did arrive and unloaded his equipment, as he needed it for his second performance in the park (he was going solo for the Idol competition). Dylan and Lauren made their way around the park, checking things out and talking with the people. This was a totally new situation for me, and I was doing good with it. Dylan finally made his way over to say hello to the family, as it was all his family in attendance. As he made the rounds and it was time for a hug for me, I whispered into his ear, "Glad to see you." He just smiled at me. Then he was gone again, which was exactly what he should have been doing.

Dylan did say as he left that he would be back to see me before he went on stage. I smiled, but I kind of got the feeling that people did not understand my nervousness for Dylan, as it completely felt as if it were my son in the competition. When Dylan returned, he sat between his dad and me for quite some time before his performance. He talked about the songs he was going to perform and his overall plans. I remembered that I was to say nothing except that it sounded wonderful. It was then time for Dylan to line up beside the stage; he hugged me and his dad, and he was gone. I was so proud of him and felt very comfortable being a spectator in the audience.

Dylan's first song was "Midnight Special," and it didn't take long for him to have the crowd in his hands. Christine and Paul went down to the front of the stage to cheer Dylan on; Paul even jumped out of Christine's arms to dance on stage with Dylan, and this was a fantastic moment, as Paul was clearly comfortable with him. Then it was time for the judges' comments. They were all mostly positive, as Dylan's dance skills and ability to move on stage were terrific. They did say that he should have kept his shoes on and that he did his little yell a bit too much, which was really a trademark and one of my favourite parts of his singing. They mentioned that he shouldn't read the words, to which Dylan replied, "I have sung this song so many times I know all the words, but I will look out into the audience more and not look as if I am not reading the words from the screen below."

Dylan made it to the finals, for which he chose a Tragically Hip song called "Boots and Hearts." This performance was so good it brought me to my feet because I just couldn't contain myself. It brought Emily to her feet as well. Dylan then returned to see us all and receive amazing feedback, as he had done a fantastic job. When it was time for the results to come forward, for some reason I had a funny feeling in my gut. I could see the people were over-the-top clapping when he was performing, much more than any of the other participants, but I felt like there was some connection with the people around the event and a relationship with some of the contestants. Something wasn't right. I also noticed that Dylan's vocal coach Anna was sitting off to the side under a tree with a very large hat on. As they all stood on stage, the first prize was given to a young woman who had a flare for opera, and then there was a tie for second between Dylan and a boy whose father was in charge of the music. I could immediately feel the uneasiness in Dylan, as this was the first time we had experienced politics and disappointment with his music. After Dylan left the stage, I could see the disappointment on his face and those of most of the people in the audience. He said to me that his gut dropped and how could that be. I said to just take it as a learning experience.

Then it was time to move forward to the next performance, which was with the young band he was playing in five hundred feet around the lake. The rest of the family headed home, and Dylan's dad and I moved to the next performance. It was truly an amazing performance with the young band, and it was perfect timing for Dylan to play with his keyboard and sing his originals songs. We received quite a bit of feedback from people saying that Dylan should have won the competition although the next day we learned that the girl who won was thinking of changing her major at school and that this win gave her encouragement to continue in music, and this made Dylan feel very happy. I just believed it was a learning experience and time to move forward as always.

Life Was Changing Again

Christine was still having a hard time in a relationship that just wasn't working, and so the question came up if she and Paul could move in with me, and of course I said yes. And so my house filled up again with family, and this time it included a twenty-month-old baby, which I totally enjoyed. I also was grateful that Christine could experience a home full of love, easiness, loyalty, and respect—a home filled with conscious behaviour. I put Christine into Kate's room, although I hesitated on this as I thought Kate needed the security of having a home with her mom and a bedroom of her own in it. But I also had the knowing that Christine and Paul needed this space, and Kate wasn't due home until Christmas, which was six months away.

Then all of a sudden I had a change in my schedule at Mama's Restaurant and I somehow managed to get weekends off, which was basically unheard of in the restaurant business. At first I was a little upset because those days were the busiest days and the owners were giving my shifts to a member of their family and so I was getting knocked off because of this. But my next instinct was to believe that this was happening for a reason, and so I placed all my trust into the universe and accepted my new schedule with joy. Now, I must say that working the four shifts in a row during the week was very tiring due to the stress that came with this type of work, but there was a prize at the end: three days off.

Saturday became a day of rest and a time to take care of myself. That first Saturday, I met up with a wonderful friend and enjoyed some cottage time, dinner out, and a fabulous hot tub later with Christine and Paul. It was a fantastic having Saturday off, and I thought to myself that this felt good and I could actually get used to it. For my Sunday off, I went to a family brunch at Stephanie's for all of us: me, Mimi, Emily and Brandon, Christine and Paul, Dylan and Lauren, and all of Stephanie's husband's family as well. The food was fantastic as always, and it was special enjoying the slowness of a Sunday.

Soon the kids grew restless and decided to play volleyball. It was a beautiful hot sunny day with a slight breeze coming off the water, and the bay had become a busy place, as it was a prime day for water activities. First, it was just the five kids who took to the volleyball court—Brandon, Emily, Christine, Dylan, and Lauren—and they were really having a great time. Then all the adults started to join in as well. It was wonderful to see how the game of volleyball brought everyone together as one, because some of us had just met that day for the first time. After a while of playing in the sun, the kids needed to go for a swim and the older crowd needed a rest.

We had to drive Lauren to a family event, so Dylan, Lauren, and I packed up, gave our thanks, and headed into Middletown. After dropping Lauren off, Dylan and I then stopped briefly to pick up fifty more CDs to burn and some that were ready to sell. I could see the joy and happiness within Dylan as he held onto his CDs and I drove to the destination for delivery, and all I could feel was pride for this talented young man.

As we headed back to Victoria Harbour, Dylan realized he had missed a call from his dad, and because we were going to be passing Dylan's dad's house, I suggested we stop for a visit. As I said the words, Dylan was saying the same thing. We pulled into the driveway and Dylan headed into the house. Gary was very happy to see both of us, and we all sat outside and enjoyed the beautiful day, wonderful conversation, and even a cold beer. This was a very peaceful moment as the three of us sat and shared what was happening in all our lives.

Later, the kids, baby Paul, and I all ended up at my house for dinner. The highlight of this moment was Dylan showing Paul how to walk on his hands and Paul trying to do it. Finally, I ended the day in my cozy bed, this becoming a time of reflection as this was one of my first Sundays off in almost two years. I thought about the fantastic brunch that included all our family and four generations, then the marvellous volleyball game that brought camaraderie to all, and finally to the delivery of Dylan's music, the visit with Dylan's dad, and dinnertime with baby Paul. And I realized once again, it was all about family!

I had spoken with Kate throughout the day, as she physically was the only person missing. But she was living her dream, spending her weekend slalom skiing and jumping, and ending it by spending her first night alone in her very own condo. I must say that I was very proud of her. I felt very thankful and blessed that I had the opportunity to experience a weekend full of friends and family.

The next day became a day to regroup a bit in the business department all across the board and for everyone. First, I took care of some personal banking, then Mimi's things, and then Dylan's stuff (such as booking vocal lessons for the next week and burning another fifty CDs). Then it was time to work on my book distribution project and to spend some time writing. The day ended with a moment of reflection, or meditation, which brought a bit more awareness. All I had to do was to sit quietly in silence, which was definitely a special time I looked forward to and something I always tried to make time for every day.

My reflections that night began with Kate, as she finally was independent and self-sufficient. What came to mind was, boy, what a struggle we had been through and how difficult it had been to get to this point. This surprised me; I would like to say that it wasn't the first thought to appear within, but it truly was. I thought about the guy in the Justin Bieber movie who said, "It was a natural progression, but it was still a lot of work." Then I realized that these were the exact words that make sense for the passage of all kids and all goals coming to fruition, and that this was perfectly okay.

Then Emily popped into my mind: she had completed two years at Queen's University, had a summer job in her field of chemical engineering, and was in a healthy relationship—all which I felt really good about. Dylan next popped into my mind because after six months of just being there and helping him, he was definitely on his way towards being independent. The transformation that he had experienced so quickly was amazing—not only due to me and my motherly role, but also through help from Neil, Garfield, and Dan in the studio. It seemed to be taking a village to create a rock star.

Christine had made a decision to be on her own and all of us were helping and supporting her. Her mom was helping with food and a car, Brandon with moving things, and from me some financial support and a loving home to be at ease within. So Christine had a good start, with lots of support from everyone around her. She also had a few months ago taken the incentive to register herself for school. It was at Georgian College in Middletown as a PSW, personal support worker—which was perfect for Christine, as she had such a gift with the people. This course also only took eight months, so she would be ready for employment in less than a year, and I knew that the care of Paul would unfold perfectly during this time of education.

Now it was time for bed and of course time to say good night to Dylan. I stopped for a second and thought, oh my, I am in a way saying good night to him and actually tucking him in through a text message every night. I then felt a little strange, as if I were a new mother with a young child. Even though Dylan was twenty-one, he was now accustomed to having a mother saying good night to him and, when I thought about it, good morning as well. Plus, I couldn't think of going to sleep without saying good night to him because he was like a son and this was just for me a natural instinct, although I did know that Dylan's dad was very loving and had certainly tucked him in. Then I remembered my mom tucking me in and I also remembered tucking my girls in and kissing them on the forehead, which I still loved to do (even knowing that Emily really doesn't like me kissing her on the forehead, and I did it anyways).

I thought how important it was for everyone to be aware that kids in their late teens and early twenties still needed families, either parents or mentors from within the community. Moreover, it was important to just be there for our kids and to remember the power we give them even when we tuck them in every night. I knew that realizing this really was the power of love, something we should respect and appreciate more within our lives.

A Night to Celebrate

It was now Friday morning, July 13, and this day started off in alignment with the superstition that surrounds all Fridays with this date. First, I endured an early 6:00 a.m. wakeup from my mom, and then I could not find Ernie, my faithful beloved cat. As I was leaving for work at 8:30 a.m., Ernie did appear and he had treats for mom (meaning me) in the form of a dead mouse and a half-eaten snake. I must say, however, that the day took a happier change of direction, beginning with a good day at work, and then later a wonderful haircut and great plans for an evening performance at The Boat House in Middletown. Emily was on her way home, Paul's dad was coming to pick up Paul for the weekend, and my friend Cathy and her lovely daughter Julie were set to come for dinner and a night of entertainment at The Boat House. It was so good to have Emily home, and she enjoyed having Christine and Paul living in our home.

I left early to pick up Dylan and his equipment, and en route received a call from The Boat House owner saying there was a fan base waiting for him, and so we were quickly on our way. As we were unloading, we noticed that the patio was packed and this was a wonderful feeling. I did manage to get a table with a perfect view of Dylan and was excited for Emily, Christine, Cathy, and Julie to arrive and join me. As I sat and enjoyed the opening songs, I noticed that I again felt a nervousness, sort of the feeling I would get when the girls were going to ski. But I just set it aside and brought myself to the now and enjoying the entertainment.

Cathy and Julie were first to arrive, then Emily and Christine came right behind them. We had a table of family, and this was great for all of us. The first hour of Dylan's performance consisted of background music while the customers were enjoying dinner and dinner conversation (although I could see Dylan's eyes moving through the audience on a constant basis, picking up on their reaction to his choice of songs). Once again, he seemed to have the ability to get into the hearts of the people. This was something I had seen many a time, but it was still amazing to watch. I was also enjoying the company of Emily, Christine, Julie, and Cathy.

About ninety minutes into Dylan's performance, the magic started to unfold. The people clearly loved him and his music, and it was as if the audience was becoming one, and this was great to be a part of. It reminded me of being in a concert setting, as the people were clapping, moving to the music, singing, filling his tip jar (a strainer that I had borrowed from Cheryl, his landlord), and buying his CDs. It was truly an amazing moment for everyone.

As Dylan took a break and moved around the audience with love and his magical glow, I sat in a moment of wow! He then returned to finish his performance and give the audience what they wanted, and this was all good. When he announced that he was going to do his last song, we all paid attention to what it was going to be—and of course, it was "Bohemian Rhapsody"! I tried very hard not to make this song about me and the gift of this wonderful son—but let me tell you, it was very hard not to as I heard him belting out "Mama." It just filled my entire soul with love. I turned to Cathy and told her a little about Penetang Idol and the reaction from the crowd, and I hit a trigger within, which then caused the most amazing flashback in time for me.

First, I was back at Penetang Idol, videotaping Dylan shaking and the crowd rising to their feet. Then I flashed to the car and the first CD from Dan's studio with "Mama," the first song recorded from the studio, and me reaching for my sunglasses and fighting back the tears. Then I went back to the restaurant in Orillia with friends and family all around, then to the Art Gallery, and finally to that current moment in time. And then came the "ah-ha" moment of how very far we had come and in such a short period of time. Yes, it was moment of, "Wow, we sure have come a long way," and it was a fantastic feeling. I then found myself present in time, hearing the ending of the song and then an encore as well. Later, when I told Dylan about my ah-ha moment, he just laughed at me, smiled, and gave me a short hug, and then returned to the people. I then smiled back and thought, yes, you are just a regular kid!

Afterwards, we just sat and enjoyed the warm summer night, the beautiful waters of Georgian Bay, and the closeness of family. Then it was time for the kids to head home, and Cathy and Julie as well. Dylan started to pack up and we loaded my truck and went to one of our regular spots, Cellarman's, for a beer and time of celebration. Dylan said that this had been the best night ever in his music career.

One of the best parts of our conversations and our time together was that we didn't dwell on any point or moment, so after a time of celebration, it was time to move to a time of reflection and consideration of what was the next step and our goals for the next few days. We talked about a vocal lesson on Monday and made a note to talk with Anna about how to maintain the quality and vocal cords themselves. Next, we talked about the radio station and if he was to have a solo presentation soon. Then we closed with the realization of how very far we had come. And then Dylan said something so brilliant I had to write it in my notes on my iPhone. It was that "OUR FORMULA" was working fabulously for him. I said out loud, "You are so very right," and without words being spoken we both knew what our formula was and I will share it with you now:

Paying attention

Following the path that is shown right in front of us

Integrity

Believing we are always in the right spot at the right time

That the correct people are always present

Goal setting

Letting life flow

Practicing

Learning through movies and books

Always doing and working towards our goals

Tight team

Trust

Respect

Communication

It's all about the people.

And faith.

It was working, and we were sticking with it!

Mothers Are the Driving Force

Sometimes there can be awareness, and it can be something that is not judgemental. Rather, it can be a fact and it can be something that just is. I was lucky enough when I was in Arizona for Kate's graduation to ride in a waterskiing boat with this wonderful woman Marianna while Kate was enjoying a slalom ski set. Marianna was in her late thirties and had taken a shine to Kate and thus was helping Kate by letting her water-ski at her home, as the lake was right at her back door. At the beginning of her set, this woman talked about how Kate had a similar path to her own, as she was also a water skier who graduated from the engineering program at Arizona State University. We then somehow started to talk about everything I had done for Kate as a mother.

I commented that both Kate and Emily had taken downhill ski lessons, dance lessons for years, piano, singing, volleyball, soccer, basketball, and of course competitive waterskiing. I then said that I had been the driving force and mostly the driver of the car as well, and that I had enjoyed playing that role. Most of all, I knew that my girls needed this involvement. Marianna then said that mothers were the driving force behind the kids, and that while dads might want things for their kids, it was usually the mother's ambition and driving force that took kids down the path of success. I thought for a few seconds about this. I then shared that while I was sure there were a few cases where dads were the driving force, at that moment I totally agreed with her.

Now, two months later (and after six months of Dylan experiencing a driving force of a mother), I could see the result right in front of us. My motherly influence was helping him in ways I don't even think we both were even aware of. It was the support and the driving force that was the gift I was giving him, and it was showing up everywhere in his life.

I do feel that being a strong mom sometimes is not recognized as much as it should be—that it is a job that is sometimes not valued as much as it should be and therefore goes unnoticed. I also know that it is the gift of love that is the most important gift and the true gift a mother can give to her children and all the other children who may come into her life. I hope that one day Dylan realizes that the greatest gift I have given him is really the gift of love.

Helping a Friend through a Difficult Time

Chrissy from Mama's Restaurant had recently become a large part of my awareness. She was at this time still focusing on a healthy relationship coming into her life—feeling a little sad about being alone but knowing down deep that the right man was on his way. However, what was happening in her life at this moment was dramatic and life changing: her older sister was dying of cancer. Chrissy was trying to be strong, but due to the ease of our relationship, she was able to be honest about what was happening with her sister. I was able to understand what she was going through, as four years earlier I also lost my sister Judy to cancer. I found during our times together that I would just hug her, listen to her, and give my support.

One warm summer night, I arrived at work to find Chrissy absent and I knew that time was moving forward for her sister. At this time, I just said a prayer for Chrissy and her family. Two days later, we were told at work about the passing of Chrissy's sister. I felt the loss of this young woman who left three sons behind. Two days later, I read the obituary in the local paper and decided to attend the wake.

The morning of Chrissy's sister's wake started off in quite a bit of turmoil in all areas of my life. First, Stephanie had taken ill and was now in Princess Margaret Hospital in Toronto, which led to upset within Christine, Emily, and myself. This morning then also began a time for me to defend Christine and Emily, as there was some judgement being portrayed against these girls, and because I was physically there when they were doing the best they could and trying to help out due to Stephanie's sickness, I found myself setting some boundaries. After this episode, I chose to release the situation and concentrate on giving my support to this bubbly young woman from work who was very special in my life.

My traveling time to the wake was no more than ten minutes, and as I pulled in the driveway I couldn't help but notice what a beautiful homestead this was and I had the knowing of being in right spot. I got out of my car and started walking towards the house, which was a country-style home with an amazing wrap-around white porch. I smiled at the people while heading towards the garage area where there was some activity taking place. I then noticed Chrissy on the porch, and as we connected and she sighted me, the most wonderful smile appeared on her face. She quickly came over to greet me at the door to the garage. We shared a hug of support, which filled my eyes with tears, although Chrissy seemed happy, peaceful, and glad to see me. She then said, "I can't believe you came!" I just smiled back at her.

Chrissy explained that they had had the service that morning at the funeral home and that they were having a lunch now and she was glad I was there to join them. I said thank you, and we then started to approach the house. Chrissy showed me the memorial pictures of her sister, which were lovely to see, and I noticed the resemblance between the sisters. We then got some food and sat under an elm tree to enjoy the food and our time of support. I was able to meet some of the family, and I could tell that it was the eldest son who was mostly feeling the extreme loss of his mother. I thought at this moment that Chrissy would become a lifeline for this young man.

We then talked about everything, even the restaurant, and there was a sense of some betrayal that she was aware of that made her concerned for me. This betrayal had to do with all the drama surrounding Dylan. After an hour had passed, it was time for me to head home and rest, as the day had been quite an emotional one.

Dealing with Rumours

The following Sunday morning, I found myself in town waiting for church to end, as my mom was in attendance at the United Church. This Sunday was unfolding differently, as most Sundays I would drive back home for the hour break. But this particular Sunday, I was going to take Mimi to The Boat House to watch Dylan, so I chose to visit Marlene and David for a wonderful cup of coffee. Our conversation started off great, talking about how the girls were, and I explained about Christine and the baby moving in. And then the conversation took a turn towards Dylan. I mentioned how wonderful everything was going with Dylan and that the past Friday had been the greatest night of his career and a time to celebrate.

As I looked across the table, there was a look of turmoil and dismay from both of them, which was a surprise to me. I was then informed by them that they found that they were continually having to defend me. They then reinforced that they found themselves in many situations where they had to defend my actions. First, they mentioned that it was in the area of me being a manager for Dylan. I stated right away that I didn't want to be his manager but that the right person had not come along yet. I was then reminded that I blew off a potential manager, and I thought, well, I don't have that much control over Dylan, and if he wanted a manager at this time he would have one. But then their next statement would alter my life forever. They told me that some of the people in our great town of Middletown were speculating that there was a romantic relationship between Dylan and myself!

It was like the bottom fell out of my life, and my eyes filled with tears. They said, "Well, isn't it good we told you?" I said, "How could people think such a horrible thing?" I then vaguely remembered detecting this type of energy just that past week and but had ignored it (when you feel something like that and you know that there is no validity in the statement, you just keep going). I then thought about my writing. I hadn't seen any evidence of such negative thoughts, but I knew I was always focusing on the good.

As this conversation continued, I found myself defending everything I had done concerning Dylan, and this did not feel right at all. All I could think about was how Dylan was like a son to me and I was just being a mother to him. There even was mention of my phone message, which stated: "Jenny and home of Dylan Lock the musician." I quickly explained that Dylan's first business cards had my phone number on them because he didn't have a phone at the time. Moreover, I received many calls about Dylan and his career, messages that I passed on.

Then I realised that the message behind this conversation was clear as day: that for my best interest, I should have much less to do with Dylan from this point forward. Well, my gut, my body, and my heart definitely did not feel good hearing this. Marlene and David also said that because I didn't have a man in my life, people were talking more, and I replied that I had just left an unhealthy marriage and I was still healing and had not found the right man yet. I then thought of my girlfriend who lost her husband and how it was six years until she found the right man.

As the conversation continued, I started to get really upset and discouraged, as no matter what I said the writing was on the wall. I did try to understand that the people who were thinking these things did not know the history of what had happened. My friends were saying things like, "Well, they only see what has happened from the time of Penetang Idol; they do not know you have been a part of Dylan's life for almost a year and the history of Dylan's life. And why should they? It truly is none of their business." I also knew it was my reputation that was at stake, and while I cared about that, it wasn't worth choosing over Dylan. I said that Dylan did love me and I could see that people could see that, but there was thirty years difference in age and there had never—and I mean never—been a slight second that the mother and son line was ever crossed.

I then said to them, "Well, what about Justin Bieber's mom and that she was by his side all the time?" But they pointed out that she had given birth to him and raised him from a child and thus deserved to be part of his life and his music career. I for sure got this message, and it was plain as day: I did not give birth to Dylan and I had only been in his life for a short time, and so I did not deserve or was entitled to be his mom or by his side as his support." I said that I had helped many kids in my life and that it was only because Dylan was now in the public eye that it was under the judgement of society.

That was it: it was judgement, and it was everywhere and all over me. I thought, I help this kid and I get crucified for it. I also immediately thought of people with fame in their lives, what they truly had to endure, and that people can really be mean. Well, I finally had had enough of this and I had to pick up my mom, so I headed out the door. I did thank my friends for being honest and letting me know what they were hearing, and I also knew not to shoot the messenger.

I was probably only two steps out the door when I burst into tears, and the only way to describe my feeling within was of complete devastation. I cried the entire way to pick up my mom and all the way home and into my living room. I had forgotten my cellphone at home and when I looked at it I saw that three of my kids were looking for me, one being Dylan. I texted him with the words, "We have a problem," and the response was, "What's wrong?" By now I was crying so hard that I could barely see the words on the screen of my phone. I tried to gently tell him what had happened, but I found that I had to say it outright: that people were thinking that we were involved in a romantic relationship. His response was simple: "That is ridiculous, absolutely ridiculous; I have a girlfriend." I told him I was upset and needed time to think and figure out what to do.

It was 12:30 p.m., and Dylan needed to get his equipment from the pool party he and Lauren had been at yesterday and get to his next performance by 2:30 p.m. I texted him and said I would pick him up, get his stuff, and take him to the performance, and then I was going to leave and so he would need to find a way home. It was a sad moment, because I had planned to take my mom to that performance—my mom who had helped Dylan so much, too. I had wanted to take her, as the performance was finally during the day and it was open to the public. I thought to myself how the horrible people were already winning with their minds being in the gutter and how could they not understand the parental connection. Moreover, I was a mess, so they were really getting the best of us.

On my way to pick up Dylan, I found it hard to fight off the tears, but somehow I managed. We really did not have much time, as we had to go to the other side of town to pick up his equipment. Lauren, his girlfriend, who really never left his side, was with us as well, which really was the irony of the situation. We talked about business and how the past day had unfolded, as I had not seen him since he and Lauren had gone to that pool party. I told him about going to Chrissy's sister's wake and what a special time we had had together. As we were unloading at the back of the restaurant, a feeling of anger came over me, as all I had ever done for Dylan was to help him and be there for him. He then turned to me and gave me a hug and a kiss and said, "I don't care what they think; you are like a mom to me." I then burst once again into tears and was thankful I had my sunglasses on. As I got into the car and started to back up, I did notice that Dylan was watching me and that he could tell that I was crying.

Emily then took over with some tender loving care and made me dinner and cookies for dessert. We then started to watch the third Harry Potter movie, which had many parallels to our situation. It was society against the people, being controlling as usual. I started to feel a little better and texted Dylan. The messages I was sending were that people who make it big have to protect the people around them, as they will always be judged, and also that the people didn't know that there was an underlying story of FAMILY! Next, I said, "We are going to have to keep our circle smaller and tighter; this way we can focus on the good xo." There was a reply of yes, and "OMG, I love you." I replied, "I love you, too, and I still believe it's all about the kids and we have to turn to faith—it is once again all about faith." However, I did have to admit that this was a tough one to deal with.

During the next few hours, I experienced waves of sadness, and it was like my heart was broken again and bleeding all over the place. I did text Dylan good night and said that I was having these waves of doubt and then would know to surrender and have faith. He replied, "Good night," and at first I was a little disappointed, and then I thought, well, he probably doesn't know what to say—therefore, it was a perfect response. I then thought, maybe I shouldn't help kids anymore, which was countered with, I was the only one who stepped up to help Dylan, and all those people who didn't have the strength or nerve to do it were the ones judging me now. I knew I had to protect myself from society. Did I have to give up on my passion and my belief because of the judgement from the people? I truly felt sick inside. So then I found my Bible, turned to prayer, and surrendered once again.

A Small Town

The benefits of living in a small town are many, as it doesn't take much time to get across town, the air is clean, the people are friendly, and the atmosphere is good. However, there is always an underlying problem within a small town and that is the hard hand of judgement. I had heard about this for years and experienced it on a small scale with my youth program, but I had never really felt its massive impact myself until the judgement occurred over my situation with Dylan. I actually felt that the people should be lined up thanking me for helping a youth in our community, because don't we want the youth to do well so that they can buy a car, a house, and even pay taxes? How fantastic would it be if the police would be rewarded for diverting a kid or saving our youth from a court system that can't even handle the overload of youth as it is? To me, it's like they don't get it!

When I told my story to a couple I was friends with, I heard them saying that this type of judgement had been in the community for the past forty years. I thought to myself, what a shame. I also decided that to deal with the judgement I needed to be in a surrendered state, meaning using my wisdom to yield to the flow of life and to remember to ignore and be. This was important, because if you were changing yourself to accommodate others, then from my experience this would put you on a collision course to destruction, with you losing yourself and losing the power of just being.

I then remembered a conversation I had had with a few of the more prominent community members I had known for years (one whom I was very fond of). I could see the judgement these people had towards the people, and it was basically a judgement that was spilling out everywhere. I thought of Oprah and how her entire business was built on the people and that the reason for her tremendous success was that she had NO judgement towards the people. I then thought that these people were smart businesspeople—why in heaven's name didn't they get it? But they didn't, they didn't get it.

The next morning I awoke with a sadness that had entered my heart once again. I reflected back on the past two years and how I had tried to just live a peaceful life and surrender to the Universe and God. I believed that I must be in the right spot, and yet I felt hurt again by the people. After sitting for a few hours, I began to feel a sense of strength. I said to myself, wait a minute here: my strongest belief is to help the people and especially the kids. I realized that I was disappointed that just because I had gotten myself out of an unhealthy marriage and just hadn't found the right person yet, that people would think that about me. I then asked myself, am I going to stop helping the kids? Am I going to live my life in fear? I thought of all the kids without parents who could use the mentoring and love from people who can and want to help. I remembered the funeral I had just attended two days ago and the three boys who now had no mother. I thought of how important it was to protect oneself, and I guessed that I hadn't done that. I thought of how distractive judgement could be and the word "dysfunction" came to mind!

Then the movie The Blind Side entered into my awareness, and I thought of the turmoil that the family and the boy had to endure when he went to the college of his choice—this being the college the people who had helped him had attended, and there was an inquiry concerning this. I remembered that it was the boy himself who set the story straight and stood up for the people who had helped him and given him a family.

I then looked to the wall hanging I had that Dylan gave me for Easter that said, "Family: the love of a family is life's greatest gift." It said it all. I realized at this time that I could not stop helping the kids and that I would sit back and still be a mother to Dylan and live my life in faith, because I knew that the most powerful thing to do was to sit back and let things unfold.

Three hours later, I received the most lovely voice message from a wonderful woman asking to book my son for a gig on August 25, and the first thing that came to mind was, I changed my message that stated "home of Dylan Lock musician" because of fear, and I shouldn't have. What was I thinking? And so I released the anger towards the ridiculousness and was officially back on track. I then spoke to this woman, booked Dylan, and messaged him all the info. I also gave her Dylan's contact information, just like I always had. And so the upset of the day before was now in the past where it belonged.

Only Human

It was now two days after I had learned of the condescending attitude people had concerning my relationship with Dylan. I was glad that I stayed home on Sunday and kept quiet and followed my instincts, which were to let things unfold. I now started to review what had been said, because it must have been for a reason and there must be lessons to be learned. As I opened up to the lessons, I then began to see them. The first thing I thought I should be aware of the judgement of the people around Dylan and in general of the people in the eye of the public. I now understood why famous people got tired of this and tried to keep their lives separate and private from the press. I also could see that judgement could be deadly, as seen in many examples over the past ten years or so.

I determined that I needed to keep our circle of confidence very tight, that I should only discuss problems with Dylan, Emily, and Christine. We needed this circle or team, as this was so important to the success of anyone and anything. I then thought that maybe it would be nice if our government or even the world worked as a team! Once again I thought of Oprah and Justin Bieber. I then had the knowing that I needed to talk to Dylan about it once again, as I wanted the message to the people to be: help our kids, all the kids.

So off I went with fifty CDs that I had just burned in hand on a mission to have a heart-to-heart with Dylan. I was thankful that Dylan respected me and thus was completely open to a talk about what had happened and what lessons could be learned from it all. I started the conversation off on a serious note, explaining the judgement that comes from some people due to fame and being in the public eye. He didn't seem too worried or concerned at all. He basically said, "Well, it just is," and he didn't feel any need to change a thing but only to be aware of it. This, I thought, was good. We also talked about the people who knew and saw the mother-and-son relationship, and how wonderful they saw it to be. Wow, I thought, focusing on the good—very well done.

Next, we talked about his music career and about how the people we were talking to were changing the story about the content of the conversations that had taken place. Once again, Dylan reinforced how great things were going, that he felt great about where his career was, and that he wanted to, once again, focus on the good. Then something interesting came forth, as after months of me protecting him, he now had the power to protect me and the ability to set the story straight. I did feel that the people around the famous person did have to be protected from public judgement, although it was sad to say. I also believed that the team had to be so close, so very close, and almost solid, so that no negativity or judgement could enter in.

All I could hear the next day running in my head was, "I get knocked down, and I get up again; you're never going to keep me down," because that was exactly the way I was feeling. Emily had often said to me that if Dylan were six years of age and we took him into our family, no one would even care if he wanted me around or if he liked to hug me. And can you imagine at the age of twenty-one finally having a mom to hug? I also thought to myself, he went twenty years without a mom to hug and give a kiss to, so there was a lot of time to make up. I could also hear his dad telling me how he taught both his kids to hug and kiss when saying hello or goodbye. The first time I heard Gary say this, I thought, wow, that is why Dylan is so loving when he's in a family situation. Then I returned back to the sadness that this parental love had been misinterpreted into something that just was not there.

Moreover, it just wasn't the romantic interlude that was falsely put forward; it was also the judgement or criticism in concern with what was happening with his music career and my role in this as well. I had found myself defending myself to my friends and saying, "Wait a minute; I have a lot of business experience." Moreover, when I talked to Dylan about it, he said everything was perfect and going great, and I agreed. I was going to make some changes and try to let Dylan be more independent, even though months ago I had let him decide when he needed me. But I knew that he knew I was always there and that this was once again exactly what I was to do—just be there for him.

So the following day, I just sat back and let life unfold. I did hear from Dylan in the afternoon with a hello and how's it going. I responded to this with a good and a hello back. Eight hours later, when I had completely surrendered and was living in trust, a text came through from Dylan with only two words. It said, "Love you." My response was, "Love you, too." I sat quietly for a moment, knowing that our mother and son connection was still intact and as strong as ever. And then the conversation continued and was just about what was happening at the time.

The next day was more of the same and mostly about business as well, and all was good. That Friday was a day to organize transportation and weekend gigs. However, by 2:00 p.m. Friday, after working all week, my strength of living in consciousness was starting to fade and I found myself sending Dylan a text with a little negative energy attached to it, which came back with exactly the same negative energy. I then noticed this and sent an apology with the awareness that I was a little off, and Dylan replied with the same comment of also being a little off. I thought, how interesting. We decided on a pickup time for Friday's performance, with a little extra time set aside for reflection.

As I arrived to pick up Dylan, I had the knowing that I was in the right spot. And after a few minutes of conversation, which mostly consisted of Dylan doing all the talking (which we know, and I will reinforce again, is the greatest gift a parent can give kids of today, to listen to them), I had confirmation that things were back to normal. We then loaded everything up and headed to The Boat House.

My wonderful friend Anne Marie had come to hear Dylan play, and besides enjoying the fantastic music, we were enjoying the time together as friends. Then the entire family showed up again: Emily, Christine, Paul, Emily's friend Margaret, and Mimi. Even Dylan's dad joined us. Dylan quite enjoyed this, as we all were having a great time as a family. After a time, I found myself the only one left at the table, as everyone had gone home and Dylan's dad was off talking with friends. At that moment, a gift came forth, and Dylan looked at me and said, "Mom, what should I play?" I was a little stunned to hear the word "mom" come forth while he was performing; it was a little strange, although when he called me mom it was as if he had called me mom forever. I just kind of said nothing but was smiling. I can remember a man from the next table looking at me with such a tender smile on his face and me returning the smile as well.

Dylan then started to play a song, and I sat there sort of frozen as my mind was racing. I knew that Dylan was now trying to protect me and set the record straight, which was something I actually deserved. Later, as I was walking to get the car to load the equipment, I passed this man who had smiled at me and said good night. I then heard him talking with his wife, and when she asked who I was, his reply was, "That's Dylan's mom." It was a moment of thank-you, which came from a confirmation of faith.

The next day became a day of family. Emily, Christine, Paul, and I headed into Middletown to pick up Dylan for an afternoon of sun and swimming at the cottage. Christine had made a great dip and cut up lots of veggies, and we were all set. I must say, it was wonderful to have three of my kids and baby Paul all together in my car as a family. There was nothing like packing up the car with the kids and heading to the cottage—it was a fantastic feeling! At this time, we were very lucky to have wonderful friends who loved to open their cottage to friends. The weather was perfect, and we swam, sat in the hot tub, and enjoyed great company. Then it was time to return home to Victoria Harbour for some supper.

That evening, Dylan and I were at another performance just like always, and something wonderful unfolded. Dylan was singing the best I had ever heard him sing, mainly because he could—which meant he wasn't in a restaurant situation where he had to control his voice. This performance was in a backyard setting with only twenty people, so he could actually let his voice out, and so he did and it was amazing. I found myself quite overwhelmed and taken aback by the power of his voice. Once again, I knew he was to perform in the Air Canada Centre, something I had been envisioning often, and I felt at this very moment how close this could actually be. We happened to be waiting to hear from Dan about a party he wanted us to attend, so Dylan stopped in the middle of singing and said, "MOM, what time is it?" I started to scramble to answer the question, but after a moment had passed, I realized that he was once again setting the story straight and protecting me, which I was very thankful for.

As we loaded up my truck and were about to leave, the parents of a friend of Dylan's were out talking to us and expressing the enjoyment of the evening and the talent they could see in Dylan. They were down-to-earth people, kind, and grateful, and it was a pleasure to have met them.

Sunday came upon us, and of course I woke up with Dylan's equipment in my truck, as he really liked it when I took it home. Therefore, I had to pick him up and deliver him and his equipment to The Boat House, which was a pleasure to do. Emily came with me, and then we headed to the store to find a baby pool for Paul. I must say, I did find it hard to leave Dylan, but I couldn't be there all the time and it was good for both of us if I was not. I told myself that I had to remember that it wasn't quite like a volleyball game or waterski tournament, as he was working as well, and who wants their mother there all the time? I did know that Dylan did want me there some of the time, but we just let it unfold. I did find it necessary to send a "xo" text, even though he was playing, and of course, a short time later I received an "xo" as well.

Getting Back on Track

Dan at this moment had reopened the practice of visioning in my life, as I had just had the most amazing vision. I saw a house in the country: eight bedrooms, a beautiful large kitchen, and a pool in the backyard. This house served a purpose; it was for the people: the kids, the women, and the men. It was for everyone! It was a safe place, a place full of love and kindness. It was a place to heal and a place to get back on track. I saw that there was going to be a charity for Dylan to contribute to and myself as well from my books. We were going to fund this wonderful home and program, a program called "Back on Track."

I messaged Dylan and told him my idea, and he was excited, already wanting to give back, help his community, and help the kids. I then saw how wonderful Christine was doing in a peaceful environment, a place without worry, and I thought that maybe Christine was going to run it! I did know that one criterion for this house would be the willingness and the desire to get back on track, as I had seen wonderful things from both Dylan and Christine once they had the opportunity.

I had heard a story on my way home from work the other night about a young girl who had been bullied, tried to commit suicide, and was having such a hard time. I asked about the parents, and it turned out that the father died when this teenager was four and her mother abandoned her, and she was living with an old boyfriend of her mother's. This story broke my heart and brought tears to my eyes, and all I could say was, I wish I had another bedroom open, as I would take this girl in as well. I then shared with Meghan from work that I had a vision of a house in the country, and it would be for kids like this girl so that she would be able to heal and then get back on track. After I dropped Meghan home, I started talking to God and saying that it was time and I was completely clear on my purpose in life.

As I woke up the next morning, I felt fantastic and I talked about this house in the country and the name once again came to me: "Back on Track." I now had the same excitement as when Dylan and I had started towards his goal, developing him into a successful rock star

A Day of Shopping

It was July, and we were experiencing a very hot and dry summer. I had thought to myself many a time that I could never live in California, as the heat would be too hard to take for my body. I then thought of Kate and the fact that she was now living full-time in California and in the desert as well, and how she really must love waterskiing to be able to live in that heat. In fact, the last time we talked she said it was 107 degrees. As I looked around my yard, I saw that the trees and the burnt grass were not happy with the heat either.

Then finally we enjoyed a day of rain. Of course, this was the day that Dylan and I had planned to go shopping. We had agreed to go to Food Basics and Wal-Mart just after 2:00 p.m., but as I checked my iPhone I realized that this was not going to happen. I then texted Dylan and said I was going to be a little late. This was all good, and I arrived to pick him up just before 3:00 p.m. and we headed to Food Basics, the local grocery store. Dylan was driving, as he really had become a great driver—he had a natural ability for it.

We got a cart and started at the right of the store in the produce department. We both enjoyed shopping together, the ease of just being and the fun of checking out the sales, the products, and of course the people as well. Dylan was shopping for himself now and I for my household. We enjoyed going down every aisle and scanning all the products. It didn't take long for us to fill the cart with great healthy produce, sale items, and necessities. I took a moment and looked at Dylan and saw the growth that had occurred in this fine young man and the happiness he was experiencing grocery shopping.

I passed a few people I knew, and they commented on the fullness of my cart and how family and the kids were still a large part of my life. I just smiled back at them and send confirmation that yes, kids and family were still a large part of my life. We spent an hour in Food Basics until I realized that it was now time to pick Mimi up. I had tried to get

Christine to get her, but this didn't work out, so Dylan and I loaded the car and headed to the church to get Mimi from bridge and bring her home to my house. We unloaded my groceries, got Mimi settled, and then returned to Dylan's to unload his things before heading towards Wal-Mart.

As we arrived and got a cart, I could see the happiness just spilling out from Dylan, as he had financial abundance for the first time in his life and it was time to do some shopping. We started at the far end, in the shampoo area, as body wash, shampoo, and all those type of items were at the top of Dylan's list. It was so much fun watching Dylan smell every one of them and decide on a smell that he liked. We then moved to the fitness section, as Dylan wanted to look at exercise equipment. We looked at bars to hang from the door and then spent quite a bit of time with the weights, which were like barbells. I started to chuckle a little, as I never thought I would be with a son in the barbell aisle in Wal-Mart and enjoying every second of it.

Next, we headed to the movie section and found a bin of five-dollar movies. I picked out The Notebook and My Sister's Keeper, and I thought how great it was that Dylan had brought the love of movies back into my life. Dylan was standing at the other side of the bin picking some movies for himself, and he started talking about the concept I had been teaching him for the past eight months: that the only way to shift the world was to set the example yourself. I looked up at him and said, "Yes, I believe this to be true and live my life by this concept." He then said that movies teach us this as well. I looked right into his eyes and said, "That is so true." Dylan then pointed out, "We go to movies to see the people who set the example of the way we would like to be." I replied, "That is brilliant. That is why true stories are the best, because it is true life setting the example."

Dylan mentioned that he wanted to find the music documentary section, and so we headed that way. We then started poking around the music aisle, which was fun, until we found the music documentary section. Dylan started slowly looking through the various films. I thought to myself how wonderful a moment this was and also how many music documentaries I had seen over the past five months. I thought back to the first two Queen movies I had watched, followed by The Doors, Rush, Michael Jackson, and many more. It seemed a little overwhelming and a little unbelievable, but here we were in Wal-Mart, Dylan and me, reading the backs of all the music videos. Dylan did find a Queen movie, and we then headed to the men's section, where it was time for t-shirts and underwear, a new experience for mom and son once again. The best part of that afternoon was that there was an ease around everything, which was amazing. At times I truly felt that Dylan had been my son forever, absolutely forever.

Next, we backtracked to the razor section, where we had a fantastic surprise. There was a young man standing there with his family: a son around six years of age, a daughter around two, and a happy and very pretty young woman as well. The young man said, "Wow, it's Dylan Lock!" Dylan said hello with a smile on his face and turned to me and said, "It's Donald." I looked at Dylan with a surprised expression on my face and then it was like a ton of bricks hit me—it was Donald, Donald who had come to the studio, Donald who I had talked with while I had driven him home. It was Donald, and he looked fantastic. I then started to smile at Donald and felt warm and fuzzy all over. I could see inside him, and his joy and happiness was everywhere. The most important thing was that Donald had lost weight and his body was at peace and the change within him gave me goose bumps all over.

Donald and Dylan immediately fell into a conversation; a question about a copy of Dylan's CD came forth and I mentioned that I had one in the car. We said we had a few more items we need to purchase and then planned to meet them in the parking lot. Dylan and I then continued to the face care section, and I lit right up. I could not believe the shift in Donald; it was as if I had just experienced a visit from God demonstrating that He was happy with the work I had done and confirming that I was on the right path. Dylan didn't say too much, just that yes, Donald looked good.

When we got to the men's face care section, I had no idea what we were even looking for. I thought to my ex-husband and what he would have used to shave, but decided that that was not what Dylan needed at all, and so I felt completely lost. I also was still shook up about seeing Donald. Then a woman and her son appeared beside us, and they were looking for a similar kit that Dylan would need. I at this time just became a spectator and watched. Dylan did pick a face care kit, and it was placed into the cart. To this day, I still don't exactly know what it all did, but Dylan was happy with it so that's all that mattered.

We then headed to the food department for cream, paper towels, and whatever else jumped at us. We found ourselves in the frozen pizza section, enjoying all the sales and trying to find our favourite kinds. We also found great sales on ice cream and other items, before heading towards the cash register with a full cart once again. Dylan was texting Donald to set up the meeting for the purchase of a CD, so I went through the cash register first then headed out to the parking lot to find Donald, as he was taking a cab with the family. I got the CD from my car and I started to look for Donald, but he had already left. I then returned to see Dylan cashing out and handing quite a bit of cash to the cashier—this is what happens when you spend two hours in Wal-Mart. As we were leaving, we found ourselves in the McDonalds line ordering Quarter Pounders because all this shopping had made us hungry, and after the large bill for Dylan, I chose to treat.

When we were loading the car, Dylan's phone rang and it was Donald still wanting a CD and asking if we could stop by, as his house was on our way. I at this time texted Donald and told him how great he looked, how happy and wonderful. He replied, "Yeah, me and Julie are doing amazing ☺." I couldn't even reply, as I had tears in my eyes, knowing that I never wanted to lose this feeling. Dylan and I quickly ate our burgers and started towards Donald's house.

When we arrived, Donald and Julie met us in the driveway. Dylan handed him a CD and Donald said to me, "I was telling Julie about your book, and Julie said that she would love to read it." Dylan then took over with the conversation, and I reached into the backseat, pulled out a book, and said, "I have one." Donald asked the cost and quickly opened his wallet and paid me for the book. Dylan then realized he was quite late, so we headed to his house. On the way to Dylan's, I couldn't believe it was almost 8:00 p.m.—where had the time gone? Dylan and I quickly unloaded and said our goodbyes, and I drove away thinking that shopping with Dylan was one of my most favourite times with him.

Dwight

The next day, I was sitting in my living room, which Christine had just rearranged—and I must say that Christine did a fantastic job and I thought at the time that she should take an interior design course—when I saw a young man walking up to my front door. My first thought was that I was not expecting anyone, and then I recognized this young man as one of the kids I had hired at the Quarterdeck Restaurant that I had managed three years ago. I then said to Christine, "Hey, isn't that a kid who worked at the Quarterdeck?" as she had also worked there. She replied, yes, that she remembered him from there as well.

I went to the door, opened it, welcomed Dwight in, and said that it was great to see him. He said, "I was just visiting Sandra where she works at Place Pizza"—another wonderful woman who had worked at the Quarterdeck—"and she said that you just lived down the street and that you would love to see me." He explained that he had followed Sandra's directions to my house and had been looking for my truck, as Sandra said it would probably be the only car in the driveway. To Dwight's surprise, when he found my truck, he also found a driveway that was full of cars. We laughed when he told us this story, as my driveway was now always full of cars. Then we reminisced about the job fair I had held for the start-up of the Quarterdeck and that Emily had been my secretary. We then remembered that Dwight had arrived at 8:40 a.m. (the start time was 9:00 a.m.) and was the first person there, and how I had hired him because of this, as he had no experience but he just seemed like he was a great kid who needed a break.

I actually wrote about Dwight in my first book, as he was the kid who had rolled a friend's truck and was afraid to tell me, as he thought I would be mad at him and have judgement towards him. However, this was not how it unfolded, as I remember saying that I was glad he was okay and simply reminding him to learn from his mistakes. Dwight had been seventeen at this time. His mom and brother lived out west and his situation at home was unhealthy, so Dwight was longing for family (he missed his mother and brother very much). Moreover, by this time Dwight and I had had many conversations about the journey of life. The Quarterdeck Restaurant also became a family for Dwight; actually, it became a family for us all.

Dwight then explained that he was out of the restaurant business and working towards his machine licence and enjoying it. He said that his boss was good to him and that he loved living in Calgary. He then mentioned that his mom had just moved back to Ontario and was living way up north. I must have had a scared look on my face, as Dwight then started to explain that his brother still lived in Calgary and that he had two kids and so he had family around him. I felt better right away, because I knew that family and the love from family was very important to Dwight, as it was for all kids. We then talked about my girls and some of the other staff at the Quarterdeck. Our visit was full of great stories, laughs, and happy memories.

As Dwight was leaving, I gave him a hug and said how glad I was that he had stopped by. As I watched him walk down the street, I thought how wonderful it was that a mere three years later this young kid was doing so well.

I then quickly got organized and headed to Dylan's to pick him up for his regular Friday night Boat House performance. I was excited for this one, as Emily and Brandon were in town. The night seemed to unfold extremely well, as the concert scene was becoming a regular event for the people. It was also great watching Emily and Brandon become a part of Dylan's performing life: sort of the music world and family becoming one. After the performance, we had our regular visit to Cellarman's, although it was a larger group than usual, as Dylan had invited Emily and Brandon. I was not sure how it was going to unfold, as things were changing for us. This was a change that was inevitable and one that needed to happen, but it was one that Dylan and I were both afraid to happen. This fear, I believe, was something that was new for both of us and something that was a mirror, as we didn't want to hurt or lose each other. This was easy to understand, as we had just found each other within the past year, where the normal progression of mom and son letting go of each other would have taken twenty years normally.

So we headed to Cellarman's, and something quickly became very wrong. Dylan enter the bar with us and then he ended up outside for our entire stay. There was something else happening in his life, something that was normal and something that needed to unfold. As Emily, Brandon, and I sat alone, I knew and understood this but still felt hurt, as I would have gone home right after the performance if I had known that he wasn't going to join us. I was deep-down tired too that night, which triggered some unhealthy behaviour, and so I reacted from the Mother Bear in all areas, as there was more than one of my children involved, and it wasn't pretty.

I knew that Dylan had a heart of gold and would never mean to hurt, but there was hurt and it was all around us. I did not deal with the situation very well, and the next morning I dropped off Dylan's equipment with a whole lot of anger and frustration of having had enough—and that is exactly what I told him.

Turmoil Was Everywhere

I was not sure what was happening in our community at this same time, but there seemed to be turmoil everywhere. We had a beautiful man beaten to death behind a downtown store, an eighteen-year-old teen who had just graduated from the same high school as Kate and Emily accidently run over by his best friend and killed, and a seventeen-year-old drowned at the beach. In all my years in this community, I had never seen such turmoil.

In addition, my wonderful friend and support Anne Marie was also going through a rough time in her life and was turning to faith and the power of surrendering. Moreover, Dylan and I were still experiencing turmoil, and this was not going well at all. I had the knowing that this was a part of all parents' and children's relationships, to have turmoil, but it hurt and felt so strange. I knew we both were upset and it was something that was just coming forward; actually, it was an underlying problem that was building, and it was time I paid attention. It must have been the combination of the visit of Dwight and the change in Donald and the enlightenment of the unfortunate judgement that came with the public eye and the life of a musician that was wearing at me, and it was like I woke up and simply wanted my life and my life purpose back. I also felt that the connection of team within Dylan's music career was not there; it just wasn't there, and it did not feel right anymore. I knew I had to pull back, that what I was doing wasn't right and it was time to wake up. I had been here before in my life and had learned a hard lesson, and it was now time to pay attention.

I then expressed some more anger towards Dylan, which I probably shouldn't have, and I was immediately sorry for it—although at least I cared enough to be a mom, but it was a strong wakeup call for me again. So I said that I would always love him as a son and that my door was always open to him. Dylan probably never had anyone as a mom express turmoil, and I don't think he knew what to do about it. So he retreated as well, and it just was.

I actually at this time felt a great sense of relief, as I had worked so hard to create a life of peacefulness, kindness, and conscious behaviour, and this was now returned and I had my life again. But I still had some anger hanging around. Then the greatest awareness came forth, and I knew it was now a time to surrender, a time to turn to faith and trust in the universe. And so this was what I did: I let it all go and I surrendered once again. I then began to work on me, and this was the best thing I could have done, as I have learned that when you work on you, everyone else falls perfectly into place! I did miss Dylan but I knew without a doubt that it was time to let go.

So I then turned to my writing. Emily and Brandon were home, Christine and Paul were also home, and Mimi, of course. I was very happy and blessed to be surrounded with the love of family.

Our Journey

I wished I had a magic answer for the situation between Dylan and myself, but I didn't. I would actually have to say that the situation was becoming worse and getting almost completely out of control, and I guessed this was the way it was to be. I just did what I felt I had to do to survive, and I guess Dylan felt betrayed once again and we had a confrontation over it. During this time, I would also ask myself quite often why. Why me? Why was I chosen to be the mother of this wonderful kid—a kid who was going to be a famous rock star one day?

I somehow managed to keep myself busy over the next few days with my book, Paul, and Christine, but my heart was broken again and I just couldn't leave it like that, so I found myself contacting Dylan just saying hi and that if he needed me this weekend I would help. Even though I knew I needed a break and so did Dylan, and that it was best for everyone if I stayed away, the mother in me took over once again. At first there was no reply. I knew Dylan missed me too, but I also knew he was setting his boundaries. I guessed he was still upset with me as one text from him had said that I left him again, and for him, it probably felt like that. But for me, I was just tired, plain old tired out, and as I thought about that, I said, "No, I didn't leave you; I just got mad at you, and moms do that." Then Dylan replied, "Thank you, but I am fine for the weekend." I said, "Great—have a good weekend!"

Saturday fell upon us, and Emily, Christine, Paul, and Heather (a girlfriend of Emily's) headed to Wasaga Beach for the morning. I had driven through Wasaga Beach many a time, but I had never been to the beachfront and neither had Emily. So we packed up the car for a forty-five minute road trip with treats, water toys, and chairs for the beach. I must say that the beach is one of my most favourite places and I was feeling very peaceful that day. We arrived early and found a great place to park and a wonderful place to sit. The beach was spectacular, and we were so very blessed to have such beauty so very close to us. As we set up our spot, Paul immediately wanted to go in the water, and it was so hot out that we all ended up in there with him. Paul was enjoying it, as it was shallow and warm, and all of us were there as well. We had a Frisbee with us too, and we just had fun being together in the water, leaving life behind on the shore.

We spent over an hour in the water, and then it was time to sit on the beach. The gang decided to go for a walk along the boardwalk, and I thought that this was a great time to just be alone. (I loved them all very much—it was just fine to be alone sometimes.) So I sat in my chair enjoying the beautiful beach, and then all of a sudden behind me live music started to play. First the music warmed my heart, and then the loss of not hearing Dylan play the night before took over. I found myself reaching for my cellphone to check on the two kids who were not with me. I first contacted Kate and asked how everything was, and a reply of good and a smiley face came back. Then I thought about Dylan and our path over the past ten months; I thought how it had been over a week since I had seen him, and of course, I thought about the unsettledness between us. I then sent him a text saying that I knew he had had a great night and that I was at the beach enjoying the water, and that I loved him because I didn't want him to feel like I had left him and wished him good luck for his performance that night. He did reply with a "Love you, too," and I then felt peaceful and more settled.

Of course, I decided I would try to do it all this first weekend off from my wonderful son, and so I next found myself on the way to Barrie after first dropping Emily and her friend Heather off at a pre-party (they were going to the club to dance later on in the evening). As I was heading to Barrie to meet Anne Marie and a friend, I realized that I was a little tired and hoped I would find my second wind.

There were three of us women looking for a night of dancing, and after checking into the hotel and having some pizza, we found ourselves on the dance floor at the local club. We were enjoying ourselves, and I am not sure what brought my attention to my cellphone, but I quickly saw that there was an incoming call from my ex-husband. I managed to answer it and then found myself on the patio trying to hear what was up and the reason for this call. There was a situation unfolding with Kate that my ex felt I should be aware of. I listened and thanked him, and then placed a call to Kate but to no avail. So I made a call to another contact, which brought more fire to the situation. I then released the situation to faith and ended up at the far side of the bar away from the excitement, as I had lost my steam.

As I was standing there feeling sorry for myself, a group of regulars entered the bar and congregated in the area that I was standing in. I must have looked as if I had lost my best friend, as this wonderful, tall, happy man named Larry leaned over me and asked how I was doing. I was a little taken back, and he said that he just noticed I needed a friend and wanted to help out. I must have looked scared, as he then said, "Don't worry; I am not trying to pick you up," which then made me laugh. Next, he said, "Let me buy you a drink." At first I said no thank you, and then I let the fear go and said sure, that I would have a Corona. As the bartender was getting my beer, he and Larry were enjoying great conversation and Larry now was hugging me. I looked again at this tall man with brown skin and a beautiful cowboy hat on, and felt like there was a friend standing beside me.

As I was drinking my beer, Larry asked me what was wrong, and I just said life was unfolding in a challenging way. He then started to say things similar to what I would say to someone just needing a friend: things like to be positive and that life was going to get better and to live in faith. I was thinking, wow, someone is doing for me what I have done for so many others, and thank you. It was then time for Larry and his group to leave, and he turned to me and gave me the biggest hug and said, "Don't forget me; don't forget me!" I just smiled and said, "Thank you, I won't."

It was a few minutes later that I received a text from Emily, and she was upset, very upset. She was at the club in Middletown, and there was a situation that was unfolding with Dylan and she felt hurt and betrayed. For me, it seemed as if my entire world was completely falling apart, and I was upset and frustrated once again and it became a time to unleash it. I sent a text to Dylan saying, "You go and talk to Emily right now!" This text went unanswered at this time, which was probably a good thing. I then said to Emily that I was sorry she was upset and that I was also upset, and then I told her about Kate. She then said that she too was sorry and that everything would be okay.

It was about an hour later that I did receive a text back from Dylan, and then we entered into an argument. It was an argument about the people, family, and how important this was. My point was valid but not delivered in the correct fashion. We never spoke in person, only by text, but it was not pretty and it was not me. But I had had enough, completely enough.

Two days later, I contacted Dylan and said that I was sorry for not speaking from a place of love and that I was upset, but really I was done. I realized that I had tried to be superwoman again and not take time for me, and thus I was falling apart once again. We truly are all only human and need to take time for ourselves and not give as much. Moreover, basically what I was giving was not good anymore anyway. Dylan did forgive me, as he said I was just human and that he knew I loved him.

Well, then this new situation between Dylan and I became the center of the gossip, and once again the light that was shining on me was not so pretty. Now I was being accused of more false wrongdoing and more judgement was being place upon me, and I knew it was a time to stay home once again. Therefore, my days were now totally filled with the writing of this book, which I had faith in, knowing that this was exactly what I was to be doing. Even though we were in contact through text—though on a much less frequent basis—I still missed Dylan. I missed the little things, like driving in the car listening to music and him singing along. I missed grocery shopping and just listening to what was happening in his life. But I knew it was time to let things unfold, to let go of him and do nothing, which was one of the most difficult things to do. I was now living in faith and truly Just Being There!

Kate was now strongly in my awareness as she was experiencing dis-ease within her life. She was living in California enjoying her job, but her personal relationship had come to an end. It was an end that I believed was inevitable but an end that was very painful. The worst part was that Kate was now alone; yes, she was completely alone and she was a five-hour plane flight away and in another country as well. I was very thankful at this time that she had her kitten to go home to every night and was doing so well at her job. Even so, it was very hard knowing that my child was alone and in pain. It was mainly at night that was difficult for her, as she was up very early in the morning going to work and she enjoyed being a civil engineer and working on the construction job site.

The main problem that came with the upset with Kate was the contact that I was now having with the past (in terms of my ex), a past that I was so very happy to have healed from. Yet it was once again knocking on my door. At first I was open to it, believing there was a chance of a different relationship, but I must say that it was about a week into this that the dysfunction returned. The best part was that it didn't hurt anymore; it just was disappointing and, for me, a place I was not going to waste any more time in. I also admired the strength within me, and this was wonderful. So I concentrated on Kate.

Survival Mode

What happens to kids when their lives become turned upside down when they experience a loss of a parent or when the home they lived in just isn't there anymore and they now are living their lives without structure? What about if they have never experienced family? Do they learn to compensate for the loss? Do they go into survival mode? Do they run away and get captured by the evil of the world? Are they looking to replace what they have lost or maybe even never had? And does this become a natural behaviour? Does it become a way of survival? Moreover, if our kids are living in survival mode, does it become a natural way of being?

I now think of how many kids are living without structure, parents, and families, and wonder if this is truly the norm in the year 2013? How many kids are in dysfunctional situations and just trying to survive? And if so, when our kids are living in this survival mode, is it anyone's fault or is it just a way of being?

If you are able to help a kid survive, give them structure or opportunity (as I believe that it is opportunity that some kids need so very much), then just step up and do it, because helping our youth is important and makes sense since they are the future of the world. Yes, they are the future of our world. Remember to be aware and have the understanding of the survival behaviour that they most likely have acquired, as this may be the only behaviour they have really ever known. Moreover, remember that the dysfunction that they have experienced throughout the past will always be with them and can at times surface to the top. Also set boundaries and keep yourself intact, as you can only help others when you are in one piece yourself. I believe this is the only way that we can help our youth—something that is of growing importance in all our communities.

I also believe that it is the power of love within the family that we need to be reminded about. Children flourish with love and truly all living entities flourish with love, and we must go back to the family to help the kids and heal the dysfunction to save our youth.

Distance

I felt as if I had been betraying myself for months, as the same problem kept happening over and over again, and it was time I stepped up to the plate. The problem seemed to be a lack of understanding of the importance of the love of the people and that there were people who were simply feeling hurt. I also noticed that there was the lack of ability to establish long term relationships with people and this was causing the hurt feelings. This I understood and saw plain as day although when brought forth the result was distance. I felt that for Dylan, it was okay for me to be the giving mom, but as soon as I started to become the teaching mom, the walls started to go up and became higher and higher. Plus I wanted to continue to teach and be a real mom to Dylan, but Dylan kept putting more distance between us.

I understood that this was something new for Dylan and understood why he would put those walls up. But there is only one way to describe this distance between Dylan and myself, and for me, it was painful, very painful. I found some nights that I would sleep with my Bible, praying for strength and for faith in the strength in our parental-child bond. I must say that the universe was answering, as it kept sending me events or things that kept me in some contact with Dylan, which I was very thankful for. It was also interesting to experience the continual line of people who kept coming into my life with the answers that I needed to hear and that I needed to understand.

One of those people was a woman named Cathy. We got into a deep discussion of our roots: meaning a person's history, passage of life, what they had experienced, and being proud of that. We came to the conclusion that this also involved understanding that this passage, even if not so pretty or natural or what one would have chosen to happen it had brought that person to this very point in their life.

I thought about myself and my life and what I had to go through to find my passion for writing and to realize my ability for insight and healing. I looked to the joy of all my children, and of course Christine, Paul, and Dylan would not be a part of my life if I had not experienced the end of my marriage. I looked to the time when I was homeless and what strength I gained from that and having to leave my family and the pain and suffering that I endured. This was something that I would not wish on anyone, but it did happen to me and it was my history and my roots and my passage and something I needed to be proud of, to be proud of where it had led me.

The understanding I gained from this is that you can leave an unhealthy life and have nothing, and when living in faith and following your path that unfolds, an amazing life can come forth. This was exactly what had happened to me: I had family, kids, a son, and a home, and my passion and my career was unfolding. And I knew that the perfect relationship was close, and most of all, that I would be able to find ultimate peace, love, and happiness.

Friday Night

Things were pretty much still at a distance with Dylan, but I decided to attend his Friday night performance at The Boat House. Everyone in my circle wanted to go to The Boat House and watch Dylan, and they wanted me to join them, so I guessed it was time for me to attend once again. It was a wonderful feeling and it brought a sense of family to the forefront: a family that seemed to be getting bigger and bigger. I did text Dylan and tell him that a large group was planning to attend and received the reply, "That's great."

Within a few hours, I found myself driving alone to The Boat House to secure a large table for the gang. I knew that Anne Marie was on her way, as well as Marilyn and John, and Cathy and family (which consisted of Joe, Emily, Roditha, Robert, and two of Emily's friends from university). I also heard that Maggie, Laura, and Alex were on their way as well. We all actually arrived there before Dylan, which I found strange as he was to start in a few minutes. Marilyn and John sat at the bar, as John was an Irish man and felt more comfortable at the bar area. Chrissy and Meghan from Mama's Restaurant also came for the show.

We all settled in at a great table with a good view of where Dylan was to play and ordered some drinks and appetizers. The weather was warm and the atmosphere was great, and we seemed to be surrounded by friends. We then notice that Dylan had arrived, and for me there was one amazing gift: Donald was helping carry in his equipment and Lauren was there as well. A big smile appeared on my face, although I immediately noticed the coldness of Dylan's energy towards me, which I thought was strange as I had just talked with him at noon and everything seemed good. Donald dropped off the equipment and immediately came over and gave me a hug and a quick hello. Then all of them left for one more final trip with the equipment. On Dylan's return, he did shake hands with Joe and says hello to Robert, as he had met Cathy and her family many a time. Dylan then sat down and prepared to play, as it was now already 7:00 p.m. Lauren and Donald stayed for a few songs and then were on their way.

I simply sat enjoying Dylan singing, as it was truly one of my most favourite things to do. I felt sadness, as there was not much eye contact between me and Dylan (in the past, I had actually at times even been in conversation with Dylan when he had been playing). But he looked good (I had not seen him in a couple weeks) and I was happy to just sit and watch him play. His voice was strong, clear, and warming to the hearts of the people. He then took a short break, and I noticed a few new young kids around and Dylan out visiting with them, and then he came back to play. At this time, I started to notice that Dylan's eye contact was mainly around the family but there was a strong sense of avoidance towards me. I was okay with it, although my close and dear friends Cathy and Anne Marie were noticing the difference and not saying a word.

Dylan then took his next break, and the people surrounded him once again. I noticed he was looking towards me; I just gave him a little wave of "come on over" and he immediately headed over to our table, greeting everyone with such love and passion. I was on the other side of the table and excited for him to make his way to me. When it was my turn for a greeting, I hugged him with such love and a whisper of how I had missed him. There was a chair open on the other side of the table by Joe and Robert, and Dylan settled in with the family. I just sat and smiled at this time. Joe then asked about business and life, and stated how great Dylan sounded. I noticed that the walls that were around Dylan were now almost down and that he was himself, shining like the star within. Maggie, Laura, and Alex arrived, and Dylan found himself in conversation with Maggie about her music career as well. It was finally time for Dylan to return to his keyboard, and the people on the patio became one again. After this set, Dylan found his way back to the family, and it was normal and peaceful, and we all were just having fun.

Maggie did ask Dylan for a song request, and Dylan asked if she had it on her iPod and could he listen to it. There became stillness at the table as Maggie found the song and Dylan placed the earphones on his ears. Emily (Cathy's amazing daughter) looked over at me as if to ask me, is this possible? I of course had seen this many a time in the little Toyota, but I just smiled and said nothing. Dylan then returned to his keyboard and played the song. I was a little surprised, because I had never seen him do this in public, although I knew that he just wanted to play the song request for Maggie. About ten minutes later, I found Dylan standing beside me asking me to get him some water and a beer. I immediately got up and got him what he needed and entered into the mother mode again with a smile on my face.

Towards the end of the evening, Dylan played "Wonder Wall," which was one of my favourites, and then ended with "Bohemian Rhapsody"—where it took all my energy to stay centered. It was then time for all of us to leave, and on the way out I saw Dylan at the inside bar and chose to say my goodbyes there. We had a hug goodbye, and I told him how very much I loved him, and the hug and love was returned. I then momentarily went back to the patio to say goodbye to Marilyn and John, and when I passed Dylan putting away his equipment, he was surrounded by at least twenty people. I was happy he was doing great and smiled to myself as I passed him. Then all of a sudden there was this tall, handsome young man cutting through the people and hugging me once again, telling me he loved me, thanking me for coming, and thanking me for bringing all the people. I hugged him back and told him how wonderful his performance was with the tears quietly running down my cheeks. He then said, "Text me tomorrow," and I said I would.

As I walked away, I thought, wow, the power of love—no matter what people said or did or how much they judged the situation, the power of the love between Dylan and myself was so much stronger. I also knew that part of the intensity was because Dylan had gone without the love of a mother for so long and people just didn't know that or understand it. Moreover, did people in our society know what to do when they saw love, natural love, and the strength and power that came with it? Our society has told us at times not to hug, not to show love, and this made me feel a little sad. So I turned to compassion for all the people who had judgement towards Dylan and my relationship. But it truly didn't matter, because whatever they did or said, the parental love was still there!

Balance

It was like a brick wall hit me the day when Emily used the word "balance" in a conversation with Dylan. As they were saying their goodbyes (as Emily was returning to Kingston and university), she said something very profound to Dylan. She said, "I understand what is it like to balance the people in your life, as I have had to learn to balance the adults in my life," and I thought, wow, she is so right.

I thought of Emily's life and how she had to balance her dad, her mom (meaning me), her sister Kate, her stepsister Heather, her boyfriend Brandon, his mom Stephanie and her new husband Bryan, her dad's new girlfriend, Heather, and her sister's boyfriend George. Next, all I could feel was compassion for Emily, as because of the divorce there was a continual sense of dis-ease within. It was something that we tried to heal but something that was still always there. It was like the kids got stuck always within the dysfunction of the adults' lives.

I then thought of Dylan and all the people he was now balancing: a new mom (being me), a birth mom, a stepmom, a dad, a girlfriend, the girlfriend's family, my kids, family and friends, roommates, and all the people who had touched his life throughout his journey. This was such a large group of people because he was never set in one spot, and so many people had been a part of his life. Moreover, there were also all the people who wanted to guide him, which was frankly almost everyone who entered into his existence. While we knew it was from a place of love, it could be a little overwhelming for him.

Kate had quite the list of people she had to balance in her life as well, while also having a full-time job and still competing as a professional athlete. Beside all that, there was Christine she had, baby Paul, Stephanie, stepdad, step-siblings, Paul's dad, her boyfriend, her other mom (being me), Emily, girlfriends, and Mimi, too.

I could see that balance was a very important word or concept, as we had to balance everything to create balance in our lives: balance within our jobs, our family, our partners, our friends, exercise, food, liquor. I believed it was a good idea for everyone to take a look at their lives and see how balanced they truly were.

As time passed, I now needed to find balance in my life with Dylan and his music career, as he was now the entertainment in most of the establishments that I had been frequenting for the past ten years. I didn't want to stay home all the time, as I missed the people, the dancing, and just having fun. So I decided to join Marilyn and John and a few other friends at The Boat House. As I arrived, I smiled at Dylan and he seemed happy to see me. I sat with my friends, listening to the wonderful music and enjoying a good glass of wine. When Dylan took his first break, he visited with the people and then came right over for a hug and a kiss. I felt extremely relieved, and it was as if no time had passed and we were surrounded with friends and family. We then enjoyed some more great music from Dylan. Interestingly, "Bohemian Rhapsody" was becoming a song of the past, although Queen could never leave Dylan's performance as it was such a gift that he could sing as well as or better than Freddy. But the new song became "Somebody to Love," which was absolutely an amazing song, and Dylan performed it superbly. This song was becoming one of my new favourites. The evening ended with Dylan enjoying his dinner at our table. I looked at him and saw that he was just a kid sitting with family. I could tell that he was enjoying the conversation and the easiness of the people.

Then Dylan asked the people at the table what their plans were for the following night. We all just look at each other, as there was no set agenda for tomorrow. He then mentioned that he was playing with a band in a small place just outside of Barrie and invited us all to attend, as it was going to be a great night filled with great music. I knew that Dylan had been playing with this band (Souled Out) for at least a year and that it was a comfortable setting for him. The members of the band were a little older and understood that this was just a steppingstone for Dylan. I had already heard them play a short performance and was pleased that Dylan was involved with such wonderful people. The consensus was at the table that we all would attend this performance with the band. I was thankful for my wonderful friends and the fact that they were showing support and were willing to travel a distance to do this.

The following night, three cars headed towards this bar that was located in a very small town outside of Barrie. The five of us decided to meet in a slightly larger town for a quick pint before the performance. As we were enjoying this time, I was in contact with Dylan concerning what time the band was going to be on stage, as he was still finishing up another performance just up the road. I was excited, as it was wonderful to be a part of his performance even though it was in a different role—a role that I was happy to be in and that was just the natural course of life. We then finished our beers and headed to the venue.

As we arrived, I saw that Dylan was already there, and I talked briefly with a few members of his band and then we all found some space at the bar. I looked over and saw that his keyboard was all set up, and I got goose bumps again. It was a feeling that was nervousness and excitement all at once. This was a feeling I had experienced many a time and a feeling I had learned to embrace, as I knew that a few deep breaths would solve it. I next saw Dylan enter the door on the other side of the room and he seemed busy. He didn't really say anything to us, and that was okay; I was just happy that we were there to support him. I then notice to my left that the woman who hosted the jam session in the basement of her house nine months ago was there. I was very happy to see her, and she was happy to see me as well. We enjoyed a warm hug and a moment of pleasantries before I headed back to my spot. I noticed that all the band members were on stage getting ready, and I started to look for Dylan and there he was right in front of me, saying a hello to the gang, giving me a quick hug, and taking his spot on the stage. I once again enjoyed a deep breath.

As the band started up, the crowd became one and the music was great, really great. I was enjoying the strength and the differences of Dylan playing in a band setting. The other members of the band were

Chris, who was a firecracker on the electric guitar, and Donna, who also sang and there was a great bass player and great drummer as well. The music was upbeat and there were some great dance tunes being played, and so Marilyn and I joined the ladies from the jam session on the dance floor. Dylan was playing well but he was not quite himself—some of that coldness had returned. But I at this time was just happy being me and enjoying the music.

Towards the end of the set, I returned to stand by the bar and watch the show. At this time, I really took notice of the people, as they were really enjoying the music. People were singing along and even dancing in the aisles. I looked to my wonderful friends and saw the excitement in all of them. As they played their final song, Rolling Stones Sympathy for the Devil the crowd became one, it was fabulous. The band (Souled Out) finished to a great show of appreciation by the crowd. There was another band up next, so Dylan's band was busy clearing the stage. Dylan then loaded his equipment, and as he was going in and out of the door and the people wanted to talk to him. He was gone for quite a while, and I started to think, well, I guess this is the way it is unfolding. Then all of a sudden I saw Dylan re-enter the building, and he was moving fast and heading right towards us. I smiled at him and gestured for him to greet the rest of our group. He did, and the response was so positive, as everyone was very proud of him and his performance. Dylan then quickly hugged everyone and me as well. I hugged him back, and as he started to leave, he turned back and said to me, "I love you. I replied, "I love you, too." He then turned quickly towards the exit.

I turned to Marilyn and she was crying. No words were said between us at first, and then she said, "I don't know why I am crying." I then just smiled. The moment was interrupted as Chris handed me the dreaded missing cord and asked me to deliver it to Dylan, which I did the next morning with love.

A Change in Season

It was now September, and there was a coolness in the evenings. Life had fallen into a routine again, which felt very good for everyone. Christine and I were in the kitchen talking about her first few classes of school, and she mentioned that the band(The Bruce Lee Band) that had played at her Mom's wedding was playing at the Middletown Legion and that a gang of people were going. My eyes then lit up and I said that I would love to join them, as I had now found my dancing shoes and needed a night of dancing. We then continued on with our day, with Christine looking after Paul and me going to pick up Mimi.

A few hours later, we enjoyed a drink at the kitchen table before heading to the Legion. As we arrived, there was an aura of fun in the air, as the people were already dancing and enjoying the music. As we found our seats near the band, we all waved at them and a comment was made that we were now their groupies. I was quite happy about this, as it was a feeling of family, belonging, and once again the power of music. We then settled in for a night of fun: Stephanie, Bryan, Stu and Adriane, Christine and Randy, Christine's cousin Dean, and me. It wasn't long before we all were out there enjoying the dance floor. Stu surprised me with a hidden talent as a great dancer, and it was fun watching him dance up a storm. The women were also enjoying the freedom of the dance floor, and a few others joined our group. The greatest part about it all was that age and gender had no influence; it was just people being people and becoming one.

I noticed that a few regulars from The Boat House were also in attendance, and I chose to visit with them. I had quite an ongoing shine for a man who was in attendance at this table: a man named Jim. As the night unfolded, I enjoyed quite a few dances with this wonderful man, and he was one of the best dancers I had danced with. We must have danced until midnight, and then it was time for a cab to take us to the next spot, which was Stu and Adrian's, for some more music and, thankfully, some great food.

The music now became country, as a Garth Brooks concert DVD was put on the TV, this being Stephanie's favourite. She started talking about the power of country music and how it was about family and the power of the words. As we were watching the DVD, it was as if the people were jumping out at me, as there were so many people and the love they had for Garth Brooks was amazing. I thought for a minute to Dylan and wondered whether he one day would find himself on a stage like this surrounded by this amazing love of the people.

Faith

As I continued to let go of Dylan and he continued to grow, the universe still seemed to put us in communication and in the same room at the same time over and over again. This might be in the form of gigs set up by Garfield that I was asked to attend, a lost cellphone, people giving me messages for Dylan, and even people continually talking to me about Dylan. And I must say, the connection was still always there. Moreover, we kept up communication on a daily basis, which was something I experienced as well with all my other children, and it felt normal and complete. Thus, my heart started to heal and the pain started to lessen, as I knew I was going to be a part of Dylan's life forever, I just knew it. This also increased my faith and strength in the saying, "Let it go, and if it returns, it was meant to be."

So this was how Dylan and my relationship sat at this very moment. We were talking on a daily basis and from a place of love. I now was able to speak whatever was on my mind and give guidance from a place of a motherly love, and the response from Dylan was from a place of a loving son. This, I realized, was a miracle in itself, as having a healthy relationship with a child is a parent's greatest gift and something to be cherished forever. I wasn't quite sure what was happening in his career, but this was okay. We had worked through the learning curves of a parental relationship that was so very new to both of us. When I looked to my calendar, I realized it had been a year—a year since that tall, thin young man had entered into my life and became one of the greatest gifts in my life.

Dylan posted a new song on Facebook and sound cloud called "Don't Stumble Your Words." I started to feel some nervousness as the song was loading onto my computer, but as I listened to it, I was thinking, this is good, really good. I could also tell that Dylan's voice was not as strong as it was now. After listening to it, I sent him a text saying what a great song but that I did notice less strength in his voice.

Dylan replied right away saying thank you and that, yes, this song was recorded in the studio with Neil before his training with Anna. I was thinking, how did I miss this song, and then I got it. When I received the very first CD that came from Neil's, there were only six songs on it. One time, we had an uncomfortable discussion when Dylan insisted there were seven songs and that he should know. I just let it go at the time, but I realized now that it was this song that I had missed.

Dylan then explained the history behind the song, which completely blew me away. He said that it was the very first song he ever wrote and that he was only thirteen at the time. He was at a camp, sitting on the top bunk writing the words as a buddy was repeating the riff he had heard in his head and taught to his friend on the guitar. He said that it took him two hours to write the song and that his buddy was losing patience, but he completed the song. He wasn't so sure about the strength of the lyrics, as he was so young, but he was more mature now and that maybe more mature lyrics would come now in his writing. I said, "Wow, I feel blessed to know the history," and then immediately went back to listen to the song again. I then found myself listening to the song quite a few times and loving every word of it, and once again I was able to see the brilliance in this wonderful kid who was in my life.

Kate was now fine, working hard at her job and enjoying having some financial abundance. Her relationship was still unsure, and I was just sitting back and being there for her. Emily and Brandon were doing great, learning to be a team and setting the example of a healthy relationship. Christine and Randy were also doing well, embracing the love between them and learning to be in a healthy relationship. Mimi was good, playing cards and healthy. Ernie the cat had returned after being missing for three days, and Jaja my other cat was here as well. Everyone and everything seemed great at this specific moment in time, and my family seemed very peaceful.

The weather this fall was beautiful, and Stephanie and I went on one of our fabulous walks with Paul. I noticed that I was experiencing a tremendous change in my essence and my energy. I wasn't quite sure what exactly it was until Stephanie started to tell this story she had just heard on the news about the man who was the founder of Boston Pizza (of course, as I have mentioned earlier, this was a place I went weekly). This man had previously been a police officer and then he had this vision of knowing to create this restaurant line called Boston Pizza. His father was a totally against this, as it was just society's influence that made most people look at life from within the box—and from this perspective, it was totally understandable that people would say this was not such a good idea. As the story continued, the answer came forth for this man (and for me as well). Stephanie said that he had the knowing: he just knew what he was to do and that success would come with it. All I could hear over and over again was he had the knowing, he just knew, and then I got it. I had had the knowing for a while, but I still didn't have the complete knowing until that very moment and then I just knew what I was to do and not to waver from it in any way. It was as simple as that.

Twists of Life

It was a Thursday night when I noticed that Christine and Randy were starting to show some signs of dis-ease within their relationship— dis-ease that I thought was just a sign of growing pains, as on the surface they seemed to be enjoying a great relationship. However, it was clear that there was an underlying pattern of dis-ease that was once again coming to life for them both and they had a lot to deal with (not unlike most relationships).

Randy and Christine did have Paul, which in my opinion should always be seen as a gift and (to me) this was always the case. But society often casts judgement on single people who have children, which saddens me, as there has been so much joy and love that has come to me from all the kids I have brought into my life. For single mothers and fathers to be embraced would create a wonderful shift in society. Now, Christine was a package; she came with baby Paul, and I sensed at times that this was also something that caused dis-ease within this relationship. Moreover, there had always been the issue of making a commitment and sticking with it and working as team.

I remained aware of the situation but kept my distance and just tried to be there for Christine. As a few weeks past, there was no longer any communication between Randy and Christine, but I still stayed in my own business, knowing that the right information would come forward, as I believe it always does. It was a Monday and Christine was at school, and we had a tentative plan for a movie night. Before she was due to get home, I took Paul for a walk, giving him a bath and getting him ready for bed. Christine arrived from school and told me that she was going over to a girlfriend's house with Paul and that they would maybe stay there for the night. I thought this was a little strange, but it was really none of my business and so I kissed them both goodbye. I then thought to myself that they must be going to Randy's and to bed I went.

The next day was busy and I wasn't really in touch with Christine, and they didn't come home once again. By Wednesday morning, I was concerned. Stephanie and I were planning a walk when Christine arrived with Paul for babysitting while she attended classes for the day. At this time, she was greeted by both her mothers, who were both looking for the truth. Christine was a little apprehensive but finally told us that she had been hanging out with Ron, the father of Paul. Stephanie and I were stunned but not surprised, as we both knew this could be a possibility.

Christine then headed out the door with the thought of, oh no, I now have two mothers to answer to, and sent a text stating this. Of course, I replied how blessed she was to have two mothers. During our walk, Stephanie and I decided to let it unfold, although we were both a little taken back at this time. Thursday passed and I heard a bit from Christine, and by this time Mimi and I were really starting to miss both Christine and Paul.

On Friday late afternoon, I had been talking to Dylan quite a bit and enjoying the ease of our relationship (which I was very thankful for). Dylan then told me that he was heading to the Harbour to visit his dad for the evening, to which I replied, "Let me know if there is a party." As I returned home from Boston Pizza with Mimi, I received a text from Christine stating that she was missing me. As I sat in the driveway returning her text, she pulled in and I was so very happy to see her. We exchange a hug and entered the house and cozied up at the island in the kitchen with a glass of wine. This became a time for Christine to let her heart out and for me to listen—which is what parents should do before an opinion or judgement is given. Christine took her time and things were making sense, and I was once again listening.

Then I noticed my phone going off and there was Dylan saying that he and his dad were going to Stephanie's for dinner and was I coming too. I thought that this was a little strange, but the next second Stephanie texted me asking if I would like to join them. Christine's phone was also going off and it was Dylan texting asking where she was. I look at

Christine and said, "Wow, you just never know how things are going to unfold. Isn't the universe powerful?" Christine and I still had some talking to do, so we left thirty minutes later for our five-minute car ride to Stephanie's, passing Dylan's dad's house on the way.

As we arrived, I sensed the warmth of Stephanie's house and family. We joined Dylan and his dad upstairs where the living room and kitchen were located. Immediately, I once again noticed a sense of coldness from Dylan; it didn't make any sense to me at all, and so I completely disregarded it. Stephanie's house had the most amazing view of the water, and Gary was enjoying every bit of it, as it was the first time he had been there. I felt a sense of love, as it was so very wonderful to be in the same room with Dylan and my family all at the same time. I was very happy to see Gary, and we quickly found ourselves in conversation about my book and how excited I was that things were moving forward.

As dusk fell, Stephanie lit the fire at the waterfront and we moved down to enjoy it. As we were enjoying conversation, I just felt the need to hug Dylan—I guess it was the mom in me just missing him. Of course, he hugged me back and we just stood there for a moment, and then everything seemed back to normal again. As I sat enjoying the fire, I thought about how these feelings and unchartered waters were at times rough between Dylan and I, but somehow I always managed to stay afloat. Christine and I then started a small rendition of "This Girl," with Dylan enjoying every second of it. We returned to the house excited for dinner, as Stephanie was a fabulous cook and she had made her famous alfredo sauce.

Christine and I had talked earlier about going to the Legion and putting on our dancing shoes, not to mention that it was also karaoke night. There was a consensus by the gang that this would be a wonderful idea. We then all got into my car (Gary, Christine, Dylan, Stephanie, Donald, and myself) and headed for Gary's house, which was right behind the Legion. As we entered the Legion and smiled at all the people, I kind of had the knowing that this group of people didn't have any idea what was in store for them.

We started with drinks, dancing, and Dylan putting his name on the list to sing a song. Stephanie, Christine, and I were doing a fantastic job on the dance floor that we had just created, and then it was time for Dylan to take the stage singing "Midnight Special," which I had heard him sing about a hundred times. We were still dancing, and all of a sudden I had a sick feeling that something was wrong as I watched my genius son reading the words from the screen. I don't know what happened to me but I found myself beside him asking why he was reading the words as he knew the words—I being, at this time, about one inch from his face. I then moved quickly back to the girls, and Dylan turned to the crowd and started to perform.

After he finished, we were talking about something else and the comment came back to me, "Don't ever tell me what to do with my music." I thought, fair enough, as I felt a little bad about what had happened and a little out of my boundaries, even as a mother. Then the coldness returned, which prompted tears to appear, and I managed to keep it together. Gary appeared by my side asking me what was wrong. I thought to myself, how do I even start to explain what I have been through to Gary, although I knew we both had something very special in common and it was Dylan. We talked for a minute, and then I found myself in the bathroom telling myself to keep it together. At this time, Dylan and Gary were having a talk outside, me being the topic of conversation. I put my thoughts on the back burner for the moment and came out determined to enjoy the people, the music, and the dance floor. And there was Dylan singing again and performing like a star with the screen to his back because he didn't need the words, but still not quite forgiving me for bringing this to his attention.

We continued throughout the night enjoying the people, the music, and the dancing. I thought to myself that this night had surely taken on another twist of fate, as I was starting to feel much better. Then there was a shift once again, and everything seemed to be okay with Dylan and I could once again see the love in his eyes. Gary was not keen on fast dancing, and so it was Dylan, Christine, Stephanie, and me really letting go, and Dylan back beside me.

Later that night, Christine and I found ourselves at my house enjoying some chips and salsa, and talking about how amazing the night had unfolded. And then a text came from Dylan saying good night and "I love you. Don't forget it!" Then he texted, "Sorry for being mean and please forgive me." My instant reply was, "Dylan, I love you and I will always want the best for you." I didn't feel to say I was sorry for what happened, as I think if I were back in the same situation I probably would do the same thing again. As we were talking, we were healing, as we seem to be doing all the time. As our relationship changed and grew, everyday something new and interesting came to light. I said to Dylan, "I just want the best for you. Darn maternal parental love, it's bigger than you and me ☺." A reply of "♥ well said" came forth, and my reply was simply "♥," and then this fabulous night was over and complete.

The Rewards of Parenting

For the first time in my twenty-two years of being a mom, I was really feeling rewarded for all the time, effort, love, money, and commitment that I had put into my kids. I had recently booked a flight to California to visit Kate, a flight I was very excited about. The closest airport to her was Palm Springs, and I had obtained a great flight at a great price—and with some Visa points, it became almost a gift of a flight.

Kate called on Saturday and said she had some fantastic news and what did I think about staying Friday night in Las Vegas, as one of her best friends from her high school years was going to be there during this time. Kate said that she would book and pay for the hotel. My first reaction was how great, as I love a road trip. I hadn't been in Vegas in twenty-two years, and spending time with Kate's friend Felicia would be lots of fun.

Then Kate said that she would treat for the hotel as a bit of an interest payment for all the money I had given her for her education. She also said that she had been saving some extra money too to be used for my visit. I said to Kate, "Wow, that would be great, and thank you," and the warmth of love flowed throughout my essence. We then talked about her plans for that weekend going skiing, as Kate was still an athlete. I thought many a time that when she got older she would stop skiing at a competitive level, especially after the horrific jump crash she had had the past year at colligate nationals that scared the heck out of me. There's nothing like the feeling of standing thirty feet away on shore watching your daughter hit the water with eighty-six inch skies and knowing she cannot breathe. I still to this day can hear the sounds of her lungs opening up and gasping for air as one of the other team member got to her very quickly. She sold those jump skies, and I thought this would be a turning point, but three months later she bought a new pair. Her passion as an athlete was still very much alive, and even though it was time to step into the real world with a job, a condo, and responsibility, Kate was still a competitive athlete.

After I said my goodbyes to Kate, I starting telling Mimi about the new plans during my stay in California, and it hit me that with Kate it was time to receive something back after all the money, time, dedication, and of course just being there for her over the past twenty-two years. I had given her a large chunk of my money from the dissolving of my marriage to give her an education, as I believe all kids deserve the education they want. Moreover, the costs that my ex-husband and I had dealt with in having an international athlete had been an over-the-top expense, but the rewards were starting to come back and this felt very good.

I had to go to work at Mama's Restaurant and then later to a housewarming party for Marilyn's daughter, who was my roommate when I first left my marriage. Rebecca had a wonderful townhouse where you could feel the warmth as soon as you walked in the door. Marilyn was there, but besides the two of us, the age range was between twenty-five and thirtyish—which was a gift to me, as I so love to talk with the youth. They have such interesting lives and are full of the clearness of life. I always seemed to find myself in the right place at the right time talking to the right person, which at this moment became Melissa, a friend from Toronto Rebecca had met when traveling. Melissa started talking to me about the greatness and also the challenges of her job, as she worked with people needing support and guidance in the court systems. This was so interesting to me considering my love for the people and my love of helping people. As Melissa was talking, I could see the strength, confidence, and joy within this young woman. We enjoyed sharing the different but similar paths of our lives, as both our lives were about being in service to the people.

The following day, Sunday, became a day of reflection, as my house was much quieter since Paul and Christine were still spending time at Ron's house—which was, I believed, the right spot for them at this very moment. However, I must say that I missed them very much already. I then thought of Emily and Brandon enjoying the ease, love, and benefits of a healthy relationship, and this brought such joy to me. I thought about Melissa and the great conversation we had had Saturday night. I thought of Dylan and how much fun we had had, and I was thankful that all was good between us. I thought of Kate and the rewards of the twenty-two years of being there and supporting her dreams and goals as much as I physically could.

I then thought about my path with kids and the people, and investing in kids who entered into my life as I had with Christine and Dylan. There were so many kids who need parental help due to the circumstances of life. This was also about building community, which I feel is everyone's responsibility. As with anything, there was pain and disappointment on this path, but it was perseverance that brought the joy in the end. What I realized at this moment was that even with helping the kids who come into our lives, we have to realize that there will be pain and upset that will come with this and that it is just part of the journey. Therefore, when you open your hearts, your home, and your life to a youth in need, you have to prepare for the upset that is part of any parental journey. Despite all that, I could not imagine a day without all my kids in my life: Kate, Emily, Brandon, Christine, and Dylan. Therefore, I would turn to faith with the knowing that the joy and, of course, the gift of love was on its way!

As I sat and savoured this moment, I noticed a picture text come through my iPhone, which brought the confirmation that life was truly full of ups and downs. It was a picture of Kate's ankle and it was all swollen up, as she had a bad fall slaloming earlier that morning. My body first felt the pain, as her ankle looked very sore. I was not sure how many times she had hurt her ankle between waterskiing and volleyball, but I knew it was a lot. You could no longer see her ankle, as the area was completely swollen up. "Oh no" was my reply. Kate was being positive, as she always was when she had an injury, but I had been around too long and knew the minimum was six weeks before any more skiing. But all trials and tribulations depend on how you dealt with them, and I knew a positive attitude would heal the wound better; I understood this lesson in life.

Everything Changed

It was Monday, and I thought the day was going to unfold in an easy way, but there was a much different plan for me this day. First, my walk time got changed to the afternoon, and then right before my walk, a call came in about a special gig for Dylan, which was great news. I took down all the details and then tried to contact Dylan but to no avail, so I left on my walk with my friend. Then Dylan's dad called all concerned because he had received a strange phone call on Sunday from Dylan's phone number and he had been trying to call him over the past twenty-four hours but to no avail. He was concerned, and then so I became concerned. I called Dylan again but there was still no answer. I then called Gary back and told him that I thought everything was okay and not to worry.

I then continued on my walk but soon stopped and said that I thought I needed to go to town, as I was really starting to worry about Dylan, and then everything blew up. There was judgement towards me from my friend, judgement from a very hard hand, and so I just walked away and followed my instincts. I drove to Dylan's house to find him sleeping at three in the afternoon. I told him about his dad's concern and then called Gary on my cellphone and he talked with Dylan. We then talked about the phone call for the new gig and I thought all was well, but I just couldn't let go and I wanted to understand what the meaning was behind the judgement that had been placed upon me and so I kept digging.

To my surprise, I was informed by my friend Stephanie of an ongoing betrayal that almost knocked me over and put me on my ass. Yep, it was like the bottom completely fell out of my life once again. I thought things had been bad before, but this was worse than I could have imagined.

I then immediately started to defend myself, as this was a place I had found myself in before and a place that was not really too comfortable.

Next, of course, came the hurt rushing forward once again, but this didn't last very long. I stopped to think and what came to mind was that I thought things were quite good over the past few weeks and that everything and everyone was back on track with Dylan and me. Therefore, I was stunned once again. But all of a sudden something changed in me; something was different within me, and I had acquired some sort of new strength.

It was like a part of me had hardened inside, and it was actually a good feeling. It was like an inner strength that was waiting to be created. All of a sudden, I thought of Jasmine, my wonderful teacher of consciousness, who was hard on me but one I kept going back to. I could hear her saying, "Jenny, get angry; be strong and powerful"— which was a word I was afraid of until this very moment. I then felt this need to let this strength out and straighten a few things out. I looked at the past as a place I would never find myself in again, a place of getting hurt and having to defend myself. I guess it was the time in my life that I decided no one else was going to take advantage of me or shit on me or walk over me ever again.

Therefore, it was now time for me to go to Dylan, as he was very much a part of this betrayal. I told him that if he had a problem with me that it would be best if he talked to me about it. He said he didn't mean to betray me but that was truly how he felt towards me. He said that I was controlling with him, obsessed, threatening, and also at the same time I had left him. I first thanked him, as I was glad he was finally talking to me about it. I also told him I was once again surprised as I thought everything was good between us. He said he was sorry that I felt betrayed. I knew there had to be some truth to this statement from Dylan, so I needed to reflect on what was happening and what had been said. Therefore, once again I backed away to regroup, although at this time I was starting to getting a little tired of the roller coaster ride that I seemed to always be on.

Nothing Made Sense

It took me four days to find the strength to be able to open up my laptop and write this next chapter. I was alone once again and dealing with the pain and turbulence of life. This was a place I hadn't been in for a few years and a place where I didn't feel so very good at all. My main problem was that every time I started to come out of this situation, I kept returning to the same place and trying to make sense of everything.

At this time, I started questioning my ability to be a good mother. I started asking, had I done something wrong? I started wondering, how did I get here? I questioned my purpose in life; I questioned whether I was to help the kids. Was I to have helped Dylan? I knew he was upset with me, but I wasn't exactly sure what was happening.

I had heard from Dylan that he was upset that I left him so many times and he was not willing to forgive me—yes, he wasn't willing to forgive me. Then he said that I had been too much involved in his life and disagreed with most of his decisions. I knew that I had done my best, but I had pulled out many times and I had finally told him what I thought I had to do as a person and as mother as well. I had gotten mad at him about not talking to Emily and her friend. But I thought everything was good. I had been busy working on my books, writing, walking, talking on and off to Dylan. We were busy in our own separate lives; we had balance. However, the message was very strong, hurtful, and clear: he wasn't happy with me in his life. I asked again why he hadn't come to me; I felt so betrayed because he hadn't talked to me. There just seemed to be a different Dylan who I was talking to. It became very painful, and this pain then set in for the next few days.

I then found myself in need of a CD of Dylan's to sell to Delia at Boston Pizza, as I had already disappointed her once. I didn't know what to do, as now there was no contact at all between Dylan and me. I grabbed my briefcase with the hope that there might be a CD in there so

I wouldn't have to lose face or explain the separation between me and Dylan, and to my greatest surprise, there was one CD left. As I sat in the chair, I was so happy and relieved that I had one copy, as this was all I truly needed. At this very moment, my eye caught the pink folder with the poem Dylan had written me for Mother's Day. I froze for a second, and my first thought was, "No, Jenny, don't do it; don't read it." I then found myself holding onto the closed folder and the words from Dylan came to mind: "Let me know whenever you want me to read it to you and I will." I next found myself opening the folder and re-reading the poem:

Mom!! :)
xoxo
For whom I have become,
for how I've grown to feel,
for why I now have faith,
for love I truly feel.

For reasons for discoveries,
for days I fall apart,
for showing me myself,
and finding me my heart.

For pain that's far diminished,
for smiles that don't frown,
for setting the example,
of standing on one's ground.

For running on our journey,
for breathing by my side,
for opening my spirit,
for understanding pride.

For shifting my own energy,
for hearing the unheard,
for actively surrendering,
to people you have cured.

For being my bright angel,
my mom and my best friend,
for finding my beginning,
while waiting at the end.

For tolerance, for patience,
for happiness to come,
I thank you for your consciousness
and for being my Mom!!

xoxoxo

Your Son,
Dylan Lock xoxoxoxo

I was now finding it difficult to breathe, as at this very moment the tears were once again flowing down my face and the pain entered every ounce of my body. I once again turned to disbelief: how did we get here? I thought back to the fact that I had surrendered and that Dylan had returned to me, and then I had the realization that now at this moment he was further away from me than ever. I also felt frustration, as I was tired of the struggle to have faith with the outcome of this situation. I was frustrated with the continual tests of life and of faith. I then realized that this was all I had to hold onto: my faith and my belief that if someone comes into your life, it is for a reason, and if they are to stay in your life, they will.

I then turned to my rock, my Emily. I truly didn't know what I would do without her, as I could almost feel her standing beside me. I texted her with my pain, and she was open to help me and the situation at hand. She said to stand back and let things unfold. (It's always nice and very interesting when they start giving you your own advice back.) I knew she was right, but I still had the feeling that something was missing and it could have to do with the setting of boundaries. She then set her boundaries by stating the fact that she was at university in her third year of chemical engineering and that she had to focus on her work. I was sad that this situation had even minimally disrupted her school time, but it had. We then talked about a trip to the hairdresser for her, as she completely deserved it.

I found the strength to get ready to pick up my mom, as she was awaiting my arrival after her regular Friday bridge game, and then we were on our way to Boston Pizza. I sent a text to Christine asking about her plans for the evening. We arrived at the pizza place and I gave the CD for Delia and Dylan's music continued to enter into the hearts of more people. Mimi and I then enjoyed our dinner, and a reply came in from Christine asking if I would like to join them at the Coldwater Fair, as it was Ron's birthday. I said that this would be fantastic. Our fabulous waitress Stephanie told me that it was the smash-up derby night and that she was planning to go there right after her shift was finished. I thought, wow, this is great, as I had not attended a smash-up derby and this would be an experience.

Mimi and I returned home, and I rested for a minute until I heard from Christine. I tried to do some meditation and release the pain that for some reason was sticking with me like glue. I then decided that a cup of coffee would be the next best thing. Kate called, and I found myself in a great conversation with her. She was also feeling lonely, betrayed, and in the turmoil of life, and I had the knowing that this was actually bringing us closer. We then experienced the strongest conversation, and I realized that she was growing up and learning what was really important in life. We then talked about the excitement of my upcoming trip to visit her in California.

I then received a text from Christine telling me that they had left for the fair and asking me to bring the stroller. I got the stroller out of the garage and tried to figure out how to unfold it to no avail, so I decided to take my SUV, which would hold the upright stroller, and head towards Coldwater. I was happy to find a parking spot right on the street, and I arranged with Christine to meet them at the merry-go-round, as Paul was enjoying a ride with Ron's mom. As I paid and entered the fair, I immediately felt the judgement of entering with an empty stroller. I guessed it was just the norm for me, as judgement seemed to be everywhere within my life.

When I saw Christine, my heart warmed. I thought how I had missed her, as we hadn't spent a lot of time together over the past few months. I gave her a big hug, and I could tell she was also glad to see me and felt her heart warming as well. We then both smiled as Paul and his grandmother passed us on the merry-go-round. I felt peace and happiness inside as I looked at Christine and began to enjoy the excitement of the fair.

As Grandma and Paul found their way off the ride, I couldn't resist holding onto Paul for a visit. Then all four of us moved over to a car ride, which I rode with Paul. He was quite excited, as he was familiar with the steering wheel and had a horn to honk as well. As I passed Christine and Paul's other grandmother, I thought how wonderful it was to be in this very spot.

After the ride, we put Paul in the stroller and walked around the fair for a bit. We found a pretty large Ferris wheel where an adult could ride with a child as long as he or she met the minimum height requirements, and Paul passed the height. Grandma said it was too high a ride for her, but I said that it was okay for me. Paul and I approached the ride, and I started a conversation with the ride operator, and of course, he started to tell me about his life, as this was a normal occurrence for me. He told me that he had not seen his newborn baby boy for the past three months as he had been on the road working. I said I was sorry and asked where he lived. When he told me, I didn't even recognize the location of his hometown.

Once Paul and I were locked in and moving, Paul said uncertainly, "Nana," and I reassured him that everything was going to be good and tried to show him the moon and the people below, as it was dark at this time. As we passed the operator, I told him one more time around and that would be good. The operator smiled at me, and as we got off the ride, I recommended that he try to find some way to Skype his new son so he could see the progress of his growth. He smiled at me and I could see him thinking, no money for a computer. I felt his pain and let it go, and brought myself back to the moment at hand.

We then all headed to the smash-up derby area, and I noticed there were a lot of people in attendance. It was dark with bright lights shining on the cars that were on the field running into each other. Paul's aunt from Ron's side took him up close to watch, and Christine and I found ourselves off to the side watching the excitement. We had a little discussion about the turmoil that seemed to be within our family. She then leaned over and said that she was glad I was here, as she could feel the support I was giving her with being around Ron's family (who were wonderful, but Christine and Ron had been apart most of the summer).

I then noticed Ron in the crowd, and he was happy to see me and came over for a hug and a visit while Christine moved over to visit a friend. I wished Ron a happy birthday and said that I was glad to see him. I could see the warmth within Ron that his family was present for his birthday celebration.

We turned our attention to the field, as the bigger cars had started a new round of the smash-up derby and the excitement had gotten much bigger. I was enjoying the action and the excitement of the fair but found myself getting a little tired. I chose to head home and so said my farewells to baby Paul and the rest of the family. I found myself leaving the fair with an empty stroller because there was no room for it in any of the other cars, but I no longer cared about the judgement that would once again be placed on me.

Unfortunately, on my way home echoes of the conversations I had had that evening about the upheaval within the family due to the Dylan situation brought frustration and anger into my awareness. I thought of the loss of my other support in my life, the judgement, everything I had been accused of with my relationship with Dylan, and now the turmoil within my family. I then remembered the story of a man who had won the largest lotto in the United States and what he had endured. He ended up losing what was important to him because of money, this being his daughter to a drug overdose. I thought, well, there is no money yet, but it was fame and being in the public eye that was bringing a lot of pain, judgement, and dysfunction to all our lives. I then thought of Prince William's new wife Kate and how she was learning this the hard way, too. I thought about how much my life had changed in helping a kid who became a part of the limelight and how maybe that was why they called it "limelight," as it was a little green at times.

I then considered Dylan's comment that I was always pulling out or, as he said, "leaving him." I had to agree with him that he was right—I was always pulling away. I asked, why was I doing that? Why did I feel I had to pull out or "leave" him, as he knew I loved him so much? I knew it was my instincts that were continually telling me to get the heck out and that I couldn't stand the negative energy that was around him or the negative energy that was aimed towards me. There was also the fact that I was wrongfully accused of a romantic connection with Dylan and that I was looked upon as a gold-digger, only after him for the money. I was criticized about being a part of his career and blowing managers off. I had people telling me when they thought I shouldn't watch Dylan perform. I was criticized if I made him chicken soup because he was sick or bought him a coat that I found for a great price. I was accused of being controlling and jealous, which was ridiculous. It was as if no matter what I did, I was criticized for it.

That night I found myself sending a Facebook message to Dylan about how hurt I was, how things had had a ripple effect, and that it wasn't fair to the people that I loved and, frankly, to me as well. I thought it was time to fight for myself and say, "Hey, this isn't right. I haven't done anything wrong, and my life is hurting and so are the people I care about." I remembered the advice given to me to stay away and this saddened me again, as I couldn't even talk to a person I felt was like a son to me. I just didn't understand and I wanted the right to come forward.

Of course, I heard nothing from Dylan, but I was glad I said something as I couldn't sit back and just be wounded and have turmoil in my family—after all, I had brought this situation to my family in the first place. Most of all, it was my reputation and my life too that was at stake. Therefore, I was glad I said what I said, and now it was time to let it unfold. I was hoping, praying, that this was the last time I would have to surrender to the universe my fate concerning my relationship with Dylan.

As the days passed, the thought of fame kept coming into my mind—is this what comes with fame? I looked to the people and how many had died due to fame, and then I thought to Justin Bieber, Oprah, and Madonna. I am not sure what order they came into my awareness, but it was these three who appeared. I sat and thought about what these three people did and what they had in common: they entertained the people, they provided love to the people, they believed in God, and they were very talented and amazing business people.

I knew over and over again that I was to just sit back and let it unfold, but I was upset that this was happening to me and I had the urge to fight back to try to change things. I thought that maybe it was good that I was to fight back, but as I started to do so, I just knew that fighting back wasn't right. I tried to get help from my support network, and there was no support, as no one wanted to get involved. I thought how sad it was that we had all gotten to this spot as well.

I remembered Eckhart Tolle's book, where it talked about this man who was wrongfully accused of fathering a child and who was given this child to raise. He took the child in and said nothing, and then a year later the mother came back to get the child and told the truth that it was not his child. I wondered why Dylan was feeling this way and who was in his head and where this was coming from. I knew I took a chance telling him about the stories I had heard and finally felt he should know about. I had tried to tell him gently and not to offend, but this was to no avail. I then thought about the night I did get mad at him and we did argue, but I thought we had healed from it, as he knew it was from a place of love and I had apologised quite a few times. I thought that perhaps he told Stephanie this because he needed some direction and that he knew down deep in his heart that I loved him as a mom.

I then remembered that it was his birthday in two days and wondered what I should do. Should I text him and just say, "Happy Birthday, I love you, and have a great day"? I had bought a present for him, and it was a great present: a leather coat. I realized that I must have something about coats as I was always buying him a coat—and then fear popped into my mind as I thought, well, I started with buying him a coat and maybe was going to end with buying him a coat. I didn't know if I should give him the coat. What was society going to say if someone said, "Nice coat, where did you get it?" and Dylan told them I bought it? Would they judge again?

I just decided to stop thinking and listen to my heart, which was saying to just sit back and have faith in the power of love and the power of parental love. This felt good and right for at least a minute. And then the reality was right back in my awareness that there was no communication at all between Dylan and me, and that there was extreme turmoil between us—and basically, there was nothing I could do about it. Yep, there was nothing I could do about it, nothing at all.

Reaching Out

I did reach out one more time to Dylan through Facebook, still with the question of what the heck happened and talking a bit about the hurt and sending him an early birthday wish, and this came with no response as well. I had lost him. I did notice he seemed happy, as a comment showed up on my Facebook newsfeed about his birthday and that he was working on a new demo CD and new videos, which made me very happy.

On the day of his birthday, I did feel very sad. I looked at the beautiful leather coat I had bought him and my heart ached. It was as if I had a hole in my heart. I actually could hear Dylan's new song playing in my head called "There's a Hole in Your Heart." I then remembered the lesson I had received on Sunday from my friend Joel Osteen about thanking God in advance, like thanking him for the rain when the grass and the flowers were dry and there wasn't a cloud in the sky. So, I thought okay and I thanked God for bringing my son Dylan back into my life.

I then thought, well, I think I will keep going and thanked God for the wonderful new man in my life, my wonderful family, the selling of my books around the world, and my fabulous career as an inspirational speaker. This felt very good, and once again I said thank you God and then continued on with my day with a smile on my face and happiness within. I had the knowing that baby Paul was soon to arrive, and I was busy getting organized around the house, as it was also our Canadian Thanksgiving that coming weekend.

Quick Results

It wasn't more than an hour later that I received a call from Kate stating that her foot wasn't getting better and that she thought it could be broken. My first thought was, oh no about the foot and what kind of health care did she have, as she was living in the United States. She then stated that it was a 3,000 dollar deductible, and I thought, oh boy, better come home. Before long, there was an agreement made and a flight was booked. I really felt the excitement and the joy of hugging Kate and just smelling her. I also thought it would be good for her to have her mom by her side at the doctors, as I had been always there. Then I realized how great it would be to have my three girls and baby Paul in my kitchen baking this 2012 Thanksgiving. I felt so much peace that I found myself sending Dylan a happy birthday wish, which felt good as today was his birthday. I also told him I had a birthday gift for him and it was at my house. I did receive a quick reply saying, "Thank you □ xo."

I then said to myself, time to let go, let things unfold, and get back into my life. So I started focusing on my books, getting my house organized for Kate to arrive, getting my shopping done for Thanksgiving weekend, working, and still running Mimi around. I was also working with Marilyn on a Face case (a diversion course from the court system for our youth) and the final circle was set for that Thursday as well. I did have a life, and it was a busy one at that!

Kate

I woke up at 4:30 a.m. the following Thursday morning and started getting ready for my trip to the Toronto Airport to pick up Kate. Even though it was very early in the morning, I could feel the excitement of having her home. I quickly made some coffee and started down the highway, hoping I had left early enough. A short time into my trip I received a text from Kate saying she had landed, and since I was only in Barrie, I still had a long way to travel. I returned the text with my location, stating that I would still be a while. I then moved into the left lane and started moving with the faster traffic. I did remember, however, that Kim the psychic had told me I had a speeding card show up so to watch my speed, as I could get a speeding ticket.

The next forty five minutes were almost a blur, as I drove as fast as I could to pick up Kate, knowing the only good thing was that I wouldn't have to wait. As I pulled up at the arrivals, I could see her immediately, so I pulled over and jumped out of my car. I did notice right away that she looked very tired and was very thin, but it was wonderful to hug her, which I did for an entire minute. Then it was time to get back in the car and head towards the Middletown hospital for an x-ray. We found ourselves in some traffic, which gave us time to catch up on everything.

We first talked about Kate and about what she had been through over the past month. I immediately could see the pain in her heart as we know that breaking up is hard to do. I could see that it was the hurt, the betrayal, and the continuing dis-ease that was still very much bothering her. Moreover, she had moved to this small town that was in a different country and knew absolutely no one else but her boyfriend and his parents, and now due to the breakup, she really had no one.

As I was listening, I thought, wow, she had now been affected by another part of life, as she was dealing with a broken heart and the concept of betrayal. This was different for Kate, as she had always had a wonderful life. She did great in high school, made all the international waterski teams, performed fabulously in university, and did great with her internship. She had pretty much lived a fairy-tale life. She then talked about how wonderful her job was and how much she loved it, and that she was learning a lot and that her employer really liked her. I reminded her of the wonderful brain she had, as we had known this when she could play bridge at the age of twelve and run seven no trump. But she still looked so sad, so wounded, so hurt, and this was a different place for me, as this was my child and she was hurting. We stopped at Tim Horton's for coffee, chocolate milk, and a bagel. As we walked through the new service center heading back to the car, I could see signs of my Kate returning as the power of love was all around her.

It was 8:05 a.m. when we entered the emergency department at the Middletown hospital. Kate sat in the triage and told them about her sore foot, and we then moved to registration and the waiting room. We were very happy to see we were the only ones waiting, and to our great surprise, we were called rather quickly and found ourselves in a room waiting for a doctor. Kate and I looked at each other, quite happy that things were moving very well. When the doctor came in, he said he was concerned that there was extreme bruising on the upper part of her ankle and said an x-ray was in order. Within five minutes, a nurse with a wheelchair popped her head in and we were on our way to x-ray. Kate and I were thankful for the amazing, wonderful healthcare system that was implemented in Canada—something that was truly good for the people.

I was standing close to the screen that showed the picture of Kate's foot and leg—it was a large screen and showed great detail—and as the x-rays were taken, I could see that everything was okay and I was relieved. As we left and said thank you to the wonderful x-ray technician, he said, "It's free and you don't even have to leave a tip." Kate and I looked at each other sort of strangely, like, "How did he know?" I then thought about the amount of tax we pay in Canada and thought, well, this is okay. I pushed Kate in the wheelchair heading back to emergency telling her that her ankle and leg were fine, as I had seen the x-rays. She responded, "Mom, I didn't know you were a doctor. Maybe we should wait to hear what he has to say," and I replied, "Well, I could see the screen as it was so large, but of course we will wait to hear what the doctor says."

Ten minutes later, the doctor came in and said everything was fine and that she must have bruised the bone, which was causing the pain. We both smiled and then headed out the front doors checking the time, and it was 9:05 a.m.—exactly one hour later and we were on our way home. I then knew that it was Kate's spirit or essence that now needed healing over the next four days.

Mimi and Kate had a special grandmother and granddaughter bond, and it was wonderful to see the excitement that occurred when we arrived home. We spent the day just hanging out, eating great food, resting, playing cards, and just being—this being so wonderful to me. I also had to prepare for my Face meeting that was to take place at 4:30 p.m. I was a little sad to leave, but Kate needed to sleep during this time because she had basically been up most of the night traveling.

At the meeting, I was the facilitator and Marilyn was the co-facilitator, and what a great team we made. As the circle took place, I was thankful for the Face program, as this was how I met Marilyn. There was healing that took place at this circle, which was really the purpose, and all was good. Most of all, we helped two more kids, their families, and our community.

I arrived back home around 6:00 p.m. and was glad to find Kate just waking up. I was extremely happy to report that the Face circle had gone very well. I reinforced that good things come from bad and that healing had taken place. Most of all, some good community building had taken place and that time to give back to the community had also come forward. Kate got up, had a shower, and then told me that two of her friends were coming for a visit, and this made me very happy. I told her how glad I was that she was home, because when she was home her friends came to visit.

Aaron and Erin soon appeared at the door, and Kate and I were both glad to see them. We then cozied up to the kitchen island for some visiting time. I could tell that Erin had noticed how fragile Kate was and that she could feel her pain. Kate did talk a lot about the upset in her life, which was also healing. We all just listened and gave support. Then it was time to go to the bar for wing night and a beer. It was great to hang out with the kids, as it was really just family.

There was one upsetting story that came with the night. Kate's best friend's brother Brad Baum was there, and he came over to say hello. I had just seen Brad and his dad Brian, as they had put in an extra cable line for Mimi in the living room just a few months ago. The Baum family was a special family, one that believed in helping others and the importance of the value of family. As Brad was talking, I noticed that he had a broken hand and I asked what had happened, and I could tell this was a touchy subject. He started to tell me that he had been down at a bar in Barrie and that he had gotten jumped and into a fight down there. I looked really surprised, as Brad was not a fighter and his character was one of a quiet peaceful guy. He then said that things had changed in Barrie since he went to school and that what had happened to him was unbelievable. I looked at him quite surprised and wondered what he was really telling me. Brad then said his hellos to Kate, as they were sort of like brother and sister.

They then began setting up the karaoke event; I had forgotten that it was Thursday night. I then knew it was time to go home, as I was tired. Kate and I then enjoyed some more time to talk and then went to bed. I must say that I love the feeling when the daughter you have missed is sleeping in the next room.

Friday came, and Kate seemed distant and the pain was everywhere, but I just kept giving the love. We took Mimi to bridge, went out for lunch, and got some last-minute shopping done. We also stopped by to see Charlene, Brad's mom, as Kate and Charlene were very close. Charlene noticed right away that Kate had lost weight and didn't quite seem herself. Kate then started to tell Charlene about the breakup and the tears started to flow, and of course, I started to tear up as well. We chit-chatted about everything else and then were on our way.

Christine was also a large part of my awareness at this time, as I knew that both her and Ron were trying hard to make it work for the sake of little Paul. I just had this knowing that it wasn't in the cards for them, but I gave them both credit for trying. Therefore, once again it was time for Christine and Paul to move back into my house. As Thanksgiving weekend began, I could see that the connection between Christine and Randy was still present. This was something that never went away and something that just was. This time, they were starting slowly, and it was the knowing that there was family all around that helped to support the transition.

As the weekend came to an end, the feeling of being wounded was sticking with me like glue and I couldn't shake it. I kept thinking of the betrayal I had experienced and I just couldn't understand why. I thought about a kid I took under my wing who so needed a mother. I thought about the fact that I couldn't go to see him play live anymore and that I was no longer a part of his life. I thought about the horrible judgement that was placed upon me and the words from Marilyn: "Shame on them." I felt like it was so unfair. I could even see Dylan looking at me with the feeling of unsafeness or question in his eyes, which cut through my heart and created a large hole there. I thought about Penetang Idol, the sub shop, clothes shopping, singing in the car, and teaching Dylan to drive. Now it was like a black cloud hanging over me; it hurt, and it was so very painful.

I began to think about how hard I had worked to get my life back on track, that it had really taken seven years to get out of my marriage, that I had left with a small bag of clothes and toiletries, and that I had lost everything: my home, my family. I then could remember walking, reading, resting, and for two years trying to heal my life. I also knew I had all the tools to deal with the pain and the loss, yet for some reason I was hurting and I was wounded once again. This was also a time when I decided to turn from the global insanity of our ancestors and start to make a difference.

I knew that the healing involved was realizing that the drama and turbulence had to stop and the only way is to stop it was to stop being the drama and learn to use our wisdom that was available all around us and yield to the flow of life's progress instead of resisting it. At the same time, it was important to remember our boundaries, maintain respect for everyone and everything, and realize the power in the simple word NO, meaning "No, thank you." We needed to feel our emotions and realize that they were reactions to our mind, which was the ego, and at this very moment to stop the thinking and follow our instinct (which was our natural, inborn sense of direction). Most of all, it was important to let the judgement in life go, as it was truly not working so well for the human race—this was the only way we were going to save our planet, our kids, and our existence.

Therefore, we needed to honour love and each other, as we are the true gifts of life. We needed to realize that the gift of love was the evidence of spirituality right in front of us, yet we still seemed to resist the power of love and the power of spirituality. It is important that we opened our hearts, lived life as the example, let go of the ego and the judgement, and made a difference. When we helped our neighbours, our kids, the gifts and rewards would be countless.

I then looked to my accomplishments, as I was a single woman supporting myself, my kids, the wonderful house I had to live in, and the wonderful family who was all around me. However, I was still hurting, and I thought to the people who had been important in my life and now were no longer in my life. I thought about the untrue stories and the horrible judgement I had experienced. I thought about the many times I had been referred to as an angel, and it was like my angel wings were broken. I kept thinking, how did this happen and why? I had a stellar reputation with helping kids and in business, and I felt that due to my helping Dylan I had lost all of that. I thought it would have been different if I had a man, but if I had, I probably wouldn't have had the time to help Dylan. Maybe if I didn't like to dance and looked older and dressed older, things could have unfolded differently. The reality was, I had lost a lot because of helping this wonderful kid who just needed someone. I still couldn't believe we were here, but we were!

As I sat in all this pain, I thought, should I just sit here or should I say again, "Hey, I am hurt"? And of course, the latter came with me sending a message to Dylan, as I had only talked to him once over the past couple weeks and I wanted him to know I was hurting. I almost felt like he should have protected me from all this stuff and set the record straight. Moreover, Dylan had asked for my help. He asked me to come watch and drive him to Penetang Idol, and he had accepted my mother role in his life with his arms wide open. And now I had lost a lot of my life because of it, which in my eyes was plainly wrong. And yet there was still no contact.

The Answers

I was still voting for Dylan, as he had entered a contest for his song "Killer and the Sin." It was a week into the contest that I noticed his song had been removed due to some breach of contract. I messaged Dylan and asked what happened, and I received the answer to my questions. First, he said that there was a problem with the contest and that he was trying to find out what had happened. He then said that he was having an independent time, a time of being on his own with no parental support, as this was what he always was used to. He also confided that there was just too much attention, too much drama, and that everyone was talking about everyone, good things and bad things, and no one was just living happily anymore.

He then followed those messages with this: "You have helped me so much and I am so grateful to have you ☺. I just want to see you happy in your life first and not because of me. I want to see you find someone ☺♥, and I love you and always will. I have been writing more and doing lots, I promise, and I almost have a music video lined up and it will be great ☺. I love you, stay happy, talk soon xoxo."

I felt sad at first in response to the line that people were saying good things and bad things, as I knew it was about me. Yes, I knew that people were saying bad things about me to Dylan and that it would be best for his career for him to stay away from me. I thought what had I done wrong and I knew I hadn't done anything wrong and why would people be saying bad things about me to Dylan? I then replied that the drama was too much for me too and it saddened me greatly that untrue stories and judgement had taken place. I also learned that there was more judgement towards me concerning the time in the studio, and he did ask, did I want to know what they were saying about me? I knew that I had realized on my own that I needed balance, and I was glad that things had changed as I was almost exhausted, and I wanted a man and the right man, no settling. I was also tired of the negative energy, and so

I replied to Dylan, "I will be cheering you on from the sidelines; good job, and I am proud of you." I also said. "My life isn't all about you, Dylan, as I have other things that make me happy: Kate, Emily, Ernie, Mimi, walking, my house, music, LA Woman, dancing, and Brandon." I explained how I was also so busy helping Christine with Paul, getting Kate through her crisis, working, cooking, and looking after Mimi, too. Then I thought, I forgot Christine in my list. I could not imagine a day without Christine, as she brought me so much joy!

I then felt like I had said everything and I felt complete. I really felt that Dylan and I had had a communication problem and that it was so great we were now at least talking about what was going on all around us. Our relationship had now changed, as were not texting at all or seeing each other at all. We still had contact through Facebook messaging, and I guessed this was the way it was to be. And so once again, I knew I had to surrender, but this time was different, as I really had to surrender. All the other times, I would surrender for a day or two and then I would be acting again and not really surrendering. I was very thankful that I finally realized it and was aware of my behaviour. I then had a little compassion for myself, as it was hard to let go of a new son who had only been a part of my life for the past year.

The next day, I found myself feeling a bit better, and I was able to write, walk, and organize my life again. I felt more like myself, and this was very good. Christine and baby Paul were doing great. Kate was getting by in California, and I was happy about that. Emily was doing great: her schoolwork was a heavy load, and she was getting ready to run her first half marathon. Brandon was at work and excited about buying his first brand-new car. Mimi and I were still hanging out, and I was getting lots of great stuff together for the next book: "Taking Care of the Golden Years." I was looking forward to attending a wedding shower for Marilyn's daughter. I was very excited for Rebecca, as she had waited and had found the most amazing man and was set to marry him in two weeks.

I realized at this time that we find family in different places and that they can become the most amazing people in your life. I believe it's not blood that creates family; it is love, and we know the power of love and the greatness that comes when we value it!

It was two days later that I found myself just missing Dylan, and I knew that I had to do something about it. I sat quietly to figure out what the heck I was going to do to heal and find myself again. I thought back to what I had learned about always needing to feed the soul with walking, resting, and reading, with the keyword being "reading." I then realized I had given Stephanie my Louise Hay You Can Heal Your Life book and that I needed another copy, and so I then found myself on the way to Coles, the local bookstore. Mimi decided she wanted to come, so we both jumped into the car and headed up to the mall.

As I entered the Coles in the Middletown mall, I headed straight towards the self-help and spiritual section, as at one time my first book A Woman's Passage to Freedom was on consignment at this very location and had sat on the shelves in this very section. As I arrived, I started scanning the shelves looking for Louise Hay and I couldn't find it. I then started to go over the section again, and there was a book that stood right out in front of me and I had the strong feeling I was to buy this book. I stood still for a moment and listened to my inner gut that was telling me to pick up this book right in front of me: The Power of Now by Eckhart Tolle. As I picked up the book, I recalled reading his first book, Finding Your Life's Purpose. I had read it before Oprah and in only two days, and I had understood all of it quite easily. I then headed to the cash register with the feeling that I knew I had the right book, and the excitement was bubbling all inside me.

Mimi was sitting in the car, and as I got in and started it, she asked, "Did you find the book you were looking for?" I said, "I sure did!" I then arrived home knowing I didn't have much time to get started on this book as it was soon time to go to work, so I just read the letter from the author. As I was reading this, I could feel the excitement, a knowing that there was something amazing within the pages of this book.

My shift at work was busy and so went pretty fast. When I arrived home, I prepared a snack and cozied up in my bed with my new book. I was only a few pages into it when I received a text from Emily saying maybe she did need me to attend the start of her half marathon that she was running in Toronto the next day. Then she said, "You would have to leave at six in the morning and some streets would be closed; you don't have to come, but it would be nice if you did." My first thought was that I wouldn't be able to read my book because I was going to have to get up very early in the morning and I needed to get some sleep. I then checked the directions, told Emily I would come, and set my alarm for 5:00 a.m. I closed my book and thought, well, this would have to wait for Monday, as I had to return from Toronto to attend the wedding shower for Rebecca that weekend as well.

For some reason, I woke up at 3:00 a.m. not wanting to miss my alarm. I thought, wow, I better get some more sleep, as this was going to be a long and exciting day. I then rolled over and tried to fall back asleep. My alarm did ring at 5:00 a.m., and I was not quite sure if I really went back to sleep, but I soon found myself in the kitchen making coffee. I looked out into the dark street and noticed the rain coming down in the light of the streetlight and thought that this could be a challenging drive. But I was a very good driver and figured that I would be okay. I got dressed thinking I was going to need a large amount of warm clothes, made my coffee to go, and gathered some snacks for the ride.

I got on the 400, which was the series of highways I was going to travel to reach downtown Toronto. It was still very dark and rainy. I arrived in downtown Toronto with time to spare, although forty minutes later I was still looking for a spot to park. At this time, I would have paid anything to just park and meet up with Emily; I wanted to give her a hug of love and support, as I was so proud she was running this half marathon, but I couldn't find a spot to park. I then chose to park in a private housing unit and wrote a note saying I would be back in twenty minutes. Then through texting I found Emily, and at this moment, I was so happy to see her. I noticed the massive amount of people that were downtown for this event. Emily told me that there were many marathons taking place this morning and thousands of people running the races. I was quite impressed and felt proud of the people. Emily was accompanied by Meg, one of her roommates from university and another strong and determined young woman.

They began to play "O Canada," which always made me feel warm and fuzzy all over. The three of us stood under an umbrella in the pouring rain, singing our national anthem. We then found Meg's mom, and the girls entered the starting area, ready to start the race. As Emily passed the starting line and waved at me, my heart was singing with joy and I reflected on the amazing daughter I have and the journey of her life that was unfolding for her. She had been talking about taking a job in Calgary starting next summer for sixteen months at an oil company—which could be a final destination for her career in chemical engineering. I already had the knowing that she would get the job because her people skills shone through during any interview. I then thought, wow, these girls were going to keep me in the air flying around the country. And then the thought hit me, did I make then too strong, and of course the answer was NO. It was wonderful how very strong they were!

I was now very thankful I was able to find my way out of the city. I knew once again that I would be returning soon to it for some reason, as I really felt my life was going to change dramatically. It was now time to focus on the rest of my family and get myself to Rebecca's shower. Gratitude once again entered into my awareness, as I was so thankful for Marilyn and Rebecca in my life and I was excited to join in the celebration of her upcoming wedding. It was wonderful to arrive at Barb's beautiful house, as Barb and her house were products of love. It was equally great to see the love between the mother and bride, special girlfriends, sisters, friends, and family. The shower was wonderful and enjoyed by all. I then get myself in the car and headed to work, which was okay. After work I returned home totally exhausted and ready for bed and rest.

On Monday morning, I cozied in with my Eckhart Tolle book and a good cup of coffee. As I read the introduction, I knew immediately that this book was going to save my life. I had had many people tell me the same thing, that A Woman's Passage to Freedom had saved their lives, and I was experiencing and understanding this concept. I then went to gratitude for the upset that actually set me to the bookstore looking for guidance. Yes, I was actually thankful for all the turbulence I had endured because it had brought me to this very moment.

First, Eckhart explained in the beginning chapters about the dysfunction of the people in the world, and the examples given really showed the insanity of the human race. He then talked about how this has been the norm for a while and that the human being has become a mind-orientation being—which I totally believe in and also state in my book A Woman's Passage to Freedom. His idea that the key and secret is within the body was something else I believed in. I found myself reading this book in its entirety within the next twelve hours. One of the most powerful messages in this book for me was about the power of just being. I sat quietly for a minute and then remembered the poem I wrote about a month ago: called "Just Being."

Just Being

As I reflect to life, I see the beauty in just being.

I feel the easiness that comes with just being.

I look to nature and see how it understands just being.

I see the power that comes with just being.

I feel society pulling on the ones who choose to just be.

I feel the strength that comes with just being.

Just being is the state of the acceptance of life.

*I know the gifts of life come to the ones
who understand just being.*

I know that just being is another way of having faith.

This was what I call an OMG moment!

When I got to the last chapter, I almost fell off my chair as it was called "The Meaning of Surrendering." I then said, "Thank you, God," as this is how I lived my life and what I believed in on an hourly basis. With all my experiences of life, I had no choice but to believe in surrendering. I then had the knowing that I just needed confirmation that I was on the right path doing the right thing—as surrendering was the essence of strength and peace, and what we had to do to save our planet. Here is the quote from this book that sums it all together: "Surrender. Is the simple but profound wisdom of yielding to rather than opposing the flow of life. Also I receive the message of the power of action less activity. Weakness is power, blessed are the gentle, and they shall have the earth for their possession."

I then thought that I would so love to meet Eckhart Tolle, as I would enjoy talking with him. I was grateful for this book and his spiritual guidance. As I closed the book, I felt a tremendous change in my essence and surrendered completely at this time and continued to live my life in faith.

Last Chapter

Three weeks later, I was locked in with Dylan for a visit to complete our monthly cellphone business, which I realized would tie us together for the next two years. I also had his birthday present ready (the beautiful leather jacket I got him) and some movies to exchange that I had thoroughly enjoyed. It was a crisp sunny day, and I was feeling a little nervous as it had been almost a month since I last saw him and a lot of water had passed under the bridge. As I pulled out of my driveway, I noticed an unusual sight. The sun was straight ahead, and there was a circular rainbow around it. I stopped the car, still in reverse, and said to myself, "You have to be kidding me." I looked closer and then looked around to see if anyone else was noticing this, but there was no one around. I then put the car into forward, drove to the next street, pulled over, and once again took a picture on my iPhone.

I then headed towards Midland thinking, okay, I get it, there is a rainbow at the end. I arrived to see Dylan on the porch talking on his phone. I was not sure what our plans were, so I decided to take in the movies and the jacket. He finished his call and gave me a hug, and it was as if we were back at Penetang Idol and he had just finished playing. I then handed him the bag with the movies and started to explain what inspiration I received from each of the movies, as this was what we had always done. Next I said, "Well, here is your birthday present," and I noticed right away that Dylan's eyes started to bulge out and he started saying, "No way, no way." I just smiled and helped him get the coat out of the bag.

As he tried on this beautiful leather coat that was his belated birthday present, he marveled at the perfect fit and the amazing look. I was also at this time marvelling at the perfect fit and noticing the shine that his entire essence took on. He then hugged and kissed me, and said thank you, before running upstairs to look in the full-length mirror. He said, "I am going to wear this jacket to all my gigs," and the smile on his face was heart-warming. We then talked about the movies once again, and another bag was filled to return back to my house, with one special one being This Is It with Michael Jackson—one that Dylan almost bought each of us a copy of. Then we began to decide if we should go for lunch or what to do, and a decision was made to go down to the liquor store to buy a couple beers and sit on the porch, visit, and enjoy the fabulous weather.

Since the liquor store was only one block away, we chose to walk. As we were talking on the way, I could feel the easiness of just being together coming back to life—an easiness that had been a part of our lives for over a year. I also noticed how great the jacket looked on Dylan; it was almost as if it had been made especially just for him. As we entered the store, I headed over to the mixed cooler area and Dylan looked around. When we met in the aisle, he hugged me and just held on and said, "I missed you." I held on too and said, "I missed you, too." As Dylan let go, he now headed over to the wine area and I was thinking, why he is going that way. I looked over and there was a full-length mirror there and Dylan was checking out his jacket. He now began jumping around like a jellybean in the store. As we got in line to purchase our treats, Dylan mentioned to me that the cashier Jayne had purchased a CD. I said that was great. Then Dylan mentioned that there was even a song that Jayne didn't like. I looked puzzled at Jayne, and she said she was just being honest and I said that's good. We then tried to figure out what song it was but to no avail. I had finished my purchase and moved just slightly off to the side when Dylan said to Jayne, "Do you like my new jacket?" and then smiled over at me. Jayne said, "Yes, Dylan, it is really nice," and they both looked over to me. I said, "It was a birthday present," and Jayne then turned to Dylan and said, "Dylan, is that your mom?" I froze completely and said absolutely nothing, not even looking to Dylan, and then the most amazing gift took place. Dylan said quickly and with love in his heart, "Yes, this is my mom." We then just smiled at Jayne as if nothing out of the ordinary had taken place and walked out of the store and up the road, continuing our conversation as if nothing had happened, knowing that things had unfolded just the way they were supposed to.

We then sat for the next two hours enjoying a special conversation, a conversation of ease, love, joyfulness, an openness of trust, and intelligence—one of business, life, and the future. The sun was shining, and I did most of the listening, which was exactly what I was to do during this conversation. This was also a time of healing and reassurance of the survival of our unique and rare relationship. When I realized it was time for me to head home, Dylan walked me to the car, giving me a hug and a kiss goodbye and saying, "I love you." My reply was, "I love you, too."

As I headed down the road, I knew everything was going to be okay. I knew that it was just a matter of time before Dylan would be a famous musician and filling Madison Square Garden. Most importantly, Dylan and I were still as close as ever, as the love never changed but our roles in each other's lives had. I had now let go of him, and I was truly, completely Just Being There.

As I was driving home, I thought of all the people and all the lives that had been affected over the past year, as it truly had been an amazing year. Nick was good at the restaurant and still with Maryanne, and Chrissy was in a healthy relationship with Eric and so very happy. Young Meghan was experiencing the growth of a seventeen-year-old and opening up to the difference a healthy relationship makes. Frank and Sandra were the same, and the hotel was doing well. I hadn't heard from Dylan's dad lately, but I had the knowing that everything was good in his life. Dan was still there helping Dylan when he needed it. Donald and his family were doing well, and Anne Marie was healing and I missed her very much. Marilyn, John, and family were great, getting ready for Rebecca's wedding. Barb and Ron were preparing to attend the Gala in Middletown where Dylan was to perform.

Kate was okay and looking forward to me arriving in a few days. Emily and Brandon were happy and in the most healthy relationship that I had ever seen in two people in their early twenties. Christine was doing great at college and in her PSW course, and baby Paul was fantastic: talking, learning, and growing every day. Mimi was as healthy as ever. My family was good and complete.

I knew that my books were close to distribution and that my destiny was to teach the people to heal from their past, which warmed my heart. I was also excited for my man to enter into my life and to enjoy a solid relationship. As I passed the Martyr Shrine, the sun was shining in the car and a single tear of joy ran down my face, and all I could hear was Dylan singing "Hallelujah" and it was beautiful, absolutely beautiful. I then had the knowing of the importance of family, that life was all about the people and the power of love. And then the feeling of happiness filled every ounce of my being.

∽ **The End** ∾

Epilogue

I would like to tell you that everything worked out great immediately within the family, but that is not the reality of what actually happened. Unfortunately, more judgement occurred and this had a ripple effect. It eventually became time for Christine and Paul to move back to Christine's mom's house. This was a very difficult thing for me to do and something I had no choice but to do. I had the knowing that it was time for me to close my doors, roll up my heart, and look after me. Christine knew that it was probably the best thing as well, and she knew that I loved her and that my door was always open and that I was here for Paul always as well. It took me a few weeks to get back on track, and what kept me going at this time was that I still had the knowing that I had done my part in the lives of these children and they were on their way, and now it was time to look after me.

I found myself at Kim the psychic's looking for direction, and confirmation was given that it was time for me and time for my career to blossom. I also knew I had had enough experience in the field of life, as I refer to it, and it was time to do the teaching and set the example: to teach surrendering with boundaries, the realization that people who judge are unhappy in their own lives, and the power of love (especially the power of parental love, as our kids need this so very much). I also had confirmation that a wonderful man was to enter into my life and to just be patient. So once again, my days were now filled with the completion of this book.

Christmastime came upon us, and the power of Christmas and the miracle within fell all around us. It started with Emily coming home for the holidays and Kate arriving with her cat Luna, and then visits with Christine and even a babysitting time with baby Paul. Then Dylan agreed to join the family for Christmas Eve dinner.

On Christmas Eve, the table was set for seven and the day started to unfold perfectly. Christine asked if we could look after Paul, as she and

Randy were back on track and needed to do some last-minute shopping. Emily then headed off to pick up Dylan with Paul, as he needed a nap (and thank God for the power of a car ride). As they returned, I managed to get Paul down for much-needed sleep time in my bed. Then a wonderful miracle happened: Kate, Emily, Dylan, Mimi, and I sat around the Christmas tree and started to open our gifts. I felt that this was a time of a new birth, the birth of a new family, which warned my heart to its fullest. We exchanged gifts of love and had a wonderful time together.

Then it was time for dinner preparations. Kate, Emily, Dylan, and I were busy in the kitchen. Emily, Kate, and I were fixing the vegetables, and Dylan was carving the turkey. Next Marilyn and John arrived, and it was time for Paul to wake up. Our Christmas table was full and consisted of me at one end, Dylan next to me, Mimi, Kate at the other end, Emily holding Paul, John, and Marilyn. We enjoyed the gift of grace given by Mimi, and the Christmas crackers as well. I gave a small speech on how grateful I was to be surrounded by family, as my family was all present at this amazing Christmas table.

After dinner, Emily ran Paul home, and when she returned we enjoyed more time with family. Then it was time for Marilyn and John to head home, and they offered to drop Dylan down the road at his dad's for a visit. As Dylan was saying goodbye, he said to me how glad he was that he came for dinner and that he was playing at The Boat House New Year's Eve and would I like to attend. This was a very special moment for me, and I knew that this was where I was to be on New Year's Eve.

New Year's Eve day was a day for reflection, a day for excitement, and a day for moving into a fresh year. Emily and Brandon were heading to Toronto for the celebration, and Christine was going to a local celebration with Randy and feeling fantastic about it. She was also enjoying a brand-new car, which her wonderful brother Brandon had helped her to secure. I must say that she looked fantastic driving that new white car! Kate was unsure of her plans, as she was single this New Year's Eve. Emily and Brandon extended Kate an invitation to join them, although that day she ultimately chose to stay home and visit with her friends in town and join me at The Boat House to watch Dylan after the clocks struck midnight.

Kate and I had a fun time getting ready for New Year's Eve. I was feeling good about life, knowing that I had come a long way over the past few years. Kate was doing great and looked so beautiful in her dress she bought when we were in Vegas. We enjoyed a card game of crib, which was one of our favourite games, and mama won.

I dropped Kate off at the home of a boy she had known since grade three, and she was excited. I then headed to The Boat House with no expected plans. I was hoping Marilyn and John would stop by, but because of my years in the bar business and my history at this great location, I was okay with entering the bar by myself. On my way in, I met Lauren's dad, who had also come to watch Dylan play. We settled in at the bar for a visit and to listen to the fantastic entertainment. A few minutes passed, and then Dylan stopped by for a hello, which was wonderful. Lauren's dad and I enjoyed great conversation, and Lauren returned with the forgotten cord, which made me laugh within and a smile was exchanged between Dylan and me. Then Dan and his girlfriend entered the bar area, and it was nice to see both of them and I was glad to see such great support for Dylan. We all enjoyed a visit with Dylan, which was great. I was happy to see Marilyn and John enter as well, and I began to release any type of nervousness that was within.

The atmosphere was full of love, as the regular customers were within the bar area having a great time. I knew quite a few of them, and Marilyn and John were regulars, too. The music, of course, was fabulous, and the dance floor was full, and we the regulars were enjoying hallway dancing as well. As I remembered and heard Dylan saying from the heart that he felt controlled when I watched him, I focused on not watching him as much, giving him his space, although

I listened to every note played. On his first break, he stopped by to ask how it sounded and received a reply of fantastic.

It was then time for me to pick up Kate and drive her to the rec center for her countdown party. I was glad to be there for her. When I returned to the bar, I started to really enjoy the people, as this was what it was all about. I saw Jim there and enjoyed a dance with him, as we had so enjoyed dancing at the Legion in October. Marilyn then informed me that she and John were heading home, and this sent a fright into me that I would be alone at this time and it was pretty close to midnight. Then all of a sudden there was a hand on my back and it was Jim, and he said, "Don't worry; everything will be okay." I felt instant relief and a smile appeared on my face. Jim and I then enjoyed another dance on the dance floor. Marilyn and John had now left, and Jim offered for me to join his table, which was full of friends and regulars from the bar. I felt a sense of warmth fill my heart. Then everyone in the bar began to prepare for midnight, with the staff going around with trays of champagne, party hats, and favours. I look at Jim and saw a wonderful man within.

Everyone now had their attention on the TV screens with the excitement of a new year on the horizon. Dylan had finished his set and was busy with the people, and then headed to the microphone for the countdown. I couldn't really see him and snuggled in with Jim. As Dylan called out the final seconds to midnight, I felt a great sense of being right where I was to be. Jim and I exchanged a kiss, and the family and friends were everywhere. Jim and I both then took the time to text our girls, as Jim also had two girls close to the age of my girls. About fifteen minutes later, a tall slim young man came to wish me a Happy New Year. Dylan took this time to reflect on what we had accomplished over the past year. A smile appeared on both our faces and then all was put aside as this moment became magical, and I finally got it and so did Dylan. We both realized at this very moment that it was the gift of parental love between us that really was what it was all about: the gift of love and the power of it. The room stopped for a second, and a hug of love was exchanged once again.

Dylan returned to finish his last set, and Jim returned to my side. Jim and I were enjoying the moment when Dylan started to play "Come Sail Away." Jim then turned to me and asked if I would like to dance. I said of course. Jim and I then enjoyed a slow dance, with Dylan playing my favourite song.

As I cuddled in with Jim, I closed my eyes and stopped hearing this song. It was replaced instead with another song now playing in my head. To me, it was like I was in a different place and the music I was hearing was Susie McNeil's "Believe."

Acknowledgment

I would like to acknowledge the four wonderful children who have touched my life in such an amazing way.

Kate, I thank you for the joy of your athletic ability, your love for cards, and your strength as my firstborn. I often look to the picture of you and your first real slalom water ski. You are six and in a Minnie Mouse wetsuit, and your slalom ski sits two feet above your head. Most of all, it is the smile that appears on your face that I carry every day in my heart, and it is this smile that I return to because today you live in the warm climate of California that remains a distance from me and I know you are fulfilling your dreams. I do miss you and love you very much! I am also very grateful for our new friendship because of the growth you have experienced. You have blossomed into a wonderful young woman.

Emily, you are the perfect example of an old soul, and I refer to you as an old soul because it is the beauty within your soul that shines with every breath you take. I know this light is seen by many others, as I see the attraction of the people who cross your path. You are such a gift, and I thank you for just being you! And most of all, I thank you for being my rock, my support, and for standing beside me through everything. You are the best! I think of you now as my Emily, and you truly will always be my Emily. I also see the strength in your aura each and every day, and your amazing light that shines throughout the world.

Christine, I look and admire the strength that lies within you every time I am honoured to be present in a room with you. It is like a beam that is shining from your soul, and it is your beautiful essence and being that I look for, something that also gives me great strength. You are an inspiration to me and to all the young women in the world. I thank you for being my support and my ear, and for giving me the love of a daughter, as this is something that is always in my heart. I would also like to thank you for the gift of your son Paul, as this has been like the love of a grandson and I love him so very much. You are so wonderful with him, and your maternal love is amazing. He seems to have an old soul like his Auntie Emily, one full of strength, love, and understanding. He is a beautiful boy.

Dylan, you are brilliant—there is no other word to describe you! Yes, your gift of piano, voice, and music is of extreme brilliance, and as time passes I see brilliance in all aspects of your being—it is just everywhere. But it is your heart, love, strength, and kindness that really stand out in front for me. You at times wear your heart on your sleeve, and this is so beautiful to see—and it is this, I believe, that brings that special passion and strength to your music. Dylan, you are also like a son to me, and I thank you so very much for the gift of love and joy that you have brought to my life. I truly could not image a day without you and your music. You have brought so much to my life that I am grateful for and, most of all, the love of a son that I cherish every day. This love is a part of my heart forever and always!

Author Bio

Jan Amos is an inspirational writer who at the age of 47 discovered her love for writing and her gift for insight. Throughout the pages of her books, she takes life's day-to-day situations and shines a light of awareness on them to create a healthier way of living. Jan is also a strong believer in the need to build our communities and strengthen our youth. She spends many hours volunteering with the youth in her homeland of Canada. Jan is very thankful for the gifts she has been given.